ID0908675

Accounting Principles for Lawyers

Many lawyers, especially those dealing with commercial matters, need to understand accounting yet feel on shaky ground in the area. This book is written specifically for them. It breaks down and makes clear basic concepts (such as the difference between profit and cash flow), and explains the accounting profession and the legal and regulatory framework within which accounting operates. The relevant provisions of the Companies Act 1985 are discussed at some length. Holgate explains generally accepted accounting principles (GAAP) in the UK, the trend towards global harmonisation and the role of international accounting standards. He then deals with specific areas such as group accounts, acquisitions, tax, leases, pensions, financial instruments, and realised profits, focusing in each case on those aspects that are likely to confront lawyers in their work. This book will appeal to the general practitioner as well as to lawyers working in corporate, commercial, and tax law.

PETER HOLGATE is Senior Accounting Technical Partner at PricewaterhouseCoopers LLP in the UK.

Law Practitioner Series

The *Law Practitioner Series* offers practical guidance in corporate and commercial law for the practitioner. It offers high-quality comment and analysis rather than simply restating the legislation, providing a critical framework as well as exploring the fundamental concepts which shape the law. Books in the series cover carefully chosen subjects of direct relevance and use to the practitioner.

The series will appeal to experienced specialists in each field, but is also accesssible to more junior practitioners looking to develop their understanding of particular fields of practice.

The Consultant Editors and Editorial Board have outstanding expertise in the UK corporate and commercial arena, ensuring academic rigour with a practical approach.

Consultant editors
Charles Allen-Jones, retired senior partner of Linklaters
Mr. Justice David Richards, Judge of the High Court of Justice, Chancery
    Division

Editors
Chris Ashworth – Ashurst Morris Crisp
Professor Eilis Ferran – University of Cambridge
Nick Gibbon – Allen & Overy
Stephen Hancock – Herbert Smith
Judith Hanratty – BP Corporate Lawyer, retired
Keith Hyman – Clifford Chance
Keith Johnston – Addleshaw Goddard
Vanessa Knapp – Freshfields
Charles Mayo – Simmons & Simmons
Andrew Peck – Linklaters
Richard Snowden QC – Erskine Chambers
Richard Sykes QC
William Underhill – Slaughter & May
Sandra Walker – Rio Tinto

Other books in the Series
Stamp Duty Land Tax
Michael Thomas, with contributions from KPMG Stamp Taxes Group;
    Consultant Editor David Goy QC
*The European Company: Volume I General editors Dirk Van Gervan and Paul
    Storm*

Accounting Principles for Lawyers

PETER HOLGATE

PricewaterhouseCoopers LLP

CAMBRIDGE
UNIVERSITY PRESS

CAMBRIDGE UNIVERSITY PRESS
Cambridge, New York, Melbourne, Madrid, Cape Town, Singapore, São Paulo

Cambridge University Press
The Edinburgh Building, Cambridge CB2 2RU, UK

Published in the United States of America by Cambridge University Press, New York

www.cambridge.org
Information on this title: www.cambridge.org/9780521607223

First published 2006

Printed in the United Kingdom at the University Press, Cambridge

A catalogue record for this book is available from the British Library

Library of Congress Cataloguing in Publication data
Holgate, Peter, 1953–
Accounting principles for lawyers / Peter Holgate. – 1st ed.
    p.   cm. – (Law practitioner series)
Includes bibliographical references and index.
ISBN-13: 978-0-521-60722-3 (hardback)
ISBN-10: 0-521-60722-1 (hardback)
1. Accounting – Great Britain.   2. Accounting – Standards – Great Britain.   3. Accounting –
Wales.   4. Accounting – Law and legislation – England.   5. Accounting – Law and
legislation – Wales.   I. Title.   II. Series.
HF5616.G7H65   2006
657′.02′434 – dc22   2005020132

ISBN-13 978-0-521-60722-3 hardback
ISBN-10 0-521-60722-1 hardback

Contents

Acknowledgements

My thanks are due to a number of people, without whom this book would not have appeared. First to Professor John Tiley of Cambridge University who did not so much plant a seed thought but watered a seed that had lain unattended for some years. Second, to Kim Hughes of Cambridge University Press for guiding me through the publishing process.

Thanks are also due to many colleagues at PricewaterhouseCoopers LLP. To the whole Accounting Technical department, for providing me with a learning environment and a stock of knowledge, much of which appears in these pages. In particular, to Barry Johnson and Helen McCann for their excellent work on the 'PwC inform' database and the two PwC Manuals of Accounting: the 'Manual of Accounting: UK GAAP' and the 'Manual of Accounting: IFRS for the UK'. Readers who need more detail than is found in this slim volume are referred to those works.

I thank Elizabeth Buckley for her extensive help in detailed review of the entire text and for drafting assistance on some sections. Thanks also to Chris Nobes for his helpful review comments.

Finally, I thank my wife, Nelda, and my son, Andrew. This book was for many months my Sunday morning job, and the need for the Holgate alarm clock to sound early on a Sunday morning was a point of some discussion on certain occasions. I thank them for their forbearance and dedicate this book to them.

The law as stated in this book is correct as at 31 March 2005.

Glossary of terms

ACCA. Association of Chartered Certified Accountants.

Accruals accounting. The method of accounting that underpins the profit and loss account and balance sheet, namely recognising transactions in the period to which they relate, rather than in the period in which the cash is received or paid. Hence (a) the charge in the profit and loss account for an expense is not (except by chance) the same as the amount of cash paid; (b) the amount recognised as revenue (or turnover, or sales) for the year, is not (except by chance) the same as the cash received from customers.

Act (or 'The Act'). Unless specified to the contrary, 'Act' or 'The Act' refers to the Companies Act 1985.

AIDB. Accountancy Investigation and Discipline Board. Part of the FRC.

AIM. Alternative Investment Market.

APB. The UK Auditing Practices Board. Part of the FRC.

ARC. Accounting Regulatory Committee (of the EU).

ASB. The UK Accounting Standards Board. Part of the FRC.

ASC. The UK Accounting Standards Committee, which set standards from 1970 to 1990, when the ASB took over the activity.

Asset. In a formal sense, the UK Statement of principles (para. 4.6) defines assets as: 'rights or other access to future economic benefits controlled by an entity as a result of past transactions or events'. Less formally, an asset is something of value that a company has; it is recognised as an asset on the balance sheet if it meets certain recognition criteria, such as whether it can be measured reliably.

Associated undertaking. An entity (other than a subsidiary or joint venture) in which another entity (the investor) has a participating interest and over whose operating and financial policies the investor exercises a significant influence. [FRS 9, para. 4]

CA 1985. The Companies Act 1985.

CCAB. The Consultative Committee of Accountancy Bodies in the UK and Ireland, which comprises:

- The Institute of Chartered Accountants in England and Wales (ICAEW)
- The Institute of Chartered Accountants of Scotland (ICAS)
- The Institute of Chartered Accountants in Ireland (ICAI)
- The Association of Chartered Certified Accountants (ACCA)
- The Chartered Institute of Management Accountants (CIMA)
- The Chartered Institute of Public Finance and Accountancy (CIPFA)

CESR. Committee of European Securities Regulators.

CIMA. Chartered Institute of Management Accountants.

CIPFA. Chartered Institute of Public Finance and Accountancy.

Combined Code. The UK code of corporate governance, the latest version of which (2003) is published by the Financial Reporting Council.

DB. Defined benefit (pension scheme).

DC. Defined contribution (pension scheme).

Debit/credit. These are bookkeeping terms. A debit entry represents either an expense or an asset (or a reduction of a liability). A credit entry represents either income or a liability (or a reduction of an asset). The application of accounting principles in drawing up financial statements involves determining which debits are to be treated as assets and which are to be treated as expenses; and determining which credits are to be treated as liabilities and which are to be treated as equity or income. As an example, a payment of cash of £100 to acquire stock is represented as: Dr Stock £100 (an increase in the asset 'stock'); Cr Cash £100 (a decrease in the asset 'cash').

Deferred tax. Estimated future tax consequences of transactions and events recognised in the financial statements of the current and previous periods. [FRS 19, para. 2]

DTI. The UK Department of Trade and Industry.

Earnings. An undefined term, broadly equivalent to profits. Generally refers to profit after tax and minority interest. More accurately, it refers to profit after tax, minority interest and preference dividend, this being the definition of earnings used in the calculation of EPS (see below).

EBITDA. Earnings before interest, tax, depreciation and amortisation. This is a measure of earnings favoured by some analysts and some companies. Depreciation and amortisation are added back because they are non-cash items. Hence EBITDA is sometimes called 'cash earnings' though this is something of a misnomer, as it still includes many items calculated on an accruals basis.

EFRAG. The European Financial Reporting Advisory Group, part of the mechanism used by Brussels to help it to consider endorsement of International Financial Reporting Standards for use in the EU.

Entity accounts. The accounts of an entity itself – for example the accounts of a single company – as opposed to consolidated accounts. See chapter 8.

EPS. Earnings per share. Broadly, earnings (profit after tax, minority interest and preference dividend) divided by the number of equity shares in issue during the year. The details are set out in FRS 22.

Equity. (1) The IASB's term for shareholders' funds. (2) An equity share, defined in section 744 of the Act as 'in relation to a company, its issued share capital excluding any part of that capital which, neither as respects dividends nor as respects capital, carried any right to participate beyond a specified amount in a distribution'. Note that FRS 4 'Capital instruments' defines non-equity shares in a way that gives equity shares for FRS 4 purposes a different meaning from that in the Act.

Equity accounting. This is also known as 'the equity method'. It is the method of accounting adopted for associated companies and in certain cases for joint ventures, as explained in chapter 8.

ESOP. Employee Share Ownership Plan.

Expense. A reduction in assets, charged in the profit and loss account. This includes non-cash items such as depreciation of fixed assets.

FASB. The US Financial Accounting Standards Board.

Financial statements. A company's annual financial statements, which comprise the profit and loss account, the statement of total recognised gains and losses, the balance sheet, the cash flow statement and various supplementary notes. They form the major part of the company's annual report; this is sent to shareholders and placed on the public record at Companies House. Can also refer to other contexts, such as interim financial statements.

FLA. Finance and Leasing Association.

FRC. The UK Financial Reporting Council, the body that oversees the regulation of corporate reporting and audit, including the UK ASB and the FRRP.

FRRP. The UK Financial Reporting Review Panel. Part of the FRC.

FRS. A UK Financial Reporting Standard, an accounting standard developed by the ASB. See also SSAP.

FRSSE. Financial Reporting Standard for Smaller Entities.

FSA. The UK Financial Services Authority.

GAAP. Generally accepted accounting principles, discussed in chapter 1.

Gearing. The relationship between debt and equity. Gearing can be calculated in a number of ways. See chapter 18 for details.

Gross profit. This is profit measured as revenue less cost of sales, that is, profit before deducting overhead expenses, interest and tax.

IAS. An international accounting standard issued by the IASC.

IASB. The International Accounting Standards Board, the global standard-setter from 2001.

IASC. The International Accounting Standards Committee, the global standard-setter until 2001.

ICAEW, ICAS, ICAI. See CCAB.

IFRIC. The International Financial Reporting Interpretations Committee, a subsidiary of the IASB.

IFRS. An international financial reporting standard issued by the IASB.

Income. An undefined term, used rather loosely. Can be used as a synonym for profit (e.g. in US parlance 'net income' means profit after tax). Sometimes also, confusingly, used to mean revenue.

Interest cover. The ratio of interest cost to profit before interest. So if profit before interest is 100 and interest cost is 25, interest cover is 4. That is, interest is covered 4 times by profits.

Interims. Interim reports published by listed companies, required by the FSA as Listing Authority.

Joint venture. An entity in which the reporting entity holds an interest on a long-term basis and is jointly controlled by the reporting entity and one or more other venturers under a contractual arrangement. [FRS 9, para. 4]

JV. Joint venture.

KPI. Key performance indicators.

Liability. In a formal sense, the ASB's Statement of principles (para. 4.23) defines liabilities as: 'obligations of an entity to transfer economic benefits as a result of past transactions or events'. Less formally, a liability is something that a company owes to a third party; it is recognised as a liability on the balance sheet if it meets certain recognition criteria, such as whether it can be measured reliably.

Listing Rules. The rules issued by the Financial Services Authority that apply to companies listed on the London Stock Exchange.

LTIP. Long-term incentive plan.

Minority interest. The interest of an outside shareholder in a partially-held subsidiary.

NASDAQ. National Association of Securities Dealers Automated Quotation system).

NRV. Net realisable value.

OFR. The Operating and Financial Review. This was for some time recommended by the ASB as a supplementary report to be given by listed companies, mainly in narrative form. It is now becoming a statutory requirement for listed companies.

Operating profit. A measure of profit after deducting all operating expenses but before adding share of results of associates and joint ventures, and before deducting interest and tax. In UK GAAP, certain exceptional items (non-operating exceptionals, or 'super-exceptionals') are also added/deducted after operating profit.

P & L. Profit and loss.

Participating interest. An interest held by an undertaking in the shares of another undertaking which it holds on a long-term basis for the purposes of securing a contribution to its activities by the exercise of control or influence arising from or related to that interest. [CA1985, section 260]

POBA. The UK Professional Oversight Board for Accountancy. Part of the FRC.

Prelims. Preliminary announcements of results by listed companies as required by the Listing rules.

Profit. A measure of the results of a business on the basis of accruals accounting (see above). (See also Gross profit, Operating profit, Profit before tax, Profit after tax.)

Profit after tax. A measure of profit after deducting all expenses including tax.

Profit before tax. A measure of profit after deducting all expenses apart from tax.

Revenue. The amount earned by an entity from selling goods and services. The terms 'sales' and 'turnover' are broadly synonymous with revenue.

Sales. See Revenue.

SAS. Statement of Auditing Standards.

SEC. Securities and Exchange Commission.

Shareholders' funds. The aggregate of a company's share capital and its reserves. Called 'equity' in IFRS.

SIC. Standing Interpretations Committee of the IASC.

SoP. Statement of principles.

SORP. Statement of Recommended Practice.

SPE. Special purpose entity.

SSAP. A UK Statement of Standard Accounting Practice, an accounting standard developed by the ASC. See also FRS.

STRGL. The statement of total recognised gains and losses. This is a statement required by UK GAAP as a continuation of the profit and loss account. Together the two statements give a more comprehensive picture of economic performance than does the profit and loss account alone. Broadly, the distinction is that the STRGL includes value changes, such as gains and losses on revaluing a property, whereas the profit and loss account deals with transactions.

Subsidiary/Subsidiary undertaking. Under IFRS, a subsidiary is 'an entity, including an unincorporated entity such as a partnership, that is controlled by another entity (known as the parent)'. For UK GAAP and UK law purposes, there is a distinction between 'subsidiary' and 'subsidiary undertaking'. Section 736(1) of the Act defines a 'subsidiary' for the general purposes of the Act but not for accounting purposes. Section 258 of the Act defines a 'subsidiary undertaking' for accounting purposes, chiefly in connection with consolidation.

Turnover. See Revenue.

UITF. The UK Urgent Issues Task Force. This is a subsidiary of the ASB.

XBRL. Extensible Business Reporting Language.

PART I

The accounting environment

1
Introduction

Aim of this book

The aim of this book is to explain accounting to lawyers. This means to some extent explaining it as one would to any group of intelligent non-accountants. But I emphasise those aspects that are particularly relevant to the work that lawyers do. For example, chapters 3 and 4 on the legal framework of accounting, and on substance over form, are more detailed than they would be for a general reader. Similarly, the specific subjects covered in Part II reflect the likely interest of lawyers. Mergers and acquisitions, leases, capital instruments and realised profits are all discussed. But the reader will find little on methods of stock valuation and methods of depreciation. Similarly, this book does not deal with accounting for special industries and sectors such as banks, insurance companies and charities.

What is accounting?

Accounting is a broad term. It is used to cover the initial recording of transactions in a company's accounting records, though this is better termed 'bookkeeping'. Given the almost universal use of computers for record keeping, even this term is itself only literally accurate either historically, when entries were made in books of account or (historically leather bound) ledgers, or in the smallest of businesses.

The term 'accounting' more properly refers to either the processes that accountants carry out, namely of aggregating and shaping information into reports that are useful to users of those reports; or to the outputs of those processes, namely accounting reports that can be used internally within a business ('management accounting') or externally ('financial accounting' or 'financial reporting'). External reporting can be seen in terms of compliance with legal requirements, for example the requirement under the Companies Act 1985 (CA 1985) to lay accounts (also called 'financial statements') before a general meeting of shareholders and to file them at Companies House. Other regulatory purposes arise, such as the role of the Financial Services Authority in connection with the supervision of various financial institutions.

Whilst this compliance aspect is important, accounting – both internal and external – is perhaps better seen as a process that serves the decision-making needs of business people and various classes of users of accounts. Thus, within a company, the board and various other unit and divisional managers need accounting information to enable them to understand and control the business on a regular basis. In most medium-sized and larger businesses, budgets and subsequently monthly management accounts are prepared for this purpose. Managers will want to know about various financial indicators, such as growth in sales, margins, level of costs, amount of funds tied up in stock and debtors and so on. All of this has the overall objective of seeking to ensure that the company achieves its profit objectives. If the management accounting information shows that budgets are not being achieved, decisions will be taken relating to matters such as pricing, level of overheads such as marketing expenditure and staff numbers, or levels of capital expenditure, to try to steer the company back on course to achieving the sales, profit and other measures set out in the budget.

External reporting also has an important decision-making focus, as well as a compliance focus. In a narrow, traditional sense, a board of directors presents to shareholders an annual report that gives an account of its stewardship of the company's assets during the year. But even implicit in that is an assumption that the shareholders will consider whether they find the performance to be acceptable. If they do not, that might lead to their refusing to reappoint some directors. So even here there is a notion of decision making.

But, in a modern context, the decision-making role is more explicit. Certainly for companies listed on a stock exchange, the board is reporting to 'the market': the analyst and fund manager community in general and not just to those who happen to be shareholders at present. The market has expectations about earnings, and if the earnings reported disappoint the market, the share price, and sometimes the directors' careers, will suffer. The fundamental decisions taking place here, of course, are concerned with whether to hold, buy or sell the company's shares.

The components of a company's annual report

An annual report, especially of a listed company, is now a very substantial document. The following are currently its main components:

- *Chairman's report.* This is given by listed companies and some other public interest entities, but not generally otherwise.
- *Operating and financial review (OFR).* This is recommended for listed and some other public interest companies by an Accounting Standards Board (ASB) statement of the same name. It is now becoming a statutory requirement for listed companies. See chapter 17.
- *Directors' remuneration report.* Certain disclosures relating to directors' remuneration are required by all companies, but in the case of listed companies these are more extensive and are presented as a separate report. See chapter 17.

- *Report on corporate governance*. This is required for listed companies, and, like the OFR and remuneration report, has been a growth area in recent years. See chapter 17.
- *Auditors' report*. This is an opinion from the auditor as required by the Companies Act. See chapter 5.
- *Directors' report*. This is a legal requirement, though the contents are somewhat arbitrary and not always interesting; hence the growth of the chairman's statement and OFR as channels of communication.
- *Performance statements*. For UK generally accepted accounting principles (GAAP) purposes, these comprise the profit and loss account and statement of total recognised gains and losses (STRGL). These are required by the CA 1985 and accounting standards respectively. The profit and loss account is the traditional way in which a company (or group) communicates its performance in the year. This extended in the 1990s to include the STRGL, which shows a more comprehensive picture of performance, including for example gains on revaluation of properties or other assets. For those reporting under international financial reporting standards (IFRS) (including listed groups), the profit and loss account is the principal statement; there is a broad equivalent of the STRGL but it is not quite so well established.
- *Balance sheet*. This sets out the company's assets and liabilities and its shareholders' funds. The balance sheet was traditionally seen as merely a collection of the assets and liabilities that were, so as to speak, left over at the end of the year following the matching of costs and revenues in the profit and loss account. More recently, the balance sheet has come to be seen as a more important statement in its own right. For example, stricter definitions of what should be treated as assets and liabilities, and the introduction of more fair valuing (see chapter 7) have increased the importance of the balance sheet.
- *Cash flow statement*. This is, almost literally, a statement of the cash receipts (inflows) and payments (outflows) during the year, categorised under various headings. It may thus correspond more closely to a non-accountant's view of performance than profit. See the next section for a comparison of the two.
- *Statement of accounting policies*. Even though much of accounting is specified, there is nonetheless scope in some areas for a company to select accounting policies. In this section of the annual report the company describes the accounting policies it has used in preparing its accounts.
- *Notes to the accounts*. Many pages of notes are presented in accordance with company law and accounting standards. In general the notes amplify what is in the profit and loss account and STRGL, the balance sheet and the cash flow statement. In addition there are notes dealing with matters such as related party transactions.

The meaning of accounting terms

A glossary of terms may be found at p. x. In this section, we discuss a single set of related terms – profit and cash flow.

A question not infrequently asked by non-accountants is what exactly *profit* means and how it differs from *cash flow*. Both are measures of what has happened to a business during a year, but they shed different light on its activities. Cash flow is a natural idea, familiar to us all as individuals. By contrast, profit is an artificial construct. Profit arises from the use of *accruals accounting*, that is, recognising transactions in the period in which they occur, rather than in the period in which the cash is received or paid; it thereby measures the performance of a business. A simple example will illustrate the point.

P Limited:

- Sells goods to customers during 2003 of invoiced value £100. Of this, P receives £50 in cash during the year (the remaining £50 is received in the following year).
- Buys goods from suppliers during 2003 of invoiced value £60. P buys on extended credit and pays nothing in 2003.
- Spends £40 cash on buying office equipment.

P Limited's cash flow statement will show the figures indicated in Box 1.1.

Cash flow statement	
Operating inflows	
Receipts from customers	50
Capital expenditure	(40)
Increase in cash during the year	10

Box 1.1

The company's profit and loss account shows an entirely different picture (see Box 1.2).

Profit and loss account	
Sales	100
Cost of sales	(60)
Depreciation of equipment	(4)
Profit before tax*	36
*Tax is ignored in this simple example	

Box 1.2

The two results happen to be quite different in amount (though in other examples they might be similar) and are quite different in principle. The profit and loss account focuses on the transactions that relate to the year in question. So, it focuses on the sales that have been made in the year (£100), and on the cost of those sales (£60), without reference to whether these amounts have been collected or paid for in cash. Also, the purchase of office equipment is for use in the business over an extended period; it is not held for resale. Hence it is described as capital expenditure and the cost is spread in accounting terms over its useful economic life, in this case assumed to be ten years.

If we assume that P Limited is a new business that started the year by issuing 100 £1 shares at par for cash, we can see that at the end of the year it will have cash of £110 (opening cash of £100 plus increase in cash during the year of £10). But, as shown in Box 1.3, its closing balance sheet will reflect all the assets and liabilities of the business:

Balance sheet	
Fixed assets (cost £40 less depreciation £4)	36
Debtors (sales made, cash not yet collected)	50
Cash	110
Less: creditors (amounts owing to suppliers)	(60)
Net assets	136

Box 1.3

These net assets are equivalent to shareholders' funds, as shown in Box 1.4.

Opening shareholders' funds	100
Profit for the year (retained)	36
Closing shareholders' funds	136

Box 1.4

This simple example illustrates a number of points. First, it shows that:

$$\text{Assets } less \text{ liabilities} = \text{Shareholders' funds}$$

This simple equation demonstrates that shareholders' funds (136 in this example) is the residual interest after all liabilities (60) are deducted from all assets $(36 + 50 + 110 = 196)$.

The second point is that the profit and loss account and the balance sheet articulate with each other. They are both prepared on an accruals basis. Third, the profit and loss account and balance sheet show a much richer set of information than the cash flow statement. This is not to say that the cash flow statement is of little or no value. Indeed it is important that a business generates cash, otherwise it will run into difficulty; hence cash flow information is useful in its own right. It is also useful as a cross check on the quality of profits (or earnings).

The example also allows us to view profit in an economic way. Profit can be viewed as the amount that a proprietor can withdraw from a business at the end of a year, such that the business can continue in the following year. We can see from the examples in Boxes 1.2 and 1.4 that the shareholders could have withdrawn the £36 profit and the business would (leaving aside complications such as inflation) have maintained its capital and been able to continue. The £10 increase in cash in the year is not a helpful indicator in these respects.

Of course, merely to speak of 'profit' is an oversimplification. A typical company's profit and loss account may include the figures shown in Box 1.5.

Sales	100
Cost of sales	(60)
Gross profit	40
Admin expenses	15
Operating profit	25
Interest payable	7
Profit before tax	18
Tax	(5)
Profit after tax	13

Box 1.5

The relatively simple profit and loss account in Box 1.5 uses four variants of the term 'profit'. Whilst they are self-explanatory, it demonstrates the need for clarity in terminology.

The use of accounting terms in legal agreements

The above example of four variants of profit illustrates an important point for lawyers. A legal agreement that refers to profit should be as specific as possible as to which profit figure is envisaged. This is not just a matter of being clear as to which of the above four figures is being used. It also needs to be clear:

- Which year's profits are intended.
- Which GAAP is intended (UK GAAP, IFRS etc. – see chapter 2).
- Whether the profit is as per the statutory accounts or whether it is adjusted in some way.
- According to which accounting policies the profit is calculated – for example, the bidder's policies or the target's policies.

Hence a reference to profit calculated according to GAAP is not helpful and can be the source of difficulty, not to say litigation.

Similarly, other terms may be used in various legal agreements, and the same general principle applies. Further examples of imprecision are the terms 'gearing' and 'interest cover' which are often used in loan covenants. This is discussed in more detail in chapter 18.

What is GAAP?

As mentioned above, GAAP refers to generally accepted accounting principles. There are different GAAPs in different jurisdictions, e.g. UK GAAP, US GAAP, French GAAP and so on. There are also international accounting standards (IASs) or international financial reporting standards (IFRSs), also sometimes called international GAAP. These aspects are discussed in chapter 2.

Although it has no precise meaning, UK GAAP is generally taken to refer to:

- Parts of company law, primarily the Companies Act 1985.
- Accounting standards (statements of standard accounting practice (SSAPs) and financial reporting standards (FRSs)).
- Abstracts from the Urgent Issues Task Force (UITF).
- For listed companies, the Listing Rules.

These are the core, compulsory components of GAAP. Each of them is now discussed in turn.

Company law. This is the foundation of accounts preparation and GAAP. The CA 1985 sets out the basic requirement for a company to prepare accounts, lay them before the members, and file them at Companies House. The Act also sets out some of the details regarding their preparation, for example, requirements as to what is a subsidiary undertaking and what should therefore be consolidated; basic accounting principles and measurement rules; formats for the balance sheet and profit and loss account; some disclosure requirements. Much of the detail is found in Schedule 4 (entity accounts) and Schedule 4A (group accounts) and this originates from the EU fourth and seventh company law directives respectively (Council Directive 78/660/EEC on the annual accounts of certain types of companies, OJ 1978 No. L222/11 and Council Directive 83/349/EEC on consolidated accounts, OJ 1983 No. L193/1).

Accounting standards. The current accounting standards in the UK are FRSs and these are produced by the ASB. The predecessor body until 1990 was the Accounting Standards Committee (ASC) which produced SSAPs, some of which are extant. Many accounting standards build on the foundations of company law. For example, FRSs 2, 6 and 7 provide further detail about how to prepare consolidated accounts. SSAP 25 deals with segmental disclosures, and adds to the basic requirements of the Act in this area. On the other hand, some subjects are not dealt with in company law at all. Examples are earnings

9

per share (FRS 22) and deferred tax accounting (FRS 19). A full list of extant accounting standards may be found in appendix 1.

UITF Abstracts. These are produced by the UITF, which is a committee of the ASB. The UITF's role is to assist the ASB in areas where an accounting standard or Companies Act provision exists, but where unsatisfactory or conflicting interpretations have developed or seem likely to develop. Hence it deals with relatively narrow issues. Examples are Abstracts on website development costs, operating lease incentives, start-up costs, pre-contract costs and certain barter transactions. Perhaps the most important Abstracts in practice are those dealing with various aspects of employee share schemes.

The Listing Rules. These rules, insofar as they deal with accounting matters, are part of GAAP only for listed companies. In terms of regular reporting (as opposed, for example, to new listings) there are continuing obligations relating to disclosures that are additional to those in the law and accounting standards; examples are directors' interests and corporate governance issues. The Listing Rules also set out the basic requirement for interim reports and preliminary announcements, to which the ASB adds non-mandatory guidance.

In addition to the above, the term 'GAAP' is sometimes used in a less formal sense to include:

- Guidance from various bodies, e.g. guidance statements from the ASB on Interim reporting, Preliminary announcements, and on the Operating and financial review; Statements of Recommended Practice (SORPs) from the ASB; and the guidance from the Institutes of Chartered Accountants on matters such as realised profits.
- Manuals and similar guidance from firms of accountants.
- Quite literally, principles that are generally accepted in practice, say in a particular industry.

Two other sources also inform the application of GAAP. One is the ASB's Statement of principles. This document is not an accounting standard as such, but is the framework that guides the ASB in its setting of standards on individual subjects. It is also useful to preparers and auditors of accounts as a guide in those areas where no specific rules are set down. Secondly, it is sometimes appropriate to look to other GAAPs where UK GAAP is silent. US GAAP is more detailed and is sometimes used as a guide to practice. Increasingly IFRSs are used in this way.

Selecting and disclosing accounting policies

It is implicit in the definition of GAAP that there will sometimes be more than one acceptable method of treating a transaction or event in a set of financial statements. Sometimes, different treatments arise in practice in areas that are unregulated by formal GAAP. Some companies are more aggressive than others in terms of recognising revenue from transactions, or in terms of carrying forward costs. However, in practice the scope to take different judgements lies in a fairly narrow band: the basic legal requirement that accounts should give 'a true and fair view' guides directors to select policies that achieve this outcome. Moreover, FRS 18 'Accounting policies' requires that, where there is a choice of policies, companies should 'select whichever of those accounting policies is judged by the entity to be most appropriate to its particular circumstances for the purpose of giving a true and fair view'.

Sometimes there are choices within an accounting standard. For example, FRS 15 on tangible fixed assets allows companies to measure assets at cost or on a valuation basis (in each case, subject to depreciation). The same standard allows a company that incurs finance cost (e.g. interest cost) in the period of construction of an asset either to write it off as an expense when incurred, or to capitalise it, that is, add it to the carrying value in the balance sheet of the asset under construction.

Partly because there are choices of policies, and partly for clarity for the reader even where there is no choice, companies are required by FRS 18 to disclose 'a description of each of the accounting policies that is material in the context of the entity's financial statements' (para. 55).

2

UK GAAP and international harmonisation

The UK Accounting Standards Board

For the first hundred years or more of the accountancy profession in the UK, there was a basic company law framework, and a body of practice, but no codification or standardisation of accounting rules. Business was relatively simple and accountants used their judgement. Increasingly, however, business was becoming more complex and it was becoming apparent that the lack of a standardised approach led to different profit figures being reported for what were essentially the same economic events. Although the US had pioneered standard-setting from 1939, the first development in this area in the UK was that the Institute of Chartered Accountants in England and Wales (ICAEW) developed 'Recommendations' to members as to suitable accounting principles. These had no binding force. Soon, it became clear that these were inadequate. Hence in 1970 the ASC was formed, as a joint activity of the six professional accounting bodies in the UK and Ireland.

The ASC developed SSAPs in the period 1970 to 1990. Some of these are still in force today. They did not have the force of law, though the Institutes said that they expected their members to comply with them. This system worked for some years as regards the majority of standards that were uncontroversial, though its weakness started to be seen from the early 1980s in relation to the attempted imposition upon the profession and companies of various systems of adjusting financial statements for the effects of inflation, including SSAP 16 'Current cost accounting'. This standard eventually had to be withdrawn.

The inflation accounting debacle showed that a reform of standard-setting was needed. Following the report of the Dearing Committee ('The making of accounting standards', Report of the Review Committee (London: Institute of Chartered Accountants in England and Wales, 1988)) a new structure was put in place from 1990. This is shown in Figure 2.1.

The Financial Reporting Council (FRC) oversees the structure and adds support from business, the profession, other regulators and government. The Accounting Standards Board is the principal standard-setter. The UITF is a committee of the ASB, which develops Abstracts; these are rulings that form part of UK GAAP but which deal with narrower issues than are the subject of accounting standards. The Financial Reporting Review Panel (FRRP) enforces compliance with standards and relevant parts of company law; this is discussed

12

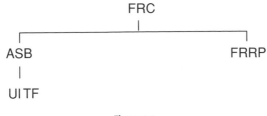

Figure 2.1

more fully in chapter 5. All these bodies were newly created in 1990; the ASB took over the work of the ASC, but the other three bodies were completely new. In 2004, the FRC took over responsibility for the Auditing Practices Board and various other bodies concerned with the supervision of the accountancy profession. The new structure that covers this wider range of activities is discussed in chapter 5.

A number of features distinguish the ASB from its predecessor, the ASC. One is more resources, including a full-time chairman and technical director, and a larger technical staff. Another was the new structure, including for the first time an enforcement arm. Perhaps less obvious, but equally important, is the fact that the ASB developed, and uses, an underlying framework of accounting. The ASB calls its framework a 'Statement of principles'. This is equivalent to the US 'Conceptual framework' and that of the International Accounting Standards Board (IASB): 'Framework for the preparation and presentation of financial statements'. These various frameworks underpin individual accounting standards with, for example, definitions of terms such as 'asset', 'liability', 'income' and 'expense' (see the Glossary of terms at p. x). Use of a framework does not make all accounting questions easy, but it does help considerably, not least in making accounting standards consistent with each other. The lack of a framework was one of the ASC's problems.

The ASB established itself during the 1990s as a successful standard-setter and made many important reforms to UK accounting in that period. These include: better information about cash flows; better presentation of performance; more rigorous treatment of acquisitions and goodwill; stricter rules on provisions; reform of off balance sheet finance; and disclosures about financial instruments. The ASB's standards are called financial reporting standards (i.e. FRSs), to contrast them with the SSAPs developed by its predecessor. These various reforms – many of which are discussed more fully in Part II of this book – did a lot to re-establish the reputation of UK GAAP during the 1990s. A full listing of UK standards may be found in appendix 1.

During the period 1990 to 2000, the ASB issued nineteen FRSs. In 2001, 2002 and 2003, no further FRSs were issued. This pause reflects a major change in the dynamics of standard-setting and a major shift in the centre of gravity to the newly-formed IASB (see under the heading 'The International Accounting

13

Standards Board', below). The ASB's role is now one of liaising with the IASB, contributing UK ideas to the debate about international harmonisation, and implementing the IASB's output in the UK. The ASB is still, nationally and internationally, an important body but its function has changed considerably. The standards published in 2004, starting with FRS 20 on share-based payment, are essentially international standards being brought gradually into UK GAAP. More international standards are likely to be brought into UK GAAP over the next two to four years. As a result, there will, by the end of the decade if not before, be little or no difference between UK standards and IFRS.

The ASB is also involved in the development of SORPs. These do not have the same status as accounting standards, and are generally prepared by specific industry groups in conjunction with the ASB. The principal industries for which SORPs have been developed are: banking, insurance, oil and gas, investment trusts, leasing, charities, pension schemes and various other public sector bodies.

International harmonisation

Systems of generally accepted accounting principles (GAAP) developed over the years in various countries. While they were similar in that they were based around the use of accruals accounting, the profit and loss account and the balance sheet, they were in many respects different from each other. There were various reasons for these differences. In some countries, the stock market was relatively important as a source of finance; hence the emphasis was on performance measurement in an economic sense. In other countries, more finance came from the banking system, and so there was more emphasis on prudence. In yet other countries the influence came from the tax system.

The existence of different national GAAPs mattered relatively little until gradually business started to become more international in its nature. In the late 1960s and the early 1970s the need for harmonisation was increasingly seen and, in 1973, the International Accounting Standards Committee (IASC) was formed. It started to develop IASs and over the twenty-seven years of its existence it became more and more important and influential.

Initially, the IASC's role was seen in relation to developing economies; for example, the World Bank often required the use of IAS by any organisation to whom it was lending. Also, it made sense for smaller, emerging economies to use IAS rather than invest in the development of their own system. Increasingly, however, the role and use of IAS changed so that, certainly by the 1990s, the principal use of IAS was in relation to the international capital markets. That is, if a company based in, say, Switzerland or Germany wanted to raise debt or equity capital outside its own country, it would be to its advantage to use IASs rather than local GAAP, as there was more chance that investors and lenders would understand the information.

As business has become more global, and as the capital markets have opened their doors to foreign companies, so the need for international harmonisation has strengthened. The fact that, say, US GAAP, UK GAAP and French GAAP report different figures for profits and net assets is now seen as, at least, a serious impediment to business and finance, and, further, it is seen as a source of some embarrassment to accountants that they cannot agree on a global basis whether – given the same set of economic facts – a company's profits are £X or £Y.

The International Accounting Standards Board

By the late 1990s it was becoming clear that the IASC, successful though it had been, was not up to the future task of leading the harmonising of accounting globally. A structural change was needed. A new International Accounting Standards Board (IASB) was formed with effect from 1 January 2001. This is an altogether more professional organisation, with a mostly full-time board, chaired by Sir David Tweedie, who had chaired the UK ASB during the 1990s. It is both a heavyweight body in its own right and is seen as a counterweight to the US Financial Accounting Standards Board (FASB). The current structure is shown in Figure 2.2.

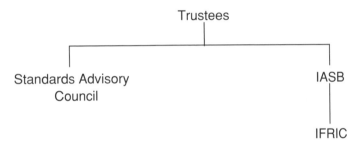

Figure 2.2

The trustees' role is to appoint the board members, raise funds, set overall strategy (but not interfere in the board's resolution of technical matters) and generally to add their weight to the board's work. The International Financial Reporting Interpretations Committee (IFRIC) acts in a similar way to the UITF in the UK. There is also an advisory council which is drawn from a wide constituency and which advises the board on its agenda and gives feedback on its proposals. The board itself (IASB) is the most important body.

On being established in 2001, the new board first debated its agenda and work programme. A considerable amount of its work comprises continuing the projects of its predecessor, the IASC. This included improving many of the existing standards, for example, to eliminate options; and improving and revising the standards (IASs 32 and 39) on financial instruments. But a key change from the previous regime involves the IASB leading the development of new accounting rules, rather than seeking to harmonise the rules of the national standard-setters. Examples of this new approach are the work on share-based payment and on insurance contracts. These and other examples serve to characterise the IASB as a leader, or co-leader, rather than a follower in the international accounting scene.

As mentioned above, the IASC developed standards called international accounting standards (i.e. IASs); and the new IASB develops standards known as international financial reporting standards (i.e. IFRSs). At present, accountants and others tend to use 'IAS' and 'IFRS' interchangeably in referring to the total package of international standards, though 'IFRS' is gaining ground.

As in the UK, many of the IASs remain in force despite the new regime, though over time some will be replaced. It is noticeable that the IASB works in much more detail than the IASC. This is for a number of reasons. Partly – literally – there is a bigger staff and a full-time board, and longer documents will automatically result. Also, the IASB needs, politically, to be seen as a valid counterweight to the FASB. This means that, whether or not the eventual standard is long, the underlying debate needs to be exhaustive. Also, business is becoming gradually more complex. It is not possible to write a short standard on accounting for financial instruments and expect it to be effective. The same can be said for insurance.

As explained more fully in the next section, the EU requires all EU companies whose securities (shares, debt etc.) are traded on a regulated market in the EU to prepare their consolidated accounts under IFRS from 2005. The IASB said that, in order to help companies plan ahead, it would impose for 2005 reporting only those standards that have been published in final form by 31 March 2004. Any standard published after that date will not be mandatory until later dates. The standards published by 31 March 2004 are:

- IASs 1–41 (i.e. all the standards published by the IASC, except to the extent they have been withdrawn or replaced; including the effect of IASB improvements of some of these standards).
- IASs 32 and 39 – the two standards on financial instruments. These are part of the inherited standards, but are worthy of special reference in that (a) the IASB has made more significant changes to them and (b) there have been significant objections to them (to IAS 39 in particular) from the banking community, and certain changes made as a result.
- IFRS 1 – first-time adoption of international accounting standards. This standard tells companies how to convert from national GAAP to IFRS, and applies to all UK (and other EU) listed companies' group accounts for 2005.
- IFRS 2 – share-based payment. This standard introduced a charge to the profit and loss account for the fair value of share-based payment; this

applies in principle to a wide range of goods and services, but in particular to employee share awards, including share option awards.

- IFRS 3 – business combinations (phase I). This requires that all business combinations be regarded as acquisitions from an accounting point of view – that is, merger accounting (also called pooling of interests) is no longer available. It also changes the accounting for goodwill away from amortisation to a method of non-amortisation with annual reviews for impairment.
- IFRS 4 – insurance contracts (phase I). The IASB has in hand a major project that would make fundamental reforms to accounting by insurance companies. IFRS 4 is the first part of this project.
- IFRS 5 – non-current assets held for sale and discontinued operations. This introduced different ways of presenting and measuring such assets and operations.

For purposes of application from 2005 in the EU, there is the further hurdle of EU endorsement, as described below. This is a particular issue with regard to the standards on financial instruments.

The EU Regulation for harmonisation within Europe

International accounting standards have no authority of their own. The IASB is a global, but private sector, body that has no power to require its accounting standards to be followed. Nevertheless, various companies around the world have decided to adopt IFRS voluntarily, and various countries have decided to base their accounting on IFRS, in one of a number of ways. In some countries such as Australia the professional bodies have decided to base their national standards on IFRS – either literally, or with an element of local adaptation. In other countries, the governments have brought in, or are bringing in, legal requirements that IFRS should be used by companies, thereby giving them the status of local law. By far the most important example of this is the 2002 initiative by the EU to require EU companies whose securities are traded on a regulated market in the EU to use IAS for their group accounts.

The context of this is that the EU wishes, from a political and commercial perspective, its capital markets to be a serious rival to those of the US. The US capital markets are very successful for a number of reasons. They are large, homogeneous and very liquid. They are subject to strong regulation by the Securities and Exchange Commission (SEC) and other bodies. In contrast, the EU capital markets are more fragmented and not generally as liquid. Neither are they uniformly regulated. In order to improve their position, the EU has a Financial Services Action Plan, which seeks to harmonise and strengthen the EU capital markets in a variety of respects. One of these respects is the intro- duction of uniform financial reporting by EU listed companies. The rule may be found in Council Regulation 1606/2002/EC on the application of international accounting standards, OJ 2002 No. L243/1. As a Regulation, this is directly effective in Member State law, without the need for national legislation.

The Regulation requires all companies with securities traded on a regulated market in the EU (estimated to be about 7,000 companies, of which about 1,200 are UK companies) to prepare and publish their group accounts under IFRS from calendar year 2005 onwards. The UK companies affected are those traded on the main market, not those on the Alternative Investment Market (AIM), which ceased to be a 'regulated market' on 12 October 2004. It is likely that AIM companies will have to use IFRS by 2007. For other entities – that is, individual entities and unlisted groups – the Regulation gives Member States a choice to allow or require adoption of IFRS. The UK has decided to make the move to IFRS optional for these other entities. The move to IFRS is a very considerable upheaval for most of the companies involved. There are some countries, such as Germany (but not the UK), where it was already permissible for companies to report under IFRS, and a limited number of companies did so. But for all other companies, a large-scale conversion exercise is required. Some of the differences between UK GAAP and IFRS are referred to in Part II of this book but, for a comprehensive treatment of the similarities and differences, reference should be made to the detailed publications of the large accounting firms.

The change to IFRS reporting will work in the following way, using the example of a company with a December year end. That company publishes its 2004 accounts under UK GAAP in the normal way in early 2005. In early 2006, it will produce its 2005 accounts. The 2005 numbers will be presented on an IFRS basis, with no UK GAAP figures. However, as is normal, there will be comparative figures for 2004. The 2004 numbers will be presented on an IFRS basis, so that they are comparable to the 2005 numbers. However a reconciliation needs to be provided in the 2005 accounts between (a) the 2004 accounts on a UK GAAP basis and (b) the 2004 comparatives in the 2005 accounts, on an IFRS basis. This reconciliation will show the nature and extent of adjustments that have been made, in converting from one GAAP to the other, to (a) the 2004 profit number and (b) the net assets as at the beginning and end of 2004.

The position is in fact a little more complex than just indicated, as UK listed companies are required by the Listing Rules to publish an interim report. Hence, the first time that IFRS information needs to be published is in the June 2005 interim results. This includes reconciliations along the lines described above.

Examples of the kind of differences likely to be encountered in the conversion exercise and therefore to appear in the reconciliations are the accounting treatment of: pensions, share-based payment, deferred tax, financial instruments, foreign currency and development costs. The conversion process, including the reconciliations required, is set out by the IASB in IFRS 1 'First time adoption of International Financial Reporting Standards'.

The Regulation is structured so as to avoid handing over sovereignty to the IASB. That is, it requires EU companies to comply with IAS but only to the extent that it has been endorsed by the EU. To assist the Commission in this regard, an Accounting Regulatory Committee (ARC) has been set up, made up of political appointees from Member States. Because of the technical nature of the work, it is assisted by the European Financial Reporting Advisory Group (EFRAG), one of whose objectives is to influence the IASB during its development of a standard, so as to ensure that the end product will be acceptable within Europe. The intention of this endorsement mechanism was seen as a safeguard for the EU, but it was intended that standards developed by the IASB would be endorsed. The first batch of standards was indeed endorsed in 2003, except that the two standards (IAS 32 and IAS 39) on financial instruments were not considered. Much of 2004 has been taken up with protracted and difficult discussions among the IASB, the banks, the European Central Bank and the EU. The outcome is that the EU has endorsed IAS 32 and a version of IAS 39 in which certain paragraphs and sentences that are problematical to some banks or regulators have been deleted. This is known as the 'carve-out' version of IAS 39.

This is a very unsatisfactory outcome, as it results in 'Euro-IFRS' being, in some respects, different from full IFRS, as set out by the IASB, and as followed elsewhere in the world. Despite the Regulation, some UK listed companies would prefer to follow full IFRS, partly because that will be more acceptable in the US and elsewhere.

Convergence with US GAAP

The US standard-setter, the FASB, has been in operation since 1973, and together with the SEC and other bodies such as the Emerging Issues Task Force, is a very active regulator of accounting in the US. The FASB has had a full-time board and large staff since its formation and has written standards on many subjects, and has written them in great detail. In many areas, US GAAP is well researched and effective. But recent events such as Enron have shown that US GAAP has its drawbacks, in particular in the area on consolidations. Also, the fact that US standards are written in great detail, taken together with the legalistic US business environment, has led to an unfortunate approach of some companies and their advisers seeking to get round the small print – a 'where does it say I can't do that?' attitude – rather than an acceptance that one should follow the spirit and intention of the standards. On the other hand, some accountants like US GAAP because it is comprehensive and clearly states what should be done in specific circumstances.

The US authorities, especially the FASB, have been involved in the IASC and now the IASB for many years but, at the same time, continued to develop US GAAP with little reference to IAS developments. Once the new IASB was formed, it became all the more important to involve the FASB in a more active way. Put simply: the US is the world's largest capital market, and if international standards are in due course accepted and used everywhere except in the US, that will be only a limited success story. On the other hand, it is not realistic to expect the US at this stage to stop developing US standards, and to adopt IFRSs in place of US GAAP.

It was therefore an important event when in September 2002 the IASB and the FASB signed the 'Norwalk agreement' under which they 'each acknowledged their commitment to the development of high-quality, compatible accounting standards that could be used for both domestic and cross-border financial reporting'. At that meeting, both the FASB and IASB pledged to use their best efforts to (a) make their existing financial reporting standards fully compatible as soon as is practicable and (b) co-ordinate their future work programs to ensure that once achieved, compatibility is maintained.

The published output resulting from the Norwalk agreement has to date been modest, though much work is going on behind the scenes. At present, a UK company, preparing its main accounts under UK GAAP, and going for a listing in the US markets, has to prepare a UK–US GAAP reconciliation. The equivalent applies to a foreign registrant from, say, France. The key practical question for companies and their advisers is whether, and if so when, the joint work will result in US GAAP becoming the same as IFRS, such that foreign registrants going into the US markets reporting under IFRS would no longer have to prepare and publish a US GAAP reconciliation statement. It is not possible to answer this question with any accuracy. Certainly, as EU listed companies move onto IFRS for their group accounts in 2005, the US requirement for an IFRS/US GAAP reconciliation remains. However, it may be, as a result of the convergence exercise, that more individual items are harmonised, such that there are fewer reconciling items. And in the longer term, it is reasonable to expect either that the two GAAPs will have become the same, or that the differences will be minor such that the US regulators will accept IAS accounts from foreign registrants. When that point will be reached, however, is difficult to forecast.

Implications for the UK

Growing convergence

International standards are clearly important to the UK in that, from 2005, UK listed companies have to publish their group accounts under IFRS. But, in many respects, the importance of IFRS is greater than that. First, a number of companies, and possibly a great many, will opt into IFRS at the entity level.

Second, even if UK companies that are subsidiaries do not decide to opt into IFRS for their entity accounts, they will typically have to provide information (often called 'group returns') to their parent companies. Where these parent companies are listed in the EU, the group returns will need to be prepared under IFRS.

Third, even where companies remain under UK GAAP at the entity level, the differences between UK GAAP and IFRS are gradually dwindling, as a result of the policy of the UK ASB of harmonising its standards with those of the IASB.

By 2005 the ASB has not entirely harmonised its standards with IFRS, but harmonisation in all significant respects looks likely to have been achieved by about 2008, based on current ASB plans. A possible exception to this is that there may remain in UK GAAP separate rules on special industries, and exemptions for defined classes of small companies.

The DTI and entity accounts

As noted above, the UK has decided to make IFRS optional at the entity level. The Department of Trade and Industry (DTI) has legislated so that, within a group, it is not possible to 'cherry-pick' – that is to have some UK subsidiaries move to IFRS and others to stay with UK GAAP. Rather, all subsidiaries should either move to IFRS or stay with UK GAAP, although there is an exemption from this where there are 'good reasons'. The exception to this rule is that it will be possible for the parent entity to move to IFRS – to be in line with its own group accounts – yet for its UK subsidiaries to stay with UK GAAP.

Tax and distributable profits

Two further important considerations for companies are what the move to IFRS at the individual entity level will mean for tax purposes and for the purposes of calculating what profits are distributable.

HM Revenue and Customs have announced that, for tax purposes, it will accept accounts prepared under IFRS as a starting point. This is helpful: if it were not the case, companies would have to prepare UK GAAP accounts as the starting point for tax assessment and, if they adopted IFRS, IFRS accounts for Companies Act purposes. However, there are special rules in certain areas, and it is important for each company to consider in detail the effect of IFRS on its tax position. See chapter 10 for further details.

Similarly, it is important for each company, in deciding whether to move to IFRS, to consider what effect the move may have on its distributable profits. Some detailed applications of this are still being considered by the Institutes of Chartered Accountants, along with counsel's advice.

3

The legal framework for accounting

The Companies Act 1985

The CA 1985 deals with a wide range of matters, and other statutes impinge on companies in a variety of ways. Most of this is lawyers' territory and the purpose of this chapter, therefore, is restricted primarily to those aspects of the CA 1985 that relate to accounting.

Part VII of the CA 1985 deals with 'Accounts and audit' and further detail is found in various schedules to the CA 1985 of which the two that most concern us here are Schedule 4 'Form and content of company accounts' and Schedule 4A 'Form and content of group accounts'.

Much of the detail in those schedules emanates from the EU company law directives: Schedule 4 represents the UK implementation of the fourth directive of 1978 (Council Directive 78/660/EEC on the annual accounts of certain types of companies, OJ 1978 No. L222/11) and Schedule 4A represents the UK implementation of the seventh directive of 1983 (Council Directive 83/349/EEC on consolidated accounts, OJ 1983 No. L193/1). The implementation of these directives resulted not only in various changes but also in a much greater degree of legal prescription of accounting. The implementation of the directives also achieved a degree of harmonisation of the accounting aspects of company law across the EU. Examples of this can be seen in the formats, valuation rules and disclosures in Schedule 4. Despite this, there is still a considerable variety of practice, either because the directives do not deal with all issues or because, even when they deal with an issue, they contain choices or Member State options; for example, there are four possible formats for the presentation of the profit and loss account.

Box 3.1 shows the matters with which Part VII of the Act deals.

The remainder of this chapter concentrates on a limited number of the above provisions, selected according to their importance in practice and the extent to which they may be relatively less familiar to lawyers.

Application of the Companies Act to UK GAAP companies and to IFRS companies

It is important to note that the Act applies in a different way according to whether a company is remaining with UK GAAP or moving to IFRS. A company's

---

Companies Act 1985, Part VII – Accounts and audit

Chapter I – Provisions applying to companies generally

Accounting records (ss. 221–2)
A company's financial year and accounting reference periods (ss. 223–5)
Annual accounts (ss. 226–32)
Approval and signing of accounts (s. 233)
Directors' report and directors' remuneration report (ss. 234–234C)
Auditors' report (ss. 235–7)
Publication of accounts and reports (ss. 238–40)
Laying and delivering of accounts and reports (ss. 241–4)
Revision of defective accounts and reports (ss. 245–245C)

Chapter II – Exemptions, exceptions and special provisions

Small and medium-sized companies and groups (ss. 246–9)
Exemptions from audit for certain categories of small company
  (ss. 249A–249E)
Listed public companies: summary financial statements (s. 251)
Private companies (ss. 252–3)
Unlimited companies (s. 254)
Banking and insurance companies and groups (ss. 255–255D)

Chapter III – Supplementary provisions

Accounting standards (UK GAAP) (s. 256)
Power to alter UK accounting requirements (s. 257)
Parents and subsidiary undertakings (s. 258)
Other interpretation provisions (ss. 259–262A)

Principal related Schedules
Schedule 4 – Form and content of company accounts
Schedule 4A – Form and content of group accounts
Schedule 8 – Form and content of accounts prepared by small companies
Schedule 9 – Special provisions for banking companies and groups
Schedule 9A – Form and content of accounts of insurance companies and
  groups

Box 3.1

---

accounting might be moving to IFRS either as a mandatory change for the consolidated accounts of a listed company, or as a voluntary move in the case of an entity or an unlisted group. In both of those cases, the company becomes subject to the EU Council Regulation 1606/2002/EC (OJ 2002 No. 243/1) and as a consequence follows IFRS instead of following the detailed accounting rules of the Act. That is, while the basic requirements of the sections in Part VII of the Act (as set out in Box 3.1) continue to apply, the detailed accounting requirements of Schedules 4, 4A, 9 and 9A are disapplied for companies following the Regulation. These changes were brought in by the Companies Act 1985 (International Accounting Standards and Other Accounting Amendments) Regulations 2004 (SI. 2004 No. 2947), which brought in changes to various sections of the Act to accommodate the move to IFRS. Perhaps the most important are the changes to sections 226 and 227, as discussed in detail below.

Accounting provisions of the Act – Part VII

Annual accounts and the true and fair view

Sections 226, 226A and 226B set out the fundamental requirement for directors, and are of such importance that they are quoted here in full:

'226 DUTY TO PREPARE INDIVIDUAL ACCOUNTS

(1) The directors of every company shall prepare accounts for the company for each of its financial years.

Those accounts are referred to in this Part as the company's "individual accounts".

(2) A company's individual accounts may be prepared—

    (a) in accordance with section 226A ("Companies Act individual accounts"), or

    (b) in accordance with international accounting standards ("IAS individual accounts").

This subsection is subject to the following provisions of this section and section 227C (consistency of accounts).

(3) The individual accounts of a company that is a charity must be Companies Act individual accounts.

(4) After the first financial year in which the directors of a company prepare IAS individual accounts ("the first IAS year"), all subsequent individual accounts of the company must be prepared in accordance with international accounting standards unless there is a relevant change of circumstance.

(5) There is a relevant change of circumstance if, at any time during or after the first IAS year—

    (a) the company becomes a subsidiary undertaking of another undertaking that does not prepare IAS individual accounts,

    (b) the company ceases to be a company with securities admitted to trading on a regulated market, or

    (c) a parent undertaking of the company ceases to be an undertaking with securities admitted to trading on a regulated market.

In this subsection "regulated market" has the same meaning as it has in Council Directive 93/22/EEC on investment services in the securities field.

(6) If, having changed to preparing Companies Act individual accounts following a relevant change of circumstance, the directors again prepare IAS individual accounts for the company, subsections (4) and (5) apply again as if the first financial year for which such accounts are again prepared were the first IAS year.

226A COMPANIES ACT INDIVIDUAL ACCOUNTS

(1) Companies Act individual accounts must comprise—
    (a) a balance sheet as at the last day of the financial year, and
    (b) a profit and loss account.

(2) The balance sheet must give a true and fair view of the state of affairs of the company as at the end of the financial year; and the profit and loss account must give a true and fair view of the profit or loss of the company for the financial year.

(3) Companies Act individual accounts must comply with the provisions of Schedule 4 as to the form and content of the balance sheet and profit and loss account and additional information to be provided by way of notes to the accounts.

(4) Where compliance with the provisions of that Schedule, and the other provisions of this Act as to the matters to be included in a company's individual accounts or in notes to those accounts, would not be sufficient to give a true and fair view, the necessary additional information must be given in the accounts or in a note to them.

(5) If in special circumstances compliance with any of those provisions is inconsistent with the requirement to give a true and fair view, the directors must depart from that provision to the extent necessary to give a true and fair view.

(6) Particulars of any such departure, the reasons for it and its effect must be given in a note to the accounts.

226B IAS INDIVIDUAL ACCOUNTS

Where the directors of a company prepare IAS individual accounts, they must state in the notes to those accounts that the accounts have been prepared in accordance with international accounting standards.'

A number of key points arise from these important sections. First, the context of this section is what section 226(1) calls the 'individual accounts'. These are also sometimes called 'entity accounts' or 'solus accounts'. In each case the contrast is with group accounts (dealt with in section 227).

Second, section 226(2) sets out the basic choice for 2005 onwards: a company may either prepare what the Act calls 'Companies Act individual accounts' (meaning accounts that comply with UK GAAP including Schedule 4) or 'IAS individual accounts'. Subsections (4), (5) and (6) provide that a move to IFRS is a one-way move, but there are exceptions.

Third, section 226A deals with the detail for those companies that are staying with UK GAAP. While it cross refers to Schedule 4, where further detailed requirements are added, it refers in section 226A(1) to the two primary financial statements – the balance sheet and the profit and loss account. That is, the law does not require a cash flow statement or a statement of total recognised gains and losses. These, although they are also primary statements, are required only by accounting standards.

Fourth, and most importantly, section 226A sets out the requirement that UK GAAP accounts shall give 'a true and fair view'. Note that the law requires *a* true and fair view – not *the* true and fair view. This is taken to mean that there is potentially more than one way in which a true and fair view may be given. For example, a company might choose format 1 or format 2 for its profit and loss account. It might choose under accounting standards to keep its assets at cost, or to revalue them. This true and fair view requirement is overriding – it is the key objective of annual accounts. Section 226A(3) is the cross-reference to Schedule 4, which contains the detailed requirements as to form and content of accounts, including note disclosures. But subsection (4) adds that where compliance with the detailed rules is *not sufficient* to give a true and fair view, further disclosure should be given. Hence, it may be that there is something unusual but important relating to a company, but there is nothing in Schedule 4 or elsewhere that requires its disclosure; yet the directors (or the auditors) believe that without additional information about it, the accounts would not give a true and fair view. Often, then, provision of this additional information will result in a true and fair view being given and that is the end of the matter.

However, there are some cases where, no matter what additional disclosure is given, the accounts would still not give a true and fair view. Indeed there is a general principle of accounting that 'disclosure of information in the notes to the financial statements is not a substitute for recognition and does not correct or justify any misrepresentation or omission in the primary financial statements' (ASB Statement of principles, chapter 7). A good example is off balance sheet finance. As discussed more fully in chapter 4, before the introduction of FRS 5, there was a practice of excluding some debt from the balance sheet but giving disclosure about it in the notes to the accounts. This was regarded as poor practice at the time and is not now regarded as acceptable. In this context, subsection (5) adds that where compliance with a detailed rule is *inconsistent* with the requirement to give a true and fair view, the directors shall depart from that rule to the extent necessary to give a true and fair view.

Subsection (6) is also important. This requires that, when the override is used, 'particulars of any such departure, the reasons for it and its effect shall be given in a note to the accounts'. It is necessary for any use of the departure to be flagged so that a reader can be aware that – albeit for good reason – something unusual or non-standard has been done. In order that a reader can compare the financial statements of different companies, it is important that there is explanation, including quantification, of the effect. FRS 18 also specifies disclosures that must be given when the true and fair override is invoked.

Subsections (4) and (5) are not used frequently but are very important to accountants. They – subsection (5) in particular – make the philosophical point that the overriding objective is to give a true and fair view. Compliance with the detailed rules is important, and in nearly all cases it will result in a true and fair view being given. But in that rare case, where this does not hold, the law is clear: if there is insufficient information, give more; and if despite that, the accounts do not give a true and fair view, depart from the detailed rules to the extent necessary. It is a very powerful concept.

Companies that follow IFRS have to apply section 226B instead. There is only one requirement in law, namely to state that IFRS is the basis of preparation. We may note that the above discussion of giving a true and fair view, and the true and fair override, were in the context of companies preparing UK GAAP accounts. IFRS uses the expression 'present fairly'. However, the two expressions are generally taken to have the same meaning, and this is confirmed by the IASB's Framework (the 'Framework for the preparation and presentation of financial statements', para. 47).

Section 227 sets out equivalent requirements relating to group accounts. Directors shall prepare consolidated accounts if, at the end of the year, the company is a parent company. Subsection (1) specifies that 'those accounts [i.e. the consolidated accounts] are referred to in this Part as the company's "group accounts"'. The terms 'group accounts' and 'consolidated accounts' are sometimes used interchangeably. Strictly, 'group accounts' is a looser term, and can mean any form of aggregation of information relating to a group of companies. Consolidated accounts, which is the form required by law and accounting standards, means a specific technique of preparing a set of financial statements for the group as if it were a single entity, by aggregating all subsidiaries and, for example, eliminating intra-group transactions.

Section 227A, which applies to group accounts prepared in accordance with UK GAAP, is equivalent to section 226A except that the cross-reference to the detailed requirements is to Schedule 4A. That is, the requirement to give a true and fair view, and the override, work in the same way in relation to consolidated accounts as they do in relation to individual accounts.

In relation to group accounts prepared in accordance with IFRS, section 227B mirrors section 226B – see above.

There are additional requirements in section 227C relating to consistency of accounting within a group. Briefly, the objective is that, within a group, all UK entities follow the same GAAP, either UK or IFRS, but there is an exception, for which see the heading 'The DTI and entity accounts' in chapter 2 at p. 21.

Approval, distribution and filing of accounts

Financial statements, once prepared, should be approved and signed by the directors (section 233), audited and the audit report signed by the auditors (sections 235, 236). The annual report and accounts should then be laid before the company in general meeting (section 241) and delivered to the Registrar of Companies (section 242). Further details are set out in the indicated sections of the Act, and further comments about the role of auditors may be found in chapter 5 at p. 61.

There are provisions in the Act for the revision of defective accounts and reports (sections 245–245C). These provisions are discussed in chapter 5 at p. 59 under the heading, 'The Financial Reporting Review Panel'.

Exemptions, exceptions and special provisions

Chapter II of Part VII of the Act contains various exemptions, exceptions and special provisions. These are not discussed in detail in this book. However, the principal categories of exemptions are:

- Relief from certain disclosures for medium-sized companies, and greater relief for small companies.
- Relief from the need to prepare group accounts for groups below a certain size.
- Relief from the need for an audit for companies below a certain size.

The law relating to exemptions and exceptions is very complex. For example, the level of exemption available for accounts for shareholders is different from that for accounts for filing. Full details are discussed in chapter 43 of the Price-waterhouseCoopers LLP, *Manual of accounting – UK GAAP* (Kingston upon Thames: CCH, 2005).

We may note also that certain accounting standards give exemptions for companies below a certain size. In addition, the ASB has developed a Financial Reporting Standard for Smaller Entities (FRSSE). This is designed to provide small companies with a single reporting standard that is focused on their circumstances. That is, companies using the FRSSE need not generally comply with other accounting standards and UITF Abstracts. The FRSSE, however, contains essentially the same requirements as accounting standards as regards recognition and measurement, although they are expressed in simpler terms. As to disclosure matters, some of those set out in the other accounting standards are omitted.

Chapter II also contains special provisions relating to banking and insurance companies and groups. The accounts of companies and groups in these categories are required to give a true and fair view, just as with the accounts of other companies. However, the detailed requirements are different. The detailed rules for the accounts of banks are set out in Schedule 9, and those for insurance companies are set out in Schedule 9A, instead of Schedules 4 and 4A for other companies. In particular, the formats for the profit and loss account and balance sheet of banks and insurance companies are different from each other and from the formats of other companies. There are differences also in the measurement rules and the required disclosures. These different rules for banks and insurance companies result from their being the subject of different EU Directives – the bank accounts directive (Council Directive 86/635/EEC on the annual accounts and consolidated accounts of banks and other financial institutions, OJ 1986 No. L372/1), and the insurance accounts directive (Council Directive 91/674/EEC on the annual accounts and consolidated accounts of insurance undertakings, OJ 1991 No. L374/7), are the harmonising directives equivalent to the fourth and seventh directives (Council Directives 78/660/EEC and 83/349/EEC, respectively) for other companies.

Accounting provisions of the Act – Schedule 4

As noted above, Schedule 4 applies only to companies that follow UK GAAP. It does not apply to those that follow IFRS.

Part I – General rules and formats

Following the EU fourth directive (Directive 78/660/EEC), UK law contains two different balance sheet formats and four possible formats for the profit and loss account. The reason for this choice is rooted in compromises necessary within the EU. In practice, in the UK, most companies use format 1 for the balance sheet (see Box 3.2); in the case of the profit and loss account, most companies use format 1 though a minority uses format 2. The others are used rarely, if at all, in the UK, but are used in other EU countries.

Section A of Part I sets out some preliminary rules relating to the formats. For example, an item can be shown in more detail than the format requires (para. 3(1)). Also there is scope for the directors to adapt the arrangement and headings for some of the items but only where the special nature of the company's business requires such adaptation (para. 3(3)). All items shall be shown if there is an amount in either the current or previous year, but not otherwise (paras. 3(5), 4(3)). There is also an important rule under which 'items representing assets or income may not be set off against amounts in respect of items representing liabilities or expenditure (as the case may be), or vice versa' (para. 5). This point is also addressed by FRS 5 'Reporting the substance of transactions', which views the point in the context of stopping companies from hiding liabilities by netting them against assets.

Balance sheet format 1 is the more common in the UK. It involves showing current liabilities separately from longer-term liabilities. Thereby, a company shows the net current assets (current assets, less current liabilities) which is a useful indicator of liquidity. The balance sheet formats in the Act look very long and complex. Format 1 is reproduced in Box 3.2.

Balance sheet formats – Companies Act 1985, Schedule 4, Part 1, Section B, format 1

A. Called up share capital not paid . . .

B. Fixed assets

   I Intangible assets

     1. Development costs

     2. Concessions, patents, licences, trade marks and similar rights and assets . . .

     3. Goodwill . . .

     4. Payments on account

   II Tangible assets

     1. Land and buildings

     2. Plant and machinery

     3. Fixtures, fittings, tools and equipment

     4. Payments on account and assets in course of construction

   III Investments

     1. Shares in group undertakings

     2. Loans to group undertakings

     3. Participating interests

     4. Loans to undertakings in which the company has a participating interest

     5. Other investments other than loans

     6. Other loans

     7. Own shares . . .

C. Current assets

   I Stocks

     1. Raw materials and consumables

     2. Work in progress

     3. Finished goods and goods for resale

     4. Payments on account

   II Debtors . . .

     1. Trade debtors

     2. Amounts owed by group undertakings

     3. Amounts owed by undertakings in which the company has a participating interest

     4. Other debtors

     5. Called up share capital not paid . . .

     6. Prepayments and accrued income . . .

   III Investments

     1. Shares in group undertakings

     2. Own shares . . .

     3. Other investments

   IV Cash at bank and in hand

D. Prepayments and accrued income . . .

E. Creditors: amounts falling due within one year
  1. Debenture loans . . .
  2. Bank loans and overdrafts
  3. Payments received on account . . .
  4. Trade creditors
  5. Bills of exchange payable
  6. Amounts owed to group undertakings
  7. Amounts owed to undertakings in which the company has a participating interest
  8. Other creditors including taxation and social security . . .
  9. Accruals and deferred income . . .

F. Net current assets (liabilities) . . .

G. Total assets less current liabilities

H. Creditors: amounts falling due after more than one year
  1. Debenture loans . . .
  2. Bank loans and overdrafts
  3. Payments received on account . . .
  4. Trade creditors
  5. Bills of exchange payable
  6. Amounts owed to group undertakings
  7. Amounts owed to undertakings in which the company has a participating interest
  8. Other creditors including taxation and social security . . .
  9. Accruals and deferred income . . .

I. Provisions for liabilities
  1. Pensions and similar obligations
  2. Taxation, including deferred taxation
  3. Other provisions

J. Accruals and deferred income . . .

K. Capital and reserves
  I Called up share capital . . .
  II Share premium account
  III Revaluation reserve
  IV Other reserves
    1. Capital redemption reserve
    2. Reserve for own shares
    3. Reserves provided for by the articles of association
    4. Other reserves
  V Profit and loss account

Box 3.2

In practice most companies do not have all the assets and liabilities that the formats, in seeking to be comprehensive, envisage. So, these lines do not have to be shown. Moreover, those items labelled with an Arabic number can be relegated to the notes to the accounts. Hence, a typical balance sheet may include, to take the example of fixed assets, only the items in Box 3.3.

Fixed assets:
    Intangible assets   W
    Tangible assets   X
    Investments $\underline{Y}$
                            Z

Box 3.3

The notes to the accounts then include the analysis of (say) tangible assets into land and buildings, plant and machinery and so on.

Two points may be noted in relation to the balance sheet formats:

- The lines of the format specify where an item should be shown if it is on the balance sheet. For example, if there is any goodwill (and note 3 to the format specifies that it should 'only be included to the extent that the goodwill was acquired for valuable consideration'; in other words, self-developed goodwill should not be shown on the balance sheet), the format shows where it should be presented: within intangible fixed assets. This does not preclude a company from adopting a different treatment under which it does not appear on the balance sheet at all. For many years, there used to be a treatment, permitted by accounting standards, of writing off purchased goodwill to reserves on acquisition, and this was not regarded as being contrary to the formats. Accounting standards no longer permit this treatment for new acquisitions.
- Accounting standards place a further layer of detail on the formats. Examples include:
  - FRS 5 introduces a 'linked presentation' under which certain liabilities are deducted directly from certain assets.
  - FRS 9 requires a 'gross equity' presentation for joint ventures, again requiring additional detail to be provided beyond what is required under the formats.
  - FRS 17 requires specific presentation on the formats of pension surpluses and deficits.

As noted above, there are four possible formats for the profit and loss account. Format 1 is commonly used in the UK and a minority of companies use format 2. The others are rarely used, if ever. Format 1 is reproduced below:

1. Turnover
2. Cost of sales . . .
3. Gross profit or loss
4. Distribution costs . . .
5. Administrative expenses . . .
6. Other operating income
7. Income from shares in group undertakings
8. Income from participating interests
9. Income from other fixed asset investments . . .
10. Other interest receivable and similar income . . .
11. Amounts written off investments
12. Interest payable and similar charges . . .
13. Tax on profit or loss on ordinary activities
14. Profit or loss on ordinary activities after taxation
15. Extraordinary income
16. Extraordinary charges
17. Extraordinary profit or loss
18. Tax on extraordinary profit or loss
19. Other taxes not shown under the above items
20. Profit or loss for the financial year

Box 3.4

Format 2 is the same as format 1 from 'income from shares in group under-takings' downwards. But it differs as regards the way in which a company's operating expenses are presented. In place of lines 1 to 6 above, format 2 requires:

1. Turnover
2. Change in stocks of finished goods and in work in progress
3. Own work capitalised
4. Other operating income
5. (a) Raw materials and consumables
   (b) Other external charges
6. Staff costs:
   (a) wages and salaries
   (b) social security costs
   (c) other pension costs
7. (a) Depreciation and other amounts written off tangible and intangible fixed assets
   (b) Exceptional amounts written off current assets
8. Other operating charges

Box 3.5

Format 1 uses the 'functional' analysis of expenses –namely cost of sales, distribution costs, administrative expenses. Format 2 uses the 'type of expense', for example it shows all staff costs together, whether they relate to costs of the factory floor or the boardroom. An effect of this is that format 2 shows a figure for depreciation, whereas in format 1 it is part of other headings, for example, part of cost of sales. Also, format 1 shows a figure for gross profit or loss, whereas this is not shown in format 2.

As noted above in connection with the balance sheet, accounting standards add to what is required by the Act. In particular, FRS 3 'Reporting financial performance' adds further requirements, as follows:

- FRS 3 requires companies to report a sub-total of 'Operating profit'. This is not part of the Act's formats, but in practice comes after line 6 in format 1, and after line 8 in format 2. Operating profit is a very commonly reported figure, for example in preliminary announcements, interim reports, operating and financial reviews and chairmen's statements.
- FRS 3 requires certain gains and losses to be reported below operating profit, for example gains and losses on sale of fixed assets. These items are additional to what the formats require.
- FRS 3 also adds requirements relating to separate disclosure of acquisitions and discontinued operations.
- Lines 15 to 18 show how extraordinary items should be presented. In fact, there are none in current UK GAAP. They were ruled out by FRS 3.
- FRS 3 takes a broader view of performance than just the items in the profit and loss account. It requires companies to present a statement of total recognised gains and losses (STRGL, pronounced 'struggle' by accountants). The accountants' modern notion of performance is that it reflects all changes during the year under review in recognised net assets, which equates to the change in shareholders' funds, apart from changes resulting from transactions with shareholders such as dividend payments and new capital introduced. Hence a revaluation of an asset is regarded as an element of performance, as is a change in the surplus or deficit in a pension scheme. But these items are reported in the STRGL rather than the profit and loss account.

As noted above, the whole of Schedule 4, including the formats, is disapplied for companies following IFRS. IFRS has some rules on presentation of items in the profit and loss account and balance sheet but they are not as detailed and prescriptive as those in the Act.

Part II, Section A – Accounting principles

Paragraphs 9 to 15 of Schedule 4 set out the Act's accounting principles. In view of their importance, they are reproduced below:

'9. Subject to paragraph 15 below, the amounts to be included in respect of all items shown in a company's accounts shall be determined in accordance with the principles set out in paragraphs 10 to 14.

10. The company shall be presumed to be carrying on business as a going concern.

11. Accounting policies shall be applied consistently within the same accounts and from one financial year to the next.

12. The amount of any item shall be determined on a prudent basis, and in particular

   (a) only profits realised at the balance sheet date shall be included in the profit and loss account; and

   (b) all liabilities which have arisen in respect of the financial year to which the accounts relate or a previous financial year shall be taken into account, including those which only become apparent between the balance sheet date and the date on which it is signed on behalf of the board of directors in pursuance of section 233 of this Act.

13. All income and charges relating to the financial year to which the accounts relate shall be taken into account, without regard to the date of receipt or payment.

14. In determining the aggregate amount of any item the amount of each individual asset or liability that falls to be taken into account shall be determined separately.

15. If it appears to the directors of a company that there are special reasons for departing from any of the principles stated above in preparing the company's accounts in respect of any financial year they may do so, but particulars of the departure, the reasons for it and its effect shall be given in a note to the accounts.'

The central provisions – paras. 10 to 14 – set out the accounting principles in a way similar to FRS 18 'Accounting policies'. The first – the principle that a company should, if appropriate, prepare its accounts on a going concern basis – is described by FRS 18 as a pervasive concept. The alternative basis is the break-up basis; that is used in the context of a liquidation or other break up but not in a continuing context. If there is a worry that the company may not be a going concern, for example due to breaching its banking covenants and having difficulty in finding replacement finance, that is usually dealt with by preparing the accounts on a going concern basis and describing the uncertainties regarding going concern. Often the auditors will modify their audit report in such circumstances.

Paragraph 11 requires that accounting policies are applied 'consistently within the same accounts and from one financial year to the next'. In practice, accounting policies are applied consistently from one year to the next – except when they are changed! It is in fact reasonably common for a company to change its accounting policies. Generally, this is in response to new accounting standards or UITF Abstracts coming into force. The Act's rule is aimed at precluding companies from changing policies at random, or without good reason.

When accounting policies are changed, FRS 18 requires certain disclosures to be given (FRS 18, para. 55); it also imposes the requirement that they can be changed only if the new policy is more appropriate than the old one.

Paragraph 12 starts by saying that 'the amount of any item shall be determined on a prudent basis . . .'. When the EU fourth directive (Council Directive 78/660/EEC), on which this law is based, was written, prudence was a more dominant accounting principle than is now the case. Prudence was sometimes used to mean the intentional overstatement of liabilities or the intentional understatement of asset values. The work of the UK ASB and the IASB over the last ten to fifteen years has gradually chipped away at the role of prudence. The focus is now more on neutral measurement, or best estimate of the amount of an asset or liability. Prudence still has a role in accounting, albeit a smaller role. For example, a contingent liability is disclosed if it is regarded as 'possible' and provided for in the balance sheet if it is regarded as 'probable'; whereas a contingent asset is ignored if 'possible'; disclosed if 'probable' and recognised as an asset on the balance sheet only if it is 'virtually certain'. Although the accounting interpretation of prudence has changed considerably, the notion still exists, and modern accounting practice is regarded as being consistent with the general principle with which para. 12 opens.

Paragraph 12(a) goes on to say that 'only profits realised at the balance sheet date shall be included in the profit and loss account'. Chapter 16 gives a fuller treatment of realised and distributable profits. However, we may note here that in general (and with a number of exceptions):

- Only realised profits are included in the profit and loss account.
- Unrealised profits, such as those arising from revaluations of assets, are presented in the STRGL.

Paragraph 12(b) deals with what liabilities should be included in a balance sheet. This wording was changed by 'The Companies Act 1985 (International Accounting Standards and Other Accounting Amendments) Regulations 2004' (SI 2004 No. 2947). Previously, the words suggested a stronger role for prudence than is part of modern accounting. Before FRS 12 'Provisions, contingent assets and contingent liabilities' was introduced in 1998, some companies had a practice of providing for alleged liabilities on a generous scale, often in order to have a cushion to absorb any future downturn. But FRS 12 applied the definition of a liability from the ASB's Statement of principles ('Liabilities are obligations of an entity to transfer economic benefits as a result of past transactions and events', para. 4.23) and thereby constrained companies' ability to provide for what were often not liabilities at all but just likely future costs. By introducing a tighter definition of liability, the ASB has changed practice. The 2004 amendment to para. 12(b) can be seen as the law catching up with a change in practice that has already occurred.

Paragraph 13 is a restatement in law of the accruals concept. Rent may be paid on 23 December but relates to the first quarter of the following year.

Hence it is charged in the profit and loss account for the following year – that is, without regard to the date of payment. If we were drawing up a balance sheet at 31 December, the amount paid for rent would be shown as an asset (a prepayment) on the balance sheet.

The law does not refer to the 'matching' principle. Matching, which is nowadays regarded as a bad word by most accountants, certainly by standard-setters, refers to matching expenses and income against each other. For example, it might be argued that certain start-up costs are incurred in setting up a new line of business. A company might wish to carry the costs forward in order to match them against the revenue that may (or may not) arise from that business. However, accounting standards would say that, unless the costs meet the definition of an asset, they should be treated as an expense and not carried forward. Modern accounting does not recognise matching as a principle and indeed rules out some potential applications of it. Matching is thus distinct from the accruals concept, which merely seeks to place an item of income and expense in the period to which it relates.

Paragraph 14 – 'in determining the aggregate amount of any item the amount of each individual asset or liability that falls to be taken into account shall be determined separately'– might appear to be obvious. What it means can be illustrated by reference to stock of goods. Assume there are two items of stock. Item A cost £50 and is worth £60. Item B cost £30 but its value has declined to £25. In aggregate the value of £85 more than covers the aggregate cost of £80. However, the Act requires that when applying an accounting policy – typically 'lower of cost and net realisable value' in the case of stock – that policy should be applied to each item, without cross subsidy. Applying the policy to each item separately gives us:

Item A – lower of cost and NRV is 50
Item B – lower of cost and NRV is 25

Hence the total carrying value for stock is 75. The gain on A is not allowed to compensate for the loss on B.

Paragraph 15 deals with departures from the accounting principles in paras. 10–14. An example of its application would be a change of accounting policy, which is an exception to the rule in paragraph 11 that requires consistency. It is very similar to the section 226A true and fair override discussed above. Disclosure of the reasons, particulars and effect is required in a similar way.

Part II, Section B – Historical cost accounting rules

The legal rules in this section and in Section C (see below) are, along with the rules in Schedule 4A on acquisition accounting, the most detailed accounting rules in the Act. Hence they overlap with accounting standards more than other parts of the Act do. The basic legal framework for accounting is the historical cost accounting rules. The alternative accounting rules in Section C may be used by companies on a voluntary basis.

The rules relating to fixed assets are found in paras. 17 to 21. The formats earlier in Schedule 4 (see above) indicate that fixed assets comprise (a) intangible assets, which include goodwill, (b) tangible assets and (c) investments. The cost of a fixed asset is its 'purchase price or production cost', and, in the case of an asset with a limited useful economic life (that is, most assets in categories (a) and (b)), this amount, less any estimated residual value, is to be depreciated over the asset's useful economic life. This is consistent with FRS 15 'Tangible fixed assets' and with the rules relating to intangible fixed assets in FRS 10 'Goodwill and intangible assets', although those standards include more detail.

Paragraph 19 requires careful analysis. Paragraph 19(1) states that 'where a fixed asset investment . . . has diminished in value provisions for diminution in value *may* be made in respect of it and the amount to be included in respect of it *may* be reduced accordingly . . .'. Paragraph 19(2) adds that 'provisions for diminution in value *shall* be made in respect of any fixed asset which has diminished in value if the reduction in value is expected to be permanent . . .' [emphases added]. Taking these together, the effect is that if there is a permanent diminution in value, this must be recognised as a loss; and this rule applies to all three categories of fixed asset – intangibles, tangibles and investments. But, in the case of a fixed asset investment, if the diminution is regarded as temporary it is optional as to whether that should be reflected in the accounts or not. This leaves an apparent gap in relation to temporary diminutions in value of tangible and intangible fixed assets. In practice, this does not cause any problems, as diminutions in value are dealt with by the depreciation rules and the rules in FRS 11 'Impairment of fixed assets and goodwill'. However, the rules in para. 19 do leave a practical problem, especially in relation to investments, in determining whether a diminution in value is temporary or permanent. There is no simple rule or formula that determines this. Directors, in considering the carrying value of investments when preparing accounts, may believe (or hope) that the value of an investment that has fallen below cost will recover within, say, a few months. But there is generally no way of demonstrating that. If, at the next year end, the value has still not recovered, the directors may again take the same view. But there is clearly a point at which an assertion that the value will soon recover lacks credibility and at that point the diminution has to be regarded as permanent. Quite when that point arises is sometimes the subject of some interesting exchanges between directors and auditors.

Paragraph 21 contains special rules relating to goodwill. They relate to 'any case where goodwill is treated as an asset'. This means that goodwill need not be treated as an asset. Prior to the introduction of FRS 10 'Goodwill and intangible assets', which requires purchased goodwill to be capitalised, it was common practice to write off purchased goodwill to reserves rather than treat it as an asset. Secondly, as explained in note 3 to the balance sheet formats, and in FRS 10, it is only purchased goodwill that can be treated as an asset; self developed goodwill – sometimes called internally generated, or inherent, goodwill – cannot be treated as an asset. Purchased goodwill means goodwill acquired as part of the acquisition of a company or unincorporated business.

Paragraph 21(2) and (3) sets out rules for depreciation of goodwill that are similar to those in para. 18 for fixed assets generally. However, there are differences and other points that arise. First, the depreciation of goodwill must be so as to write it off over the useful economic life. That is, it is not permissible to reduce the charge for goodwill amortisation by bringing in a residual value. This is logical, as goodwill by definition cannot be sold separately, without selling the business as a whole. Second, there is a conflict between the basic legal rule requiring amortisation and the permission in FRS 10 that goodwill need not be amortised in special cases, that is, where it is demonstrable that there is no diminution in value of the goodwill. At present, these special cases are handled by means of the true and fair override. In future it is likely that UK accounting standards will be reformed (following the IASB's recent change in IFRS 3) to make non-amortisation, supplemented by regular impairment testing, the basic rule. This will give rise to a more obvious conflict with the Act, which the future standards will have to address. Third, and as already reflected in this paragraph, it may be noted that accountants use the word 'amortisation', rather than depreciation, when referring to goodwill and other intangibles. The word 'depreciation' is used in relation to tangible fixed assets. Apart from this different application, the meaning of the two words is the same.

Goodwill is considered further in chapter 9: see pp. 106–7.

Paragraph 23 applies to current assets, such as stock, work-in-progress, debtors and cash. The basic measurement rule is cost – that is, purchase price or production cost, as with fixed assets. However, rather than depreciation, which applies when assets are consumed over a period, the approach in the Act, and in accounting standards, is that current assets are carried at the lower of cost and net realisable value. For example, if stock was bought for £100 and the original intention was to sell it for £140, but the market has deteriorated such that it can only be sold for £90, the stock would be carried at £90. In other words, the loss is recognised as soon as it becomes apparent, rather than waiting until it is sold.

Part II, Section C – Alternative accounting rules

The alternative accounting rules are an optional regime, introduced into the EU fourth directive (Council Directive 78/660/EEC) and hence the Act to permit the practice developed by accountants of revaluing certain assets. Accounting practices and accounting standards in this area are constantly evolving. There has been a practice of revaluing some tangible fixed assets, and this continues in a few companies, especially with land and buildings. But the emphasis currently is on applying a 'fair value' basis to financial instruments, which broadly means fixed and current asset investments, cash balances, debtors and certain liabilities (see Section D below).

Paragraph 31 permits various categories of assets to be revalued as follows:

- Intangible fixed assets, other than goodwill, at current cost.
- Tangible fixed assets at market value at the date of their last valuation, or at current cost.
- Fixed asset investments at (a) market value at the date of their last valuation, or (b) 'at a value determined on any basis which appears to the directors to be appropriate in the circumstances of the company'.
- Current asset investments at current cost.
- Stocks at current cost.

The following points arise:

- Goodwill cannot be revalued. This is consistent with FRS 10.
- Other intangible assets can be revalued under the Act. However, FRS 10 severely restricts companies' ability to revalue intangibles. In practice, it is very rare to revalue an intangible.
- For tangible fixed assets and for fixed asset investments, there is explicit recognition that the valuation determined under the rules may not always be up-to-date. From an accounting point of view, a valuation gives more useful information than historical cost. But this is undermined if the valuation is out of date. Hence accounting standards require up-to-date valuations.

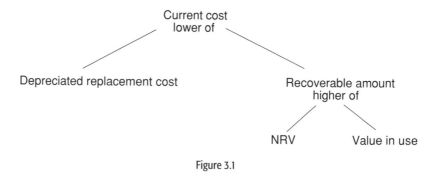

Figure 3.1

'Current cost' certainly implies an up-to-date value. However the term is not defined in the Act. In accounting standards its meaning is depreciated replacement cost or recoverable amount, if lower. This can be shown diagrammatically as shown in Figure 3.1.

Where:

- Depreciated replacement cost means current replacement cost of a similar new asset, adjusted for depreciation to reflect the extent to which the asset is not new. This is the measure of current cost, unless the recoverable amount is lower, in which case the asset is recorded at the lower recoverable amount.
- Recoverable amount simply means the amount that can be recovered from the asset, either by sale (net realisable value: NRV) or use in the business (value in use). The greater of these is taken as the relevant measure, reflecting the assumption that a company will either sell or use the asset, according to which will generate the greater value.
- NRV is net realisable value, meaning the amount that will be achieved from a sale of the asset, net of expenses.
- Value in use is the present value of the stream of future net cash flows that it is expected the asset will generate if kept and used in the business.

The remainder of Section C is concerned with various consequences of adopting a valuation approach. Paragraph 32, in conjunction with the depreciation rules in FRS 15, in effect requires that, for depreciable assets, the depreciation charged in the profit and loss account should be based on the revalued amount of the asset, not on its historical cost.

Paragraph 34 deals with the revaluation reserve. When an asset is revalued, the gain so recognised is not included in the profit and loss account, but rather in the STRGL, reflecting the fact that it is not a realised profit. Consistent with this, the revaluation gain is credited to the revaluation reserve, the balance on which is unrealised. The effect of para. 34 is that the revaluation reserve should generally carry a balance appropriate to the assets currently held at a valuation. That is, when such an asset is disposed of, the relevant amount of the revaluation reserve is released to the profit and loss account reserve. Similarly, when the asset is depreciated, an appropriate amount of the revaluation reserve is released. The effect of this is that:

- the profit and loss account (the performance statement) is charged with depreciation on the full carrying value (the revalued amount of the asset); whereas
- the profit and loss account reserve, after the transfer from the revaluation reserve, is reduced only by the depreciation on the historical cost. Put another way, the effect on distributable profits, as reflected in the profit and loss reserve, ends up being the same as if the asset had not been revalued.

In rare circumstances, the revaluation reserve may not carry a balance appropriate to the assets currently held at valuation. This arises when the revaluation reserve is used to fund a bonus issue or to fund a permissible capital payment.

Part II, Section D – Fair value accounting

This section has recently been added by the Companies Act 1985 (International Accounting Standards and Other Accounting Amendments) Regulations 2004 (SI 2004 No. 2947). Its purpose is to permit companies to state certain financial instruments at fair value. Without it, there would be a conflict between the cost-based Act and the fair value-based rules on financial instrument accounting that were introduced into UK GAAP from IAS 39 in late 2004 by means of FRS 26.

Part III – Notes to the accounts

Paragraphs 35 to 58A, which form Part III of Schedule 4, are primarily requirements for disclosure of information supplementary to the balance sheet and profit and loss account. Examples are information about share capital and debentures, fixed assets, investments, guarantees, turnover and staff. In many cases, accounting standards duplicate, and generally add to these requirements. For example, the 'particulars of turnover' required by para. 55 are a modest amount of segmental information. SSAP 25, 'Segmental reporting', adds further requirements, such as segmentation of profits and net assets, for many companies.

Paragraphs 36 and 36A deal with accounting policies. Paragraph 36 requires disclosure of the accounting policies adopted, and, in a similar way to segmental information, this is elaborated in FRS 18, 'Accounting policies'. Paragraph 36A is somewhat different. This requires a statement of 'whether the accounts have been prepared in accordance with applicable accounting standards and particulars of any material departure from those standards and the reasons for it . . .'. This is the route by which UK accounting standards are given legal recognition. Note that the Act does not require companies to follow UK accounting standards as such, but requires a statement as to whether they have complied. Of course, compliance is the intention and a statement of non-compliance is likely to be noticed and acted upon by some or all of the auditors, the press, the Listing Authority or the Financial Reporting Review Panel, as appropriate.

Part VII – Interpretation of Schedule 4

Various terms are interpreted in Part VII, most of which require no elaboration. The exception is materiality, on which para. 86 states: 'amounts which in the particular context of any provisions of this Schedule are not material may be disregarded for the purposes of that provision'. This gives legal recognition to the well-established accounting principle of materiality. Materiality is the subject of guidance from the ICAEW and is also discussed in the ASB's Statement of principles (SoP). The SoP defines materiality in the following way: 'an item of information is material to the financial statements if its misstatement or omission might reasonably be expected to influence the economic decisions of users of those financial statements, including their assessment of management's stewardship' [SoP, para. 3.28]. In practice, this means that if information is not material, it need not be given – and arguably should not be given, as a clutter of immaterial information can impair the understandability of the other information provided.

Accounting provisions of the Act – Schedule 4A

Introduction

As noted above, section 227 sets out the basic requirement to produce group accounts in the form of consolidated accounts, and, for companies preparing accounts under UK GAAP, section 227A (3) mandates compliance with the detailed requirements in Schedule 4A. Certain details, described below, are included in Schedule 4A, though much more detail is found in accounting standards – FRS 2 'Accounting for subsidiary undertakings', FRS 6 'Acquisitions and mergers', FRS 7 'Fair values in acquisition accounting' and FRS 9 'Associates and joint ventures'.

Schedule 4A is additional to Schedule 4. So, for example, the formats for the balance sheet and profit and loss account apply to consolidated accounts, just as they apply to individual accounts. However, Schedule 4A supplements them, for example, by specifying where in the formats minority interests are to be included.

Schedule 4A, para. 1(1) requires that 'group accounts shall comply so far as practicable with . . . Schedule 4 . . . as if the . . . group . . . were a single company'. This expresses the basic model of consolidation. Paragraphs 2 and 3 put this into operation by requiring that the accounts of subsidiaries should be aggregated, subject to any adjustments authorised or required by Schedule 4A or by GAAP. Also, uniform accounting policies should be used in preparing consolidated accounts. Note that there is nothing that requires the accounting policies of individual members of a group to be the same – indeed it may not be possible for a subsidiary overseas to adopt the same policies as the group. Indeed it is even possible for the parent entity to have different policies from those used in the group accounts: para. 4 requires that, where this is the case, the differences shall be disclosed and explained. In practice, it is very rare for the accounting policies of a parent to differ from those of the consolidated accounts of the parent's group. These comments are in the context of UK GAAP. As noted above, if the parent is listed, its group accounts must be under IFRS and the parent has the choice of preparing its own entity accounts under either UK GAAP or IFRS.

Elimination of group transactions

One of the techniques of preparing consolidated accounts is to eliminate intra-group transactions and balances. This is done in order to show the position as if the group were a single entity. Put another way, the resulting accounts show the transactions and balances with third parties, and exclude those that are internal. Paragraph 6 deals with this. Some adjustments affect only what the Act calls 'debts and claims' and 'income and expenditure'. That is, if subsidiary A has sold goods to subsidiary B, and the amount remains outstanding as a debtor in A's balance sheet and a creditor in B's balance sheet. The two are eliminated against each other as, from the group's perspective, they are internal balances. Similarly, part of the sales figure of A will (assuming B has sold the goods on to a third party) have an equivalent cost of sales figure in B's profit and loss account. Again, the two are eliminated against each other. If this were not done, the sales figure in the group accounts would include more than the total revenue earned from sales to third parties, and would overstate the level of business transacted by the group.

Paragraph 6(2) recognises that there may be a profit effect arising from intra-group transactions, and requires this to be eliminated also. For example, assume the sales made by A to B were as shown in Box 3.6.

A's books:	
Cost of sales	60
Sales to B	100
B's books:	
Purchases from A	100
Box 3.6	

If, in preparing the consolidated accounts, we were to eliminate merely the sale from A to B, that would leave in the group profit and loss account the profit of 40 made by A. This would be appropriate only if the group as a whole had sold the goods to a third party. Conversely, if the goods were still held in stock by B, there would be no external sale, and it would be necessary to eliminate the profit of 40, giving the effect that the stock is held in the consolidated balance sheet at cost *to the group* of 60. The sale by A to B has the effect of increasing the entity profits of A without increasing the group's profit.

Acquisition and merger accounting

The routine of preparing consolidated accounts can be technically difficult in a complex group but does not generally give rise to controversy or surprises. The same cannot be said for determining when the consolidation should be prepared using acquisition accounting and when it should be prepared using merger accounting. This is dealt with in paras. 7 to 16 of Schedule 4A. This subject has been the source of controversy in the accounting profession for the last forty years or so. However, after much discussion, the merger method is being gradually withdrawn. In IFRS, a revised standard, IFRS 3, was introduced in March 2004 which had the effect of banning merger accounting for third party transactions. Merger accounting still has a role in accounting for intra-group reorganisations. A standard equivalent to IFRS 3 is likely to be introduced into UK GAAP at some stage, though the UK ASB is for the moment retaining its own standard (FRS 6) which allows merger accounting in limited circumstances as well as for intra-group reorganisations.

The Act's detailed rules remain relevant for companies that prepare consolidated accounts under UK GAAP. The rules set out: what the acquisition method is; the conditions for using merger accounting; and what the merger method is. Paragraph 8 in effect makes merger accounting optional if the criteria are met. Paragraph 9 describes acquisition accounting briefly. The main features, which are elaborated in FRS 6, are:

- The identifiable net assets of the undertaking acquired are included in the acquiror's group accounts at their fair values at the date of acquisition. In other words, up to date values are placed on the assets when they join the group.
- 'Identifiable' is defined in such a way as to exclude goodwill.
- The subsidiary's income and expenditure are brought into the profit and loss account of the acquiring group from the date of acquisition only.
- An offset is carried out between (a) the fair value of the consideration given by the acquiring company – such as cash or shares that it issues to the vendors of the target company, and (b) the aggregate of the fair values of the identifiable assets (the Act calls this 'the interest of the parent . . . in the adjusted capital and reserves of the undertaking acquired', but the effect is the same).
- The difference arising from this exercise is goodwill. Goodwill is typically positive but can be negative. Negative goodwill – called 'negative consolidation difference' by the Act – implies that the business has been bought at a discount.

Paragraph 10 sets out the Act's criteria for being allowed to use merger accounting. Briefly, these state that at least a 90% holding of relevant shares is held; the consideration given must be almost entirely equity shares; and 'adoption of the merger method of accounting accords with generally accepted accounting principles or practice'. This last condition still has a role in that merger accounting is recognised by FRS 6. However, when IFRS 3 is brought into UK GAAP, the adoption of the merger method will no longer accord with GAAP, and so the part of Schedule 4A that makes merger accounting permissible in law will be otiose.

Paragraph 11 describes merger accounting briefly. The main features, which are elaborated in FRS 6, are:

- The assets brought into the group are not restated at fair value, but kept at previous book value.
- Income and expenditure of the undertaking brought into the group are included for the entire financial year, including the period before it joined the group.
- The comparative figures for the previous year include the new subsidiary as if it had been part of the group in that year, even though it was not.
- An offset exercise is carried out but, because the amounts involved are not fair values, the result is not goodwill. It is merely adjusted against reserves.

In other words, in merger accounting, there is no attempt to show one company acquiring the other. The presentation seeks to show how the figures would have looked, had the companies always been together. This is clearly a notional presentation.

Further details of acquisition accounting and merger accounting are set out in chapter 9 at pp. 91–109.

Minority interests

Paragraph 17 deals with minority interests, that is, interests in the share capital and reserves of subsidiaries that are held by third parties, not by the parent. Minority interests arise because the general model for consolidation is full (not proportional) consolidation. For example, if a parent acquires 75% of a subsidiary's share capital, it will generally control that subsidiary and so will consolidate it in full. But because the group owns only 75% of the subsidiary, there has to be shown an amount in respect of the other 25% that is owned by the minority. This is generally shown next to shareholders' funds. Under IFRS, the presentation is slightly different: minorities are shown within equity, albeit separately from parent shareholders' funds.

In the profit and loss account, again a partly owned subsidiary is fully consolidated because the parent controls it. Hence 100% of its sales and expense lines, and hence profit before and after tax, are presented. But, before arriving at the profit attributable to parent shareholders, an amount is deducted being the minority's share of the profit of the subsidiary in question.

The rules in para. 17 give detailed guidance on where minority interests should be presented on the balance sheet and in the profit and loss account.

Joint ventures and associates

The final paragraphs of Schedule 4A deal with the way in which joint ventures and associates are included in consolidated accounts. Further detail is added by FRS 9.

Paragraph 19 permits proportional consolidation for certain types of joint venture. Proportional consolidation means, literally, that if a venturer holds

50% of the capital of JVCo, it should include in its consolidated accounts 50% of each line item. That is, in the profit and loss account, it should include 50% of JVCo's sales, 50% of each expense line item and therefore 50% of the profit. Because the accounting exactly reflects the percentage held, there is no minority interest to adjust.

Although the Act permits proportional consolidation in defined circumstances, this has little practical effect at present as UK GAAP does not permit its use for JV entities. However, it is one of the methods allowed by the international standard, IAS 31.

The Act requires joint ventures that are not accounted for by proportional consolidation to be accounted for using equity accounting.

Paragraphs 20 to 22 deal with associated undertakings. An associated undertaking is an undertaking in which an undertaking included in the consolidation has a 'participating interest and over whose operating and financial policy it exercises a significant influence . . .'. Paragraph 22 specifies the equity method for associates. This involves including in the consolidation the relevant percentage of the results and net assets. So if A has a 25% interest in B, and the definition of associate in FRS 9 is met, A would include in its profit and loss account 25% of B's profit; and would include in its balance sheet 25% of B's net assets. Accounting for associates is further elaborated in chapter 8 at pp. 88–90.

4
Substance over form

Form v. substance

Financial statements drawn up under the Companies Act 1985 are in many ways legal documents. In a literal sense they are required to be produced by law, and to be filed at Companies House. In another sense, too, they must comply with the many detailed requirements of the Act. Yet, there is a strong notion of 'substance' in accounting. This has become stronger in the last twenty years or so. In earlier, simpler, times, following the legal form of a transaction generally gave an appropriate accounting result. But, as business transactions have become more complex, there have been an increasing number of transactions in which legal form and economic substance have diverged from each other; gradually, it became clear that following the legal form did not properly reflect the commercial transaction.

To accountants, the basic legal requirement that accounts must give a 'true and fair view' (discussed in chapter 3 at pp. 26–7) means that they must reflect the economic substance of a transaction and not just its legal form. This is not stated in law; it is merely the accepted view of accountants.

Early examples

For some years, there were examples of substance over form being applied to common transactions, almost as second nature, rather than by applying a specific rule or even consciously applying the substance over form principle. One example is accounting for an asset being 'bought' under hire purchase. The legal analysis is that the asset is being hired (or leased) for the term of the agreement. There is then an option for the lessee to purchase the asset, generally for a nominal sum such as £1. In almost all circumstances, the option to purchase is exercised, and the commercial effect of the transaction is that, from the start, the asset is being purchased on deferred payment terms. Hire purchase transactions were accounted for in this way, that is, the asset being hired/bought was treated as capital expenditure and the obligation to pay instalments was shown on the balance sheet as a liability. No accounting standard was needed in order to require this treatment; it was done as a matter of professional practice.

Subsequently, the principle of substance over form, and the practice established for hire purchase, were extended to accounting for leases (see chapter 13).

Another example is goods sold subject to reservation of title. In these transactions, goods are sold but title stays with the vendor until the purchaser settles the amount due. The substance of these transactions is that a sale is being made on credit. The reservation of legal title is merely a technique to give the vendor more security so as to reduce any losses that might occur as a result of insolvency of the customer. Following the Romalpa case (*Aluminium Industrie Vaassen BV* v. *Romalpa Aluminium Ltd*. [1976] 1 WLR 675, CA), the Institute of Chartered Accountants in England and Wales published guidance later in 1976 which advised members on the accounting treatment to be adopted. The advice was that 'the commercial substance of the transaction should take precedence over its legal form where they conflict'.

Emergence of the off balance sheet industry

Throughout the 1980s, more transactions were developed in which the legal form and the economic, or commercial, substance conflicted. Among these were so-called 'non-subsidiary subsidiaries'. These were companies that were in substance subsidiaries of a parent, in that they were for all practical purposes controlled by the parent, and brought benefits to the parent. But they did not meet the legal definition of subsidiary company, usually through establishing some unusual or artificial feature such as weighted voting rights for certain classes of shares. Accountants faced some difficulty here, as they were unsure whether it was appropriate to consolidate entities that were not, in a legal sense, part of the group. Hence the off balance sheet industry was born. Various other structures were developed with a common aim of keeping entities, or assets (and, more importantly, the liabilities that financed them) off balance sheet. The Institute responded with guidance, but it had no force, and the practice of off balance sheet finance flourished through the 1980s and was a major contributor to the worsening reputation of accounts and accountants in that period.

FRS 5 'Reporting the substance of transactions'

The situation was largely rescued by two events. One was the Companies Act 1989 (consolidated into the 1985 Act, principally Schedule 4A) which implemented the EU seventh company law directive (Council Directive 83/349/EEC on consolidated accounts, OJ 1983 No. L193/1). This introduced new rules relating to consolidated accounts and, in particular, new, wider definitions of the parent/subsidiary relationship. The parent/subsidiary relationship is explored more fully in chapter 8 (see pp. 82–4).

The second was the establishing in 1990 of the new Accounting Standards Board to replace the old Accounting Standards Committee. The ASB

49

acknowledged that it needed to develop an effective standard dealing with the off balance sheet problem. The result of the ASB's work on off balance sheet finance was FRS 5 'Reporting the substance of transactions'. This was first issued in April 1994. It is hard to underestimate the importance of this standard. FRS 5 is a complex standard in some respects, for instance its rules on when assets, such as securitised assets, can be derecognised, but at its heart it is very simple. The main principles can be summarised as follows:

- Financial statements should report the substance of transactions.
- To determine substance, consider the effect of a transaction on assets and liabilities.
- All aspects and implications should be identified and greater weight should be given to those more likely to have a commercial effect in practice.

There is, of course, much more to it than that. But accountants frequently come back to these basic principles when considering the appropriate accounting treatment of complex transactions. Some examples are given below.

Linked presentation

FRS 5 also introduced a new type of balance sheet presentation called 'Linked presentation'. This is used as a method of portraying those transactions where an asset is to some degree being sold, but a sale has not quite been achieved.

Example of linked presentation

Debts subject to financing
arrangements:
    Debts (after providing for expected   99
    bad debts of 1)
Less: non-returnable amounts received   (90)
                           9

In terms of balance sheet presentation, the 9 is shown among the assets (for example within current assets, if, as in this example, the asset is debtors). The 99 and the 90 are additional information that has to be shown on the face of the balance sheet, but the 90 is not presented as a liability.

Box 4.1

Nevertheless, an amount has been received from another party and that amount is not refundable, except out of the proceeds of sale of the related, or 'linked' asset; hence it is not appropriate to treat the amount received as a liability. The presentation is shown in Box 4.1.

Quasi-subsidiaries

A further key part of FRS 5 has been its provisions relating to 'Quasi-subsidiaries'. These are defined in FRS 5: 'A quasi-subsidiary of a reporting entity is a company, trust, partnership or other vehicle that, though not fulfilling the definition of a subsidiary, is directly or indirectly controlled by the reporting entity and gives rise to benefits for that entity that are in substance no different from those that would arise were the vehicle a subsidiary.'

This definition of quasi-subsidiaries has often been used to pick up, for inclusion in the consolidation, trusts, and companies owned by trusts, some of which carry the label 'special purpose vehicles' (or 'special purpose companies'), a term which, post-Enron, attracts less admiration than previously.

The importance of the FRS 5 rules on quasi-subsidiaries is now reduced, following the 2004 change of law (the Companies Act 1985 (International Accounting Standards and Other Accounting Amendments) Regulations 2004 (SI 2004 No. 2947)), under which an undertaking can be a subsidiary undertaking even though the parent does not have a participating interest in it. Hence some of what were identified for consolidation only by virtue of being quasi-subsidiaries may now be included as legally being subsidiary undertakings.

Other specific applications

FRS 5 includes guidance on a number of specific applications, in the form of 'Application notes'. The current notes are:

- A Consignment stock
- B Sale and repurchase agreements
- C Factoring of debts
- D Securitised assets
- E Loan transfers
- F Private finance initiative and similar contracts
- G Revenue recognition.

Application notes A to F are merely specific examples of the general principles outlined above. For example, if amounts receivable from customers are sold to a factoring company, and cash is received equal to 95% of the face value of the debtors, what is the appropriate accounting treatment? Application Note C explains that it hinges on the extent to which the originator (i.e. the party that sells the debtors) retains the risks and rewards relating to the debtors or, on the other hand, transfers the risks and rewards to the factor. The risks are primarily bad debt risk and slow payment risk; the rewards are primarily the future cash flows from the debtors settling the amounts due. The possible accounting treatments, depending on the facts of each case, are:

- Debtors remain on balance sheet; amount received from factor is shown as a liability.
- Debtors taken off balance sheet; amount received from factor regarded as proceeds of sale of the asset (debtors).
- Linked presentation (see Box 4.1) – a half-way house that reflects the partial transfer of risks and rewards to the factor.

If, for example, the amounts received from the factoring company had to be repaid to that company, together with interest, by a specified date irrespective of how many of the debtors had paid by that date, the risks and rewards of the debtors would remain with the originator and thus the debtors would continue to be recognised on the balance sheet, with the amount received from the factoring company being shown as a liability.

Application Note G is different in nature to the others. The ASB wanted in 2003 to put in place some interim rules on revenue recognition, pending the outcome of a longer-term IASB/FASB project. The ASB did not want to present it as a full accounting standard in its own right. Because the recognition of revenue is driven, to some degree, from changes in assets and liabilities, an Application Note was a convenient alternative method of promulgating the rules.

Examples of FRS 5 in practice

Presented here are examples in which accountants use the FRS 5 principle of substance over form to determine the appropriate accounting treatment.

Failed sale of an asset

In the example in Figure 4.1, we are concerned with the financial statements of the B group, which includes its subsidiary C. C has a property that it wishes to sell. A represents a holding company, or a group of investors who own B. A third party purchaser (TP) is in prospect, but no sale has been agreed, and any sale to TP is unlikely to be completed until year 2. B wants to reflect the sale of the property in year 1.

There already exists, or A sets up for this purpose, P, a property company. P has no significant assets. It is arranged, just before the end of year 1, that C sells its property to P. The terms are that the sale price is expressed as £6m., but this amount is provisional, in that if the sale to TP realises less than this, say £5m., the price in the sale contract between C and P will be adjusted accordingly; similarly if the price paid in due course by TP exceeds £6m., the excess is passed on to C again by means of a price adjustment in the contract between C and P. Further, the consideration of £6m. is not paid in cash but is left outstanding on inter-company account.

The accounting analysis of this transaction is that the B group has not effected a sale of the property (neither has C in its entity accounts). The primary

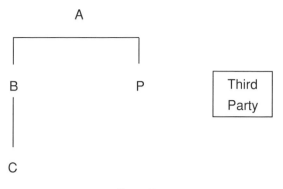

Figure 4.1

reason is that the B group has not passed on to P the risks and rewards relating to the asset. B group still has the upside potential, that is, it will gain if on a sale to TP the property is found to be more valuable. Similarly, B group will lose if the property is sold to TP for less than £6m. The conclusion is strengthened by the fact that P does not settle the price, but leaves the amount outstanding on inter-company account. However, this feature is not necessary: the same view would most likely be taken even if the consideration were paid in cash, because the key feature – that the risks and rewards have not been transferred to another party – remains present. In effect, what is happening here is a parking or warehousing of an asset, ostensibly outside the reporting entity (the B group), but no transaction of substance has taken place. The B group would report a sale when P sells the property to a third party in a way that transfers the risks and rewards of ownership to that third party.

It is important to stress that the fact that P is owned by the same parent, or investor group, as B is not an obstacle to recognising a sale by B. It is the structuring of the sale terms and the lack of transfer of risks and rewards that is the key feature. Hence if the B group were to make a clean sale of the property to P for a fixed price of £6m., and the price were to be settled in cash, or left outstanding but to be settled in the short term, the B group would validly report a sale of the property in its financial statements. It is true that there would be no sale in any consolidated accounts prepared for the A group as a whole: in that context there has just been a sale from one subsidiary to another. But our context is the consolidated accounts of the B group, and the B group has made a sale.

Warehousing of stock

A similar example is that a company may operate in an industry where the stock holding period is long, and hence have a significant holding of stock. It may wish to get the stock off its balance sheet. A variety of techniques were

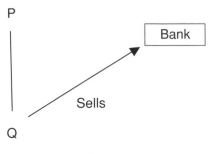

Figure 4.2

developed to achieve this, mostly pre-FRS 5, though sometimes they recur. See, for example, Figure 4.2.

Q is the operating subsidiary of the P group. The P group wishes to raise finance. Rather than borrow secured on the stock, P group arranges that:

- Q will sell the stock to the bank.
- The stock will remain in Q's warehouse, or at a third party location controlled and paid for by Q.
- The bank will sell the stock back to Q whenever Q so requests.
- If Q has not called for the stock within one year, the bank will be entitled to sell the stock back to Q.
- The bank is not entitled to sell the stock to a third party, except under Q's specific instruction.
- The price at which the stock is sold back to Q is the price of the original sale plus an interest rate applied for the period in which the bank has held the stock. For example if the annually agreed interest rate is 8%, and the stock remained with the bank for six months, the repurchase price would be 104% of the original sale price.

The substance of the transaction is that, despite the transfer of legal title in the stock to the bank, the stock remains under the control of Q, Q retains the risks and rewards relating to the stock, and is in substance borrowing from the bank. The bank's role is that it is lending money to Q, earning a lender's rate of return and not taking possession of, or risk in relation to, the stock. Hence Q's accounting, and therefore the accounting in the P group, is that the stock remains an asset, the amount received from the bank is shown as a liability, and an interest cost is shown in the profit and loss account.

Trusts and SPVs

A variety of structures is found in which either trusts alone, or trusts that own companies, are set up, often in tax havens. These structures are sometimes used in connection with securitisations or other transactions in the financial services industries, but can also be found, for example, in the area of film finance. It is often argued that the trustees of the trust perform a significant role and act independently of other parties. Accountants often doubt such claims, and take the view that trustees in these circumstances are acting in a predetermined manner and do not have any significant decision-making power or, if they do have such power, they do not exercise it in practice. Accountants therefore often seek to identify another party that controls any assets that are held in such trusts, or in companies held by such trusts. Often, in accounting analysis, such trusts are regarded as quasi-subsidiaries (see above) of one of the major players in a transaction.

The future of FRS 5

Despite the importance of FRS 5 to UK accounting, we are likely to lose it to some extent. The IASB framework refers to substance but the notion is not as strong as in UK GAAP. Certainly there is no international standard equivalent to FRS 5. Some of the applications of substance will survive, for example IASB literature includes a publication of the Standing Interpretations Committee of the IASC (SIC): SIC 12 'Consolidation – special purpose entities', which is broadly equivalent to the UK rules on quasi-subsidiaries. But the broad use of substance is likely to be lost, at least to some degree. Most UK accountants regard this as a retrograde step, though it is unclear at this stage exactly what effect it will have.

5
The accounting profession and the regulatory framework for accounting and auditing

The accounting profession

There are currently six major accountancy bodies in the UK and Ireland:

1. The Institute of Chartered Accountants in England and Wales (ICAEW)
2. The Institute of Chartered Accountants of Scotland (ICAS)
3. The Institute of Chartered Accountants in Ireland (ICAI)
4. The Association of Chartered Certified Accountants (ACCA)
5. The Chartered Institute of Management Accountants (CIMA)
6. The Chartered Institute of Public Finance and Accountancy (CIPFA)

The vast majority of practising members of the profession are in one of the first three Institutes. The ICAEW is the largest, although ICAS is proud to be the oldest body. ACCA includes some practitioners and many members overseas. Many of the members of these four bodies, having trained in the profession, work in industry and commerce, and members of CIMA do so almost exclusively. CIPFA members work almost entirely in the public sector.

These bodies to some extent compete with each other – not least for students and, therefore, for members. They also co-operate on some matters through the Consultative Committee of Accountancy Bodies (CCAB). Setting accounting standards and auditing standards used to be in the domain of the CCAB – the Accounting Standards Committee and the Auditing Practices Committee were CCAB bodies from the 1970s for about twenty years. However, in 1990, the accounting standards activity was moved away from the profession and the new Accounting Standards Board (see below) was formed. Similarly, a new Auditing Practices Board was formed in April 2002, thus removing a second important role from the professional bodies.

The accountancy bodies have a number of important roles. One is education and training – training students, admitting new members and overseeing their continuing professional education. The Institutes also set professional and ethical rules. And, despite losing the important roles of setting accounting and auditing standards, the Institutes have a number of technical committees that are active in both generating and debating new ideas and in producing guidance for the profession. A recent example of guidance is TECH 7/03 'Guidance on the determination of realised profits and losses in the context of distributions under the Companies Act 1985' which is discussed in detail in chapter 16 at pp. 165–73.

The Financial Reporting Council

The Financial Reporting Council, which is separate from the profession, was formed in 1990, following the Dearing Report ('The making of accounting standards', Report of the Review Committee (London: Institute of Chartered Accountants in England and Wales, 1988)). This was primarily concerned with the decreasing reputation and effectiveness of the former Accounting Standards Committee, and proposed a new structure primarily with accounting standard setting in mind. The structure initially involved a standard-setting arm – the ASB and, under it, various committees such as the UITF – and alongside an enforcement arm, the FRRP. In 2004, various additional functions were created or transferred to the FRC structure, so that it is now as shown in Figure 5.1.

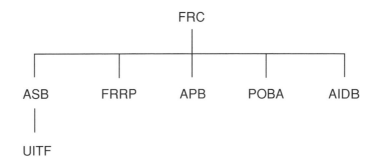

Key:

FRC	Financial Reporting Council
ASB	Accounting Standards Board
UITF	Urgent Issues Task Force
FRRP	Financial Reporting Review Panel
APB	Auditing Practices Board
POBA	Professional Oversight Board for Accountancy
AIDB	Accountancy Investigation and Discipline Board

Figure 5.1

The Financial Reporting Council

The FRC oversees all the bodies shown under it in the diagram in Figure 5.1. It is responsible for raising finance, making appointments and setting overall strategy. It does not become involved in the detail of, for example, setting accounting standards: the board of the ASB issues them under its own authority, having undertaken appropriate public consultation.

The FRC has a wide membership, drawn from senior ranks of the profession, industry and commerce, government and others.

The Accounting Standards Board

As noted above and in chapter 2, the ASB took over in 1990 from the ASC. The ASB has a full-time chairman and technical director plus, currently, another seven part-time board members. It also has a technical staff. It was very active in the 1990s in setting UK standards (FRSs 1–19 – see appendix 1) but since the IASB was formed in 2001, the ASB has moved into a different phase, in which it is mostly concerned with influencing the IASB and harmonising UK practice with the international standards.

The authority of accounting standards stems from the Companies Act. Section 256(3), inserted by the Companies Act 1989, around the time the new FRC structure was being put in place, states that 'The Secretary of State may make grants to or for the purposes of bodies concerned with (a) issuing account-ing standards, (b) overseeing and directing the issuing of accounting standards, or (c) investigating departures from such standards or from the accounting requirements of this Act and taking steps to secure compliance with them.' The regulations made under this section are the Accounting Standards (Prescribed Body) Regulations 1990, SI 1990 No. 1667 and they, in conjunction with sec-tion 256(1), result in accounting standards being defined as those issued by the ASB.

Under the ASB are a number of committees of which the best known is the UITF, described below. Others are concerned with the application of accounting standards to smaller entities, to the public sector, and to specialist areas such as the financial services industry.

The Urgent Issues Task Force

The UITF is a committee of the ASB, formed of sixteen members, the majority being from professional accounting firms. 'The UITF's role is to assist the ASB with important or significant accounting issues where there exists an accounting standard or a provision of companies legislation (including the requirement to give a true and fair view) and where unsatisfactory or conflicting interpreta-tions have developed or seem likely to develop.' (Foreword to UITF Abstracts, para. 2). In practice, this means that it is concerned with producing 'Abstracts', as its output is known, in a shorter timescale than a full accounting standard, on narrower issues than would be dealt with in an accounting standard.

The Abstracts are developed entirely by the UITF but are approved, and formally issued, by the ASB. They are regarded as part of GAAP, in the same way as accounting standards themselves, and, like accounting standards, are subject to enforcement by the FRRP. The Abstracts are listed in Appendix 1.

The Financial Reporting Review Panel

While the accounting standards produced by the ASB during the 1990s did much to improve accounting in that period, the formation and operation of the FRRP is an important second leg. Prior to 1990 there had been no effective enforcement of accounting standards (or indeed of the accounting requirements of the CA 1985), and the appearance of the Panel did much to change attitudes towards compliance.

The legal context for the Panel is sections 245–245C of the CA 1985. Specifically, the Panel is recognised under section 245C by the Companies (Defective Accounts) (Authorised Person) Order 1991, SI 1991 No. 13.

Under section 245, a company may voluntarily prepare revised accounts if it appears that the accounts do not comply with the Act. In practice, it is not common for directors to prepare revised accounts in this way – other than after a dialogue with the FRRP – though there are occasional examples. What is more common is that, when a company is preparing accounts for the following year, the directors may realise that the accounts of the previous year were not correct. There are procedures in accounting standards (FRS 3) for the correction of errors of that kind.

By agreement with the DTI, the Panel deals with enforcement of accounting standards and the accounting requirements of the Act relating to public companies (including listed companies) and large private companies. In practice, nearly all its cases have been against listed companies. The Panel had until 2004 been reactive. That is, it would enter a dialogue with a company where there was adverse press comment, or an allegation from, say, a shareholder or other interested party, that the accounts did not comply with the Act or accounting standards. The Panel would then discuss the matter with the company, through correspondence and/or formal meetings. In some cases, the directors persuaded the Panel that the treatment adopted was in fact appropriate; the case was then dropped. In other cases, the Panel was not so persuaded. In these circumstances, the Panel does not have the power to force the company to change its accounts. But it does have the power to refer the matter to the court. In the fourteen years since the Panel was formed, no cases have gone to court. In all these cases, the directors of the companies in question have seen the merit of acceding to the Panel's view and changing their accounts 'voluntarily'.

From 2004, as part of a wider picture of post-Enron reforms, the Panel has moved on to being pro-active in its work. That is, it continues to respond to complaints but it also reviews accounts as a matter of routine. Initial indications are that the Panel is concentrating its reviews on the accounts of the top 350 listed companies. It is likely, therefore, that the Panel will be taking more cases against companies, and this may lead to more restatements of accounts. The extent of this remains to be seen.

The move to pro-active enforcement is part of a wider European initiative. The Committee of European Securities Regulators (CESR) is seeking to put in place an enforcement mechanism in all EU countries. This will be a particularly big step forward in those countries that have had no enforcement activity at all.

The Panel's work hitherto has been in relation to UK GAAP accounts of UK companies. In future, the Panel is expected to extend its work to include also the enforcement of IFRS accounts for UK listed groups and for other UK entities that decide to adopt IFRS.

Professional Oversight Board for Accountancy

The Professional Oversight Board for Accountancy (POBA) is a new body and has three main roles. These are explained in the FRC's 2003 annual report (at p. 11) in the following terms:

> 'First, the government plans to bring forward legislation to delegate to it the statutory functions the Secretary of State for Trade and Industry currently exercises in relation to audit by authorising the professional accountancy bodies to act as supervisory bodies and to offer a recognised professional qualification. Secondly, it will establish and oversee an independent Audit Inspection Unit to monitor the audit of major listed companies and other public interest entities, including both the audit process and the decisions taken by auditors. Thirdly, it will oversee the regulatory activities of the individual professional accountancy bodies, including education and training, standards, professional conduct and discipline.'

The Audit Inspection Unit – the second of the roles of the POBA – is a new body but takes over an existing monitoring role previously carried out by the Joint Monitoring Unit, which was part of the Institutes. The 2004 restructuring takes away from the Institutes the role insofar as it relates to listed companies and other public interest entities. But the role in relation to other companies remains with the Institutes.

The Auditing Practices Board

The Auditing Practices Board (APB) was moved to be part of the FRC structure in 2004. Prior to this it came under the Accountancy Foundation and, prior to that, it was part of the profession through the CCAB. The APB issues auditing standards and guidelines for the profession. Its responsibilities have recently been extended to the development of ethical standards relating to the independence, objectivity and integrity of auditors. Many of the standards and guidelines are concerned with methodology and are not discussed here. However, the next major section deals with the law, auditing standards, and practice in the area of standard, modified and qualified audit reports.

Accountancy Investigation and Discipline Board

The Accountancy Investigation and Discipline Board (AIDB) is a new body though its role is not. The role is to investigate public interest cases involving accountants and to discipline as appropriate. This is seen by the government as one of the priorities for the FRC.

Audit reporting

Perhaps the most visible part of auditors' work is the audit report that is published as part of a company's annual report. The Act (sections 235–7) sets out the basic requirements. Under section 235, the auditors' report shall state whether, in the auditors' opinion, the annual accounts have been properly prepared in accordance with the Act, and in particular whether a true and fair view is given of the state of affairs at the end of the financial year and of the profit or loss of the company for the financial year. Certain more limited responsibilities of the auditor exist in relation to the directors' report and other information presented with the audited financial statements.

The Statement of Auditing Standards (SAS) 600, deals with audit report wording. There is a reasonably standardised wording for audit reports. The majority of audit reports use standard wording, namely that the accounts are properly prepared under the Act and give a true and fair view. This is known as an unqualified audit report (sometimes informally called a 'clean opinion'). It should be noted that the requirement of the Act and auditing standards is for the auditor to express an opinion. The auditor does not prepare the accounts and does not give a certificate. References are sometimes heard to 'audit certificates' but these represent an incorrect understanding of the role of the auditor.

Where an auditor is not satisfied that the accounts are properly prepared and give a true and fair view, he should modify or qualify his report. There are a number of possible ways in which this can be done, as shown in Box 5.1.

There are other types of non-standard wording that do not count as 'qualified' opinions, but are called 'modified' audit reports. The most common situation where these are used is in circumstances where the going concern status of the company is in doubt. In these circumstances, the directors need to give disclosures about the uncertainty. If the auditor regards the uncertainty as 'inherent' rather than 'fundamental', and the directors' disclosures are adequate, there is no modification to the audit report.

However, if the auditors regard the uncertainty as 'fundamental', they should include a paragraph in their report headed 'fundamental uncertainty', or similar, and refer to the uncertainty in their report. A fundamental uncertainty is defined in SAS 600 as an inherent uncertainty, the magnitude of whose potential impact is so great that, without clear disclosure of the nature and implications of the uncertainty, the view given by the financial statements would be seriously misleading.

In the 'fundamental uncertainty' paragraph the auditors explain that in forming their opinion they have considered the adequacy of the disclosures in the financial statements concerning the possible outcome of the uncertainty, and they describe the uncertainty, the possible outcome and its effect. Having made comments about the fundamental uncertainty, however, the auditor then adds words such as 'our opinion is not qualified in this respect'.

Nature of circumstances	Qualification	Reason
Limitation on scope of audit work	Disclaimer of opinion	Possible effect of the limitation is so material or pervasive that auditors cannot express an opinion
Limitation on scope of audit work	'Except for' opinion	Possible effect of the limitation is material but not so material or pervasive that auditors cannot express an opinion
Disagreement	Adverse opinion	The effect of the matter giving rise to the disagreement is so material or pervasive that the financial statements are seriously misleading
Disagreement	'Except for' opinion	The effect of the matter giving rise to the disagreement is material but not so material or pervasive that the financial statements are seriously misleading

Box 5.1

The role of accountants in transactions

Although this book is concerned with accounting rather than with the full range of what accountants do, the role of accountants in transactions still merits brief mention.

The word 'transaction' is often used rather loosely to mean a capital markets transaction such as:

- the raising of share capital which could be a new listing of shares (an Initial Public Offering – IPO) or a further issue of shares by a company that is already listed;
- a secondary listing of shares, for example when a company already listed in London seeks a US listing;

- the raising of capital in the form of a debt issue;
- a merger or acquisition involving a listed company.

Accountants carry out much behind the scenes advisory work in relation to transactions such as these. For example, they carry out investigations of varying degrees of depth in connection with potential acquisitions; these are often called due diligence exercises.

6

Communicating accounting information

Background

The Companies Act 1985 requires that all British companies prepare annual accounts, send them to shareholders and file them on the public record at Companies House. There are some exemptions from these basic requirements; for example, certain smaller companies can file abbreviated information at Companies House.

However, this chapter is primarily concerned with listed companies. In addition to the requirements of the Companies Act, they have to comply with the Listing Rules. In connection with periodic financial reporting, their requirements include:

- Selected additional disclosures, for example relating to corporate governance matters.
- Release of interim results, generally for the first six months of the year. (Companies listed in the US have to publish interim results every quarter.)
- Release of preliminary announcement of annual results (often referred to as the 'prelims').

The corporate reporting supply chain

In practice, many groups of people are involved in the reporting process for listed companies – or the 'corporate reporting supply chain', as it has been called by the recent book, Di Piazza and Eccles, *Building public trust: the future of corporate reporting* (New York: John Wiley & Sons Inc., 2002). This may be shown as indicated in Figure 6.1.

Figure 6.1 illustrates the roles and relationships among the various groups and individuals involved in the production, preparation, communication and use of corporate reporting information. Company executives and boards of directors have responsibility for preparing or approving the information that companies report. In a UK context, a company's audit committee, which is a committee of the board, has an important part to play. This is described in the Combined Code. Audit committees of listed companies comprise independent non-executive directors who should work with the external auditors and challenge management with regard to the draft annual report as a whole, including the statutory accounts. An audit committee also typically reviews interim results

Figure 6.1

and prelims. Recent years have seen audit committees perform a stronger and more independent role in this area, though practice in this respect is still mixed.

Other terms used to describe participants in the corporate reporting supply chain deserve clarification:

- *Independent auditors* are firms of auditors in their capacity as auditors. Companies may also use their audit firm, or indeed other accounting firms, for other work, for example accounting or tax.
- *Information distributors* are data vendors that consolidate reported information and provide it for others to use. This group also includes news media, web sites, and other communications media that provide commentary on company information.
- *Third-party analysts* are those who use the information reported by companies, usually in combination with other information and research, to evaluate a company's prospects and performance.
- *Investors and other stakeholders* are the ultimate consumers of corporate reporting information. Investors include company shareholders but may also refer to potential shareholders. Other stakeholders include employees, business partners, customers and suppliers, community members, social and environmental groups and non-governmental organisations.
- *Standard-setters* most obviously include bodies such as the ASB and IASB. Professional accounting bodies also have a role here.
- *Market regulators* includes national government agencies, and regional equivalents (e.g. EU). It includes both those that regulate companies and those that regulate stock markets.
- *Enabling technologies* are primarily internet technologies and Extensible Business Reporting Language (XBRL), a language that enables electronic standardisation of information from all companies so as to ease search and analysis.

The reality of the 'earnings game'

While Figure 6.1 shows the major players in the corporate reporting supply chain, there is a different, more pragmatic, description that can be given.

65

Much of recent accounting reform has been directed at making it difficult for management to present smoothed results. Definitions of assets and liabilities have shifted the emphasis away from smoothed income numbers to the balance sheet, as explained in chapter 7 at p. 73.

A related reform has been to try to reduce the focus on 'the bottom line' – an undefined term, generally taken to mean the profit attributable to shareholders, that is the profit after tax, and after minorities. Earnings, another figure of considerable focus by the market, is similar to the bottom line as defined above but also after deducting preference dividends. Earnings per shares (EPS) is earnings expressed on a per share basis. The ASB has tried, for example in FRS 3, to introduce the idea that the whole of the performance of a company in a year cannot realistically be condensed into a single number. Rather, the ASB argues, there should be presented a series of measures, such as operating profit, profit before and after tax, and total recognised gains and losses (which includes, for example, revaluations of assets, and is shown outside the profit and loss account in the Statement of total recognised gains and losses). Despite the ASB's argument, there is still considerable focus on a single bottom line earnings number.

Prior to these changes, and to some extent still, it has been the desire of some managements to present a smooth time series of numbers, characterised at the extreme by 'the chairman is pleased to report the 27th year of uninterrupted earnings growth'. Whilst this type of reporting did lack a certain credibility, analysts and other commentators find it both comforting to receive results announcements of that type and easy to deal with them. In contrast, earnings numbers that jump around from year to year in a seemingly random pattern make it very difficult to understand, and therefore value, the company concerned.

Against this background, there has developed in recent years the so-called 'earnings game', in which management:

- seek to deliver a track record of consistent earnings growth
- manage earnings expectations carefully
- aim to slightly beat market expectations
- make business decisions to meet or beat expectations.

Analysts, for their part:

- hammer stocks that fail to meet expectations
- listen carefully for the 'whisper number' (that is, a unofficial management forecast of earnings)
- hammer stocks that fail to meet the whisper number.

Whilst this description is perhaps an oversimplification, there is some truth in it. There are also a number of disadvantages arising from it. The desire to meet earnings expectations can lead to suboptimal business decisions. For example, a potential acquisition or new product development may be clearly worthwhile in the medium or longer term, but reduce EPS in the short term. If it is not done because of short-term earnings considerations, that is a poor business decision. The desire to meet earnings expectations can also lead to pressure on the financial reporting process. Many conversations between company management and auditors are based around the desire to (for example) carry forward an item of cost, or recognise some revenue early, in order to meet a target profit number and thereby not to disappoint the market.

Nonetheless, the combined effect of accounting standards that lead to more volatile results, better governance within companies (e.g. better audit committees), and better auditing have resulted in more volatile – that is, more realistic – profit numbers being reported. This has opened up another development: that of reporting adjusted, or non-GAAP, or pro-forma, earnings numbers.

Adjusted earnings numbers

Partly in response to the pressures outlined above, some companies have developed the practice in recent years of publishing adjusted earnings numbers, sometimes called 'non-GAAP' or 'pro-forma' numbers. Whether this practice is valid or not depends on how it is done.

Companies' objectives in this area are more often based on a desire to stabilise reported earnings, rather than merely to increase them. Sometimes the objective is to focus on earnings numbers that are close to operating cash flow. Hence one tends to see, as well as the required GAAP numbers, non-GAAP earnings numbers such as:

- Earnings before goodwill amortisation (goodwill is added back because it is a non-cash item; also because goodwill is rather nebulous in nature).
- Earnings before exceptional items (exceptional items are, or are supposed to be, one-off items that potentially distort the underlying trend).
- EBITDA (earnings before interest, tax, depreciation and amortisation); this is regarded by some companies as being a stabilised version of operating cash flow.
- Earnings at constant exchange rates (that is, showing what the earnings would have been if last year's exchange rates had been applied to this year's earnings of overseas subsidiaries).

These adjusted numbers are sometimes presented in additional columns (for example, columns showing pre-exceptional, exceptional, total), additional rows that show subtotals such as operating profit before goodwill amortisation, or shaded boxes that have similar objectives.

While each of these has its own logic, the danger with them is that different companies adjust their earnings numbers in different ways; as a result there is little comparability among the adjusted results. Moreover, especially in preliminary announcements, interim results, and in the 'front half' of annual reports (that is, in highlights statements, chairman's statements, and operating and financial reviews) sometimes more prominence is given to these adjusted earnings numbers than to the required GAAP numbers. This is a practice that concerns auditors. Reflecting this, the APB has issued guidance to auditors pointing out, among other things, that the GAAP numbers should be at least as prominent as the adjusted earnings numbers; that any adjusted earnings numbers should be properly explained and reconciled to the GAAP numbers. At present, there are no equivalent requirements of companies although it appears that the Financial Services Authority (FSA) may introduce rules in this area. Some improvement in practice is likely to emerge as the jurisdiction of the FRRP is being extended to include the OFR as well as the statutory accounts.

Users and analysis of accounting information

Users of accounts look to accounts for a variety of purposes. Nevertheless, it is generally accepted that the prime users of accounts are investors, or shareholders, including potential shareholders. The requirements of accounting standards are based on this assumption. A key underpinning of accounting standards is that investors want information that will allow them to forecast cash flows. This is key to valuation of companies and therefore of shares. But suppliers, bankers and employees are also very interested in information from which they can forecast cash flows, as they wish to predict whether the company will be able to pay them, repay loans, and pay salaries respectively.

Having said that, there are specific uses of accounts and specific pieces of analysis that need to be carried out. For example, a loan agreement may include clauses under which the company has to keep certain ratios within defined bounds. For instance, gearing (see glossary) should be not more than X% or interest cover (see glossary) should exceed Y times. In the event that these ratios, or 'covenants', are not satisfied, the loan becomes immediately repayable. For this purpose, there has to be clarity as to exactly how the numbers that contribute to those ratios are defined. This is explored in greater detail in chapter 18.

7
Current trends in accounting

Why all the change?

The financial reporting environment and the financial reporting rules that have to be applied are in a constant state of flux. The annual report of a UK listed company now looks very different from its equivalent of ten or twenty years ago. The same is true to a lesser extent for an unlisted company. The main factors that underlie the changes are:

- developments in business
- activities of standard-setters
- responses to scandals.

Developments in business

Business transactions continue to be innovative and become more complex. Over the last twenty or thirty years, for example, the leasing industry has changed from being clearly in two halves – lessors who rent out equipment for the short term, and subsidiaries of banks who provide finance through finance leases – to an industry where a variety of players offer leases with varying degrees of risk for different parties, thus blurring the traditional clear divide. This has led to pressure to update the lease accounting rules to reflect contemporary business. A more obvious example is the whole area of financial instruments, including derivatives, which has witnessed an explosion in volume and sophistication in the last twenty years or so.

New industries also emerge and bring new accounting challenges. Revenue recognition – primarily the question of when (i.e. in which accounting period) revenue should be recognised – was not a problem when factories made goods, put them on a lorry and delivered them. The day the goods left the factory gate coincided with the date of invoicing and that was the date the revenue was recognised. But in the software industry, a supplier may develop software at its own expense, and then secure a customer who buys: (a) a piece of software; (b) an agreement to upgrade it for up to two years; (c) a helpline and maintenance support service running for five years. If this compound sale is made for a single price (say £1m.), the software house has to consider whether and how to disaggregate the revenue into parts and when to recognise them. If there are market values for the separate supply of each of the three components, that task is made somewhat easier, but this is not always the case.

Accountants and others sometimes complain that accounting rules are becoming too complex and seek to lay the blame at the door of the standard-setters or the profession. However, to a large extent the increasing complexity merely reflects business developments.

Activities of standard-setters

In the UK, the first accounting standards were developed in the early 1970s. By 1980, the annual compendium of UK accounting standards was 320 pages long. The equivalent 2003/4 edition is 2,534 pages long of which 118 pages comprise a discussion paper on the reform of lease accounting to reflect the developments described above. A further 204 of its pages consist of proposals to implement the international rules on accounting for financial instruments – recently converted into FRSs 25 and 26.

Accounting standard-setters are now an established part of the institutional framework. There is no sense in which they are soon likely to have finished their work, having written all the accounting rules that are necessary to deal with varied and uncertain practices that need to be standardised. New issues continually emerge and, such is the depth of the subject, there is no shortage of issues to which an active standard-setter can usefully turn its attention.

The strong focus on global convergence of accounting rules strengthens this: even if an accounting issue might be clear in, say, a UK context – perhaps through an established industry practice – there may be divergent practices in other countries. Hence the standard-setters see this as a harmonisation challenge.

Response to scandals

Many pieces of legislation or other rules stem from scandals. Indeed, in the UK, the accounting standards programme was originally started partly in response to differences in accounting treatment that emerged in the GEC/AEI take-over in the late 1960s. More recently, calls for strengthened accounting standards on financial instruments followed reports of certain banks and corporates incurring large-scale losses from derivative operations, at a time when the transactions were not (by current standards) being accounted for properly, and were not even being disclosed. The new international standard (IFRS 2) on share-based payment has been developed partly because it is an area where accounting was simply not giving realistic answers. But it was given considerable fillip by the scandals about the size of executive remuneration packages in which share options played a large part and yet were not reflected in the profit and loss account.

The new millennium has of course been characterised by numerous corporate scandals, starting perhaps with Enron and WorldCom in the US. Parmalat in Italy in early 2004 showed that the capacity for things to go seriously awry in the corporate world was not restricted to the Americas. The reaction to these scandals has followed the traditional pattern in which governments and other regulators demand action and new, tougher rules in order that 'the same should not be allowed to happen again'. This is naïve: many years ago, laws were established forbidding activities such as robbery and murder, yet we may note that they continue. This is not to say that it is pointless to react to such scandals. Indeed it is good to take the opportunity to improve specific rules that were found to be weak. The risk is that people will mistakenly expect that there will be no further difficulties. The risk also is that new rules place a further burden of cost and process that hits the 99% of companies that are good citizens. This is the case with much of the US reaction to Enron: the rules coming into force under the Sarbanes-Oxley Act and from the Public Companies Accounting Oversight Board that Sarbox established in the area of internal control procedures and reporting are a good example. On the other hand, one of the very good effects of Enron was that it crystallised an improvement in the US accounting rules for determining when special purpose entities (SPEs) should be consolidated, and by whom. Prior to this, the FASB had had a project on reforming the rules for consolidations that had set something of a record by being active, if that is the right word, for 18 years without resolution.

Current trends in thinking

Greater disclosure

Throughout society, and in particular throughout the business environment, there is a trend towards greater disclosure and transparency. Many of the current and recent changes in corporate reporting can be seen as examples of that. From an accounting point of view, this is often described as allowing shareholders and other users of accounts to see the business through the eyes of management. A good example is segment reporting. Companies are required to give analyses of turnover, profit, net assets and some other measures according to a line of business and a geographical segmentation. The information – certainly in the international and US rules – is to be based on the form of analysis that is provided internally to the chief decision makers.

As well as accounting changes in a narrow sense, there are many other examples: greater disclosure of corporate governance arrangements; greater disclosure of directors' remuneration packages; earlier disclosure of price-sensitive information and so on.

Principles v. rules

One of the recent and continuing issues in the accounting profession has been the so-called 'Principles v. rules' debate. Those on the principles side say that: as professionals they understand accounting principles, and are taught to analyse and apply judgement; to have rules imposed upon them is unnecessary both because their principles work well enough and because not all circumstances are the same and hence the application of judgement gives better results than a straitjacket of rules; and, inevitably, transactions will arise that are outside the detailed rules but would be within the principles. Those on the rules side say that: principles are too vague to result in consistent application; judgement too often means flexibility and acceding to management's wishes; comparability of reporting is very important and that can only be achieved by standardisation.

This debate is likely to continue. The IASB and the UK ASB argue, with some justification, that their standards set out principles in contrast to the US approach which is more detailed and prescriptive. This is certainly true in relative terms; but, meanwhile, more and more detailed rules continue to be written by all standard-setters.

Use of fair value

An important current trend is towards the increased use of fair values in accounting. As described in chapter 3 at pp. 37–42, the principal UK legal framework is based around historical cost accounting, with permission to state certain assets at current cost, market value or fair value (these terms are broadly synonymous). However, current thinking is that, for an increasing number of assets and liabilities, fair value provides more relevant information than historical cost to users of accounts. This is even though it may be less reliable than the equivalent historical cost information. The relevance/reliability trade off depends on the asset or liability in question. For example, shares in companies listed and actively traded on the London Stock Exchange have an easily determined fair value. An investment in an unlisted start-up company is altogether harder to value.

As the following examples illustrate, UK and international accounting currently use a 'mixed model', that is, some assets and most liabilities are stated at cost but others are stated (or may be stated) at fair value.

- Tangible fixed assets (called 'property, plant and equipment' in IFRS) may be stated at valuation. In practice, it is properties that are sometimes revalued; other categories, such as plant, are valued only occasionally.
- Investment properties, however, are required to be stated at current valuation in UK GAAP (SSAP 19). This is because it is widely accepted that, for properties held for rental income and capital growth, value is much more relevant than cost. A well-developed valuation profession in the UK helps this to work. In IFRS, however, there is an option: either cost or valuation may be used for investment properties. This reflects two factors. First, the valuation profession is not so well developed in some other countries. Second, in IFRS the only required statement that reports performance is the profit and loss account, whereas in the UK there is the STRGL which enables UK GAAP to report value changes separately from realised gains and losses. International reporting of the components of performance is under review.

- Financial instruments, as explained in chapter 15 at pp. 157–9, is a complex area where part of the debate is the question of how far fair value should be applied. The international standard, IAS 39, which is becoming part of UK GAAP through FRS 26, is a pragmatic, and somewhat unsatisfactory, example of the mixed model, with some assets fair valued and others carried at cost. There is also an option to fair value certain instruments.
- Perhaps a less obvious example is agriculture, but the international standard has recently applied fair value accounting to this area too, based on the greater relevance of the information.

As may be noted, some of these examples require the use of fair value accounting while others permit it. Moreover, in some cases, the gains and losses arising from fair valuing are presented in the profit and loss account, while others are reported in the STRGL, in UK terms, or in equity (shareholders' funds) in IFRS. It is a very mixed picture, but the direction of change – towards increased use of fair value information – is clear.

Some of the moves towards the increased use of fair value, especially in the area of financial instrument accounting, have been contrary to the original version of the CA 1985. There are similar obstacles in other EU Member States, as their laws too stem from the EU fourth directive (Council Directive 78/660/EEC on the annual accounts of certain types of companies, OJ 1978 No. L222/11). To allow the pre-2004 IAS 39 rules on financial instruments to be consistent with national law, the EU, through the fair value directive (Council Directive 2001/65/EC amending Directives 78/660/EEC, 83/349/EEC and 86/635/EEC as regards the valuation rules for the annual and consolidated accounts of certain types of companies as well as of banks and other financial institutions, OJ 2001 No. L283/28), developed certain changes to the fourth directive. These changes have been enacted in the UK as part of the Companies Act 1985 (International Accounting Standards and Other Accounting Amendments) Regulations 2004 (SI 2004 No. 2947) (see chapter 3, p. 42).

Smoothing v. volatility

An important trend in accounting over the last few years is that it is becoming increasingly difficult for companies to report a smooth time series of results. The trend is towards greater volatility.

As noted in chapter 6, it has long been an objective of some managements to report a smooth profits trend. In the 1970s and 1980s this was generally not too difficult to achieve. However, in the 1990s the UK ASB brought in a number of accounting standards – many of which have international counterparts – that challenged this approach to reporting. The ASB made the point that businesses go through economic cycles, rates of interest vary, foreign exchange rates fluctuate and it is artificial to somehow report results as if the company were in a very stable situation. The ASB achieved a change of approach by altering the focus of accounting from the profit and loss account to the balance sheet. It put the main focus on properly identifying the assets and liabilities at the start and end of the year, and measuring them appropriately. For example, FRS 12 (and IAS 37) on provisions made it no longer possible for a company to provide for a cost that is likely to be incurred in the following year, unless it can be shown that it is an actual liability at the year end. Previously, especially where a company had unusually good results for the year, it would sometimes provide for certain future costs, even though it was not committed to incur them at the year end. The effect would be to reduce profits of the earlier year and thereby protect the profits of the later year.

A second example is FRS 11 (and IAS 36) on impairment of fixed assets and goodwill. The objective of these standards is to ensure that such assets are not carried at above their recoverable amount, and that any impairments are identified and reported in the right period. Impairments, of tangible and intangible assets and of goodwill, can be large expenses that can dominate results announcements.

These two standards to some extent remove managements' discretion as to when expenses should be recognised. The result is that they lose some control over the trend line of their results, and hence the results become more volatile.

A similar effect arises from the trend, described above, towards more use of fair values. This is especially the case where the changes in the fair values are reported in the profit and loss account. The leading example of this is accounting for financial instruments, where financial assets and liabilities held for trading – and some others according to choice – are treated in this way. Reported profits can thus be affected by swings in interest rates and foreign exchange rates as well as by changes in the underlying value of investments, e.g. arising from an equity investment becoming more valuable.

There is a very practical effect arising from the inclusion of fair value changes in profit measurement, namely that it will not be possible until the year end to know what the profit is likely to be. It has been a source of some comfort for boards, and for analysts, to have, say a month before the year end, a good idea of the likely results for the year. This is now much harder to achieve.

PART II
Some specifics

8
Individual entity accounts and consolidated accounts

The distinction between entity accounts and consolidated accounts

General distinction

There is an important distinction between the accounts of an individual entity, such as a company, and the consolidated accounts of a group. An individual entity could take a number of forms. The most common example is a single company, but an entity for accounting purposes could be a partnership or joint venture – that is, it does not need to have separate legal personality. A group typically comprises a parent company and a number of subsidiary undertakings.

Entity accounts, sometimes called 'individual', or 'solus' accounts, are the accounts of the entity itself. Thus, where a company transacts much of its business through subsidiaries rather than directly itself, its entity accounts will record an investment in one or more subsidiaries in its balance sheet and will record dividend income in its profit and loss account. The trading transactions will be included in the individual entity accounts of the subsidiaries themselves and are not reflected in the parent's individual entity accounts.

It is generally accepted that the individual accounts of a parent entity, while they have some uses, do not properly reflect the parent's results, assets and liabilities. For example, where much of the business is carried out in one or more of the parent's subsidiaries, this would not be reflected in the entity accounts of the parent. Hence, for many years, it has been the practice to prepare 'group accounts' for groups of companies, albeit with exceptions as discussed below. Group accounts now almost exclusively take the form of consolidated accounts. In practice, the terms 'group accounts' and 'consolidated accounts' are used interchangeably.

Consolidated accounts aim to present a picture of the group as a whole as if it were a single entity. Hence the entire turnover, expenses, profit, assets and liabilities of the group are shown in aggregate, irrespective of whether they sit in the parent entity or in a subsidiary, and reflect the transactions of the group with parties outside the group. Subsidiaries are consolidated based on a control criterion, whether they are wholly owned or partly owned, and whether they are domestic or foreign. There are a number of qualifications and exceptions to these general statements as discussed below.

Distributable profits

One of the most important applications of the distinction between entity accounts and consolidated accounts lies in the field of company distributions. Simply put: it is entities (not groups) that make distributions. It is entities to which the legal rules on distributions apply. The details about realised and distributable profits are discussed in chapter 16, but for simplicity let us assume that a company's accumulated distributable profits equate to the balance on its profit and loss account. It might be that the balance sheet of a parent entity and the consolidated balance sheet of the group that it heads are as shown in Box 8.1.

	Parent entity	Consolidation
Share capital	100	100
P & L account (retained profit)	50	(20)
Shareholders' funds	150	80
Net assets	150	80

Box 8.1

One might expect that the consolidated balance sheet would be stronger than that of the parent alone, and indeed this is often the case. However, a situation such as the above is by no means rare. One common underlying reason is that the parent may have made an acquisition, of which a large element was goodwill, and, in the consolidated accounts, the goodwill was written off the reserves, as was permissible prior to 1998, thus superficially weakening the consolidated balance sheet. Alternatively, the subsidiaries might have made losses. The key point is that when the parent considers whether it can make a distribution, it refers to its entity accounts. These show that it has profits available for distribution of 50. The fact that there is a deficit in the group does not affect the parent's ability to make a distribution.

Conversely, the parent's entity accounts might show a much smaller balance on the profit and loss reserve (say 10) than is shown in its consolidated accounts (say 150), for example because the subsidiaries have not passed their profits up to the parent by way of dividend. If the parent wishes to pay a large dividend to its shareholders it must first receive a dividend from its subsidiaries.

Entity focus for tax purposes

Another key application of entity accounts is for tax purposes. Again, the Inland Revenue assesses tax on the taxable income of entities, not on a group basis (though this is subject to various exceptions). So for example, if a parent sells goods to a subsidiary during the year for 100, including a profit of 40, and those goods remain unsold by the subsidiary at the year end, the 40 is taxed in the parent entity, even though the goods are unsold by the wider group. As discussed below, adjustments are made in the consolidated accounts to eliminate this intra-group profit.

When to consolidate

General approach

UK law, UK accounting standards and IFRS are relevant in this area. The way they interact is as follows. Whether a UK company has to prepare consolidated financial statements is determined by considering whether, at its balance sheet date, it is a parent under section 227 of the Companies Act 1985. When the parent is required to prepare consolidated financial statements by reference to the CA 1985, there are three possibilities:

- If, on its balance sheet date, its securities are traded on a regulated market, it is then required to apply EU-adopted IFRS for its consolidated financial statements. Where this is the case, Schedules 4 and 4A (and 9 and 9A) of the Companies Act 1985 do not apply, but the other provisions of the Act do still apply. The group's consolidated financial statements must comply with IFRS including IAS 27 'Consolidated and separate financial statements'.
- If its shares are not traded on a regulated market, but it opts to apply IFRS, the above bullet again applies.
- If its shares are not traded on a regulated market, and it opts to stay on UK GAAP, Schedules 4 and 4A (and 9 and 9A) of the Companies Act 1985 continue to apply along with the other provisions of the Act. The UK standard FRS 2 also applies.

Duty to prepare consolidated accounts

As discussed in chapter 3, at p. 27, section 227 (1) sets out the basic requirement that directors shall prepare group accounts in the form of consolidated accounts if, at the end of the year, the company is a parent company. However there are certain exemptions from this requirement.

Exemptions for intermediate parents

A major exemption from this requirement stems from EU law. Under section 228, 'a company is exempt from the requirement to prepare group accounts if it is itself a subsidiary undertaking and its immediate parent undertaking is established under the law of a member State of the European Economic Community' in defined circumstances. This exemption is subject to various conditions, set out in section 228(2), notably that the UK subgroup must be included in the consolidated accounts of a larger (EU) group and those accounts are prepared under the EU seventh directive – that is, law that is equivalent to the UK law relating to consolidated accounts. The effect of this is that a UK subgroup held by a (say) French (or, of course, UK) parent need not prepare consolidated accounts, as it is included in the consolidated accounts of the overall French group.

As a result of a reform in 2004 (the Companies Act 1985 (International Accounting Standards and Other Accounting Amendments) Regulations 2004 (SI 2004 No. 2947)), this exemption is extended. Section 228A provides exemption from the need to prepare group accounts if a company 'is itself a subsidiary undertaking and its parent undertaking is not established under the law of an EEA State' in defined circumstances. Among these circumstances is section 228(2)(b) which states that the accounts of the larger group must be drawn up in accordance with the EU seventh directive (Council Directive 83/349/EEC on consolidated accounts, OJ 1983 No. L193/1) or in a manner equivalent. There is still discussion in the profession as to whether, for example, accounts drawn up under US GAAP would be regarded as 'equivalent'.

Exemptions for small groups

The second major exemption is that 'a parent company need not prepare group accounts for a financial year in relation to which the group headed by that company qualifies as a small or medium-sized group and is not an ineligible group' (section 248). Note that it is the group as a whole that needs to qualify as small or medium-sized in order to avoid the need to prepare consolidated accounts. It is not sufficient merely for the parent to be small or medium. The definitions of small group and medium-sized group are set out in section 249.

What to consolidate

The spectrum of interests in other companies

This chapter is primarily concerned with groups and subsidiaries. Nevertheless, it is useful to consider the spectrum of interests in other companies and to contrast the accounting treatment in the consolidated accounts for different levels of investment. The following distinctions are made in accounting:

- *Investment*. Where a company holds a stake of up to 20% in another, that is normally accounted for as an investment. It is assumed at this level that the investor does not significantly influence (let alone control) the investee. The UK accounting treatment is that the investment is held on the balance sheet either at cost or at a revalued amount; and the income recognised from the investee is merely the dividends received or receivable. In IFRS, an investment of this type would be a financial instrument, for which there are a number of possible accounting treatments, as discussed in chapter 15, at p. 159.

- *Associate.* Where a company holds a stake in the range 20% to 50% in another, that is normally accounted for as an associate. It is assumed at this level that the investor has 'significant influence' over the investee. For example, an associate holding would normally be accompanied by a seat on the board of the investee. However, the 20% threshold is an indication rather than a rule. For example, a holding of 18% could give rise to significant influence if accompanied by a seat on the board. A holding of 22% might not give rise to significant influence if there was a dominant majority shareholder holding between 51% and 78%. The accounting rules for associates are set out in FRS 9 (UK) and IAS 28 (IRFS). These rules are similar to each other and can be summarised as follows: (a) the investment in the associate is held on the consolidated balance sheet at cost plus the investor's share of the associate's post-acquisition retained profits; (b) in its consolidated profit and loss account, the investor recognises its share of profits of the associate.

- *Joint venture.* A joint venture (JV) may well involve an investment in the 20% to 50% range but is distinguishable from an associate by virtue of the arrangements between the investing parties. The accounting rules for JVs are set out in FRS 9 (UK) and IAS 31 (IRFS). These rules are broadly similar to each other. FRS 9 defines a JV as: 'An entity in which the reporting entity holds an interest on a long-term basis and is jointly controlled by the reporting entity and one or more other venturers under a contractual arrangement'. The basic accounting approach is similar to associates; for example, the share of profits of the JV is included in the investor's consolidated profit and loss account, and the consolidated balance sheet carrying value is determined in a similar way. However, in general, JVs are more important to an investor than associates and this leads to more detailed disclosure requirements in respect of JVs. In the UK (but not in IFRS) this includes showing the investor's share of the JV's turnover along with the group turnover, and on the balance sheet there is shown the investor's share of the JV's gross assets and gross liabilities. In IFRS an alternative method of accounting for JVs is proportional consolidation.

- *Subsidiary.* A subsidiary arises when one company takes control of another, and this leads generally to full consolidation of that subsidiary. Consolidated accounts are discussed in this chapter. When the company first becomes a subsidiary, acquisition accounting or merger accounting is used as a method of bringing the new subsidiary into the consolidated accounts. The details of accounting for acquisitions of, and mergers with, subsidiaries are set out in chapter 9.

Participating interest (section 260)

A phrase that is central to definitions of associate is 'participating interest'. This is defined in section 260 as 'an interest held by an undertaking in the shares of another undertaking which it holds on a long-term basis for the purpose of securing a contribution to its activities by the exercise of control or influence arising from or related to that interest'. The Act adds that 'a holding of 20 per cent or more of the shares of an undertaking shall be presumed to be a participating interest unless the contrary is shown' (section 260(2)); and that an interest in shares includes: (a) an interest which is convertible into an interest in shares; and (b) an option to acquire shares or any such interest (section 260(3)). FRS 9 'Associates and joint ventures' amplifies this, saying that the investor's interest must be a beneficial one and the benefits expected to arise must be linked to the exercise of its significant influence over the investee's operating and financial policies.

Until the Companies Act 1985 (International Accounting Standards and Other Accounting Amendments) Regulations 2004 (SI 2004 No. 2947), this phrase used to be an important part of the definition of a subsidiary also.

Definitions of parent and subsidiary undertaking

The key to determining what should be included in consolidated accounts is the definitions in section 258 of 'parent undertaking' and 'subsidiary undertaking'. The key parts of this section are as follows:

'(2) An undertaking is a parent undertaking in relation to another undertaking, a subsidiary undertaking, if:
  (a) it holds a majority of the voting rights in the undertaking, or
  (b) it is a member of the undertaking and has the right to appoint or remove a majority of its board of directors, or
  (c) it has the right to exercise a dominant influence over the undertaking:
      (i) by virtue of provisions contained in the undertaking's memorandum or articles, or
      (ii) by virtue of a control contract, or
  (d) it is a member of the undertaking and controls alone, pursuant to an agreement with other shareholders or members, a majority of the voting rights in the undertaking.
(3) For the purposes of subsection (2) an undertaking shall be treated as a member of another undertaking—
  (a) if any of its subsidiary undertakings is a member of that undertaking, or
  (b) if any shares in that other undertaking are held by a person acting on behalf of the undertaking or any of its subsidiary undertakings.
(4) An undertaking is also a parent undertaking in relation to another undertaking, a subsidiary undertaking, if—
  (a) it has the power to exercise, or actually exercises, dominant influence or control over it, or
  (b) it and the subsidiary undertaking are managed on a unified basis.'

The common theme underlying these definitions is that of control. Control often goes with ownership but, as the notes below explain, the two are not necessarily coincident.

Of the above, it is section 258(2)(a) that most frequently gives rise to the parent/subsidiary relationship. Often, of course, a parent will hold 100% of the voting rights of another company, thus making it its subsidiary undertaking. The minimum holding to be effective under this subsection is a bare majority, that is, 50% plus one vote, and this gives effective control assuming there are no special or weighted voting rights.

Subsection (2)(b) is also relevant reasonably often in practice. Company A might have (say) only one share in company B, but B will be the subsidiary undertaking of A if A has the right to appoint or remove a majority of the board.

Subsection (2)(c) and (d) are less common in practice in the UK. Subsection (3) merely points out that the holding need not be direct.

Subsection (4) is important in practice in the UK. It was included in the seventh directive (Council Directive 83/349/EEC) as part of the objective of identifying for consolidation any companies that might otherwise be 'off balance sheet'. Until the 2004 amendment to the Act, the notion of 'participating interest' used to be part of subsection (4). It now identifies as a subsidiary undertaking any company where the parent controls it in one of two specified ways. The first method of control is that the parent 'has the power to exercise, or actually exercises, dominant influence or control over it'. This is not defined in the Act, but is defined in FRS 2 'Subsidiary undertakings' as follows:

> '*The actual exercise of dominant influence* is the exercise of an influence that achieves the result that the operating and financial policies of the undertaking influenced are set in accordance with the wishes of the holder of the influence and for the holder's benefit whether or not those wishes are explicit. The actual exercise of dominant influence is identified by its effect in practice rather than by the way in which it is exercised.' [FRS 2, para. 7(b)]

> '*The power to exercise dominant influence* is a power that, if exercised, would give rise to the actual exercise of dominant influence as defined in paragraph 7b.' [FRS 2, para. 7(c)]

The second method under which a company might become a subsidiary undertaking under subsection (4) is where 'it [the parent] and the subsidiary undertaking are managed on a unified basis'. Again this is defined in FRS 2:

> 'Two or more undertakings are *managed on a unified basis* [emphasis added] if the whole of the operations of the undertakings are integrated and they are managed as a single unit. Unified management does not arise solely because one undertaking manages another.' [FRS 2, para. 12].

83

The 'managed on a unified basis' route does not apply very frequently, though it has been applied in the context of some dual listed companies. The former – the power to exercise or the actual exercise of dominant influence – is more common. It often serves to identify as subsidiary undertakings those companies where control and ownership do not converge. For example, where A owns 25% or 49% of B but in practice controls it (actually exercises a dominant influence over it), B will be A's subsidiary undertaking. In such circumstances there are often other arrangements, such as management fees, or special dividend rights, that give A a greater economic interest than the 25% or 49% holding would suggest.

Prior to the 2004 amendment to the CA 1985, actual exercise of dominant influence alone was not sufficient for the entity to be a subsidiary undertaking – it had to be accompanied by a participating interest in order for the definition of a subsidiary undertaking to be met. Consequently, it was left to FRS 5's definition of quasi-subsidiary to require consolidation of entities controlled by the reporting entity but in which the reporting entity had no participating interest. Now the changed CA 1985 definition will catch many of what used to be quasi-subsidiaries.

The 2004 amendment also introduced the concept of the power to exercise a dominant influence, in addition to the existing actual exercise of dominant influence. This will result in a few more entities meeting the definition of subsidiary undertaking.

These definitions are drawn from the EU seventh directive (Council Directive 83/349/EEC), hence the definitions in other Member States will be similar. They will not necessarily be exactly the same, as there are options in the directive and various Member States have made different choices in implementing the directive.

'Subsidiary' and 'subsidiary undertaking'

The previous section discussed the definitions of parent and subsidiary undertaking drawn from section 258. These apply (see section 258(1)) in Part VII of the Act on accounts and audit. For other purposes, it is the section 736 definitions that apply. Section 736 includes the following, narrower, definition of subsidiary:

> (1) ' A company is a "subsidiary" of another company, its "holding company", if that other company—
> (a) holds a majority of the voting rights in it, or
> (b) is a member of it and has the right to appoint or remove a majority of its board of directors, or
> (c) is a member of it and controls alone, pursuant to an agreement with other shareholders or members, a majority of the voting rights in it,
> or if it is a subsidiary of a company which is itself a subsidiary of that other company.

(2) A company is a "wholly-owned subsidiary" of another company if it has no members except that other and that other's wholly-owned subsidiaries or persons acting on behalf of that other or its wholly-owned subsidiaries.

(3) In this section "company" includes any body corporate.'

A company that meets the definition of a 'subsidiary' will also meet the definition of a 'subsidiary undertaking', but the converse is not necessarily true.

Exclusions from consolidation

Where a parent undertaking is preparing consolidated accounts, and it has identified all subsidiary undertakings, the next step is to consider whether there are any grounds for excluding a particular subsidiary undertaking from consolidation. Section 229 of the Act and para. 25 of FRS 2 deal with this point. The basic rule is that all subsidiary undertakings are included in the consolidation. The exceptions are subject to different rules as between the Act and FRS 2, as shown in Box 8.2.

Possible ground for exclusion	Act	FRS 2
Disproportionate expense or delay in obtaining necessary information	Permits exclusion (s. 229 (3)(b))	Does not permit exclusion (para. 24)
Severe long-term restrictions over the rights that make it a subsidiary undertaking	Permits exclusion (s. 229(3)(a))	Requires exclusion (para. 25(a))
Held exclusively for resale	Permits exclusion (s. 229(3)(c))	Requires exclusion (para. 25(b))
Inclusion of subsidiary undertaking is not material	Permits exclusion (s. 229(2))	Permits exclusion (accounting standards need not be applied to immaterial items)

Box 8.2

It can be seen that FRS 2 removes the choices in the Act; it either requires inclusion or requires exclusion. This is typical of the role of an accounting standard – that is, increasing comparability by standardising on one treatment.

In IFRS, there are no grounds on which a subsidiary should be excluded from consolidation. In particular, consolidation is required even where there are severe long-term restrictions (except that there is probably no control), or where a subsidiary is held for resale. IFRS 5 'Non-current assets held for sale and discontinued operations' applies in the latter case, and requires a different form of consolidation for such subsidiary undertakings.

Although the CA1985's exclusions from consolidation continue to apply to companies adopting IFRS, there is no clash with IFRS as the CA 1985's exclusions are permissive.

FRS 5 and quasi-subsidiaries

The discussion so far in this chapter has been about consolidation of subsidiary undertakings as defined in the Act and FRS 2. However, FRS 5 'Reporting the substance of transactions', introduced a further class of entities called quasi-subsidiaries, which it defines as follows:

> 'A quasi-subsidiary of a reporting entity is a company, trust, partnership or other vehicle that, though not fulfilling the definition of a subsidiary, is directly or indirectly controlled by the reporting entity and gives rise to benefits for that entity that are in substance no different from those that would arise were the vehicle a subsidiary.' [FRS 5, para. 7]

The category of quasi-subsidiaries was introduced as part of the general fight against off balance sheet finance. Prior to the introduction of FRS 5, it had been a common practice for groups to design entities that were in practice controlled by and for the benefit of the group but which were not legally subsidiary undertakings. FRS 5 thus extended the net of entities that were brought into the consolidation. FRS 5 requires that quasi-subsidiaries be included in the consolidation in a similar way to subsidiary undertakings. As noted above, following the 2004 changes to the Companies Act, there are likely to be more entities classed as subsidiary undertakings and correspondingly fewer quasi-subsidiaries.

There is no notion of 'quasi-subsidiaries' in IFRS, though an interpretation, SIC 12 'Consolidation – special purpose entities', has similar objectives.

Exemption re holding company profit and loss

Where a company is a parent company and produces consolidated accounts, those accounts are the accounts of that company. However, the consolidated accounts include both information about the group and some information about the parent company itself. For example, there has to be published the balance sheet of the entity as well as the balance sheet of the group, and many note disclosures have to be given for both the entity and the group. However under section 230, a parent company is permitted to not publish the profit and loss account of the parent entity, so long as the profit or loss for the financial year is disclosed as a single figure. The entity profit and loss account should still be prepared, and approved by the board; the exemption is merely from publication.

Techniques of consolidation

The techniques of preparing consolidated accounts involve, especially for a large and complex group, details that are beyond the scope of this book. This section restricts itself to an overview of the techniques.

Changes in composition of a group

From time to time, a group may acquire new subsidiaries or dispose of them. On the purchase of a new subsidiary, the question arises as to whether acquisition accounting or merger accounting should be used. This used to be a major and controversial question. However, merger accounting has recently been banned in the US and in international standards. It is still available in UK GAAP, though its days are numbered. Acquisition and merger accounting are discussed more fully in chapter 9 at p. 91.

In the context of both acquisitions and disposals, the results, assets and liabilities are included in the consolidated accounts while the company in question is a subsidiary of the parent. The date an entity becomes or ceases to be a subsidiary hinges on when control is gained or lost.

Full and proportional consolidation

Subsidiary undertakings are consolidated in full, even if they are not wholly owned. This is because the concept underlying consolidation is control, not ownership. Hence if a subsidiary undertaking is held 60% by its parent and 40% by another party, the parent will consolidate 100% of its assets and liabilities and 100% of its revenues and expenses, and therefore its profit. It will then allow for the 40% that it does not own, by an adjustment called 'minority interest'.

There is another approach, called 'proportional consolidation', whereby the parent consolidates the percentage that it owns – in the above example, 60% – of the assets and liabilities, revenues and expenses. In this way, no minority interest adjustment arises. This method is not permitted for accounting for subsidiaries. Though permitted by the Act, it is not permitted by UK standards. However, it does have a place in international accounting standards (IAS 31) in accounting for some joint ventures. For example, if the above company, held 60% / 40% by two parties, was structured as a joint venture, and assuming it was not a subsidiary of the 60% investor, then each party, if using proportional consolidation under IAS 31, would include their respective percentages of each line item in their consolidations.

Minority interests

As noted above, minority interests arise when a subsidiary is not wholly owned. A minority interest arises both on the balance sheet and in the profit and loss account. On the balance sheet, it represents the proportion of the net assets of fully consolidated subsidiaries that are owned by third parties (i.e. not owned by the group). The minority interest is thus distinct from the shareholders' funds of the parent, but can be regarded as a different type of ownership interest – a partial interest of some shareholders in the assets of certain subsidiaries.

In the profit and loss account, the minority interest represents the part of the group results that is not attributable to the parent shareholders. One hundred per cent of the results of subsidiary undertakings are consolidated, but, using the figures above, only 60% of the results are owned by (or attributable to) the parent shareholders. The other 40% of the results of that subsidiary undertaking are removed from the group profit and loss account in order properly to measure the results attributable to the parent shareholders.

There are detailed rules in the Act regarding where, in the formats for the profit and loss account and balance sheet, minority interests should be shown (Schedule 4A, para. 17). IAS 27 also specifies where minority interest should be presented on the balance sheet.

Elimination of intra-group transactions

The overall objective of consolidated accounts, as noted above, is to present financial statements as if the group were a single entity. Hence there is no place in consolidated accounts for numbers representing intra-group transactions. Put another way, a sale from one subsidiary to another is a non-event for the group as a whole. Such transactions, therefore, need to be eliminated in preparing consolidated accounts. This may result in removing the relevant sales figure from the selling company and the equivalent expense figure in the buying company. Where there is a profit to the selling company, that has to be eliminated if the purchasing company retains the asset at the year end; this is because no profit has been earned on an external transaction. It is also necessary, in preparing the consolidated accounts, to eliminate items on the balance sheet such as balances owing from one group company to another, as they are not valid assets and liabilities from a group point of view. Schedule 4A to the Act refers briefly to the need for elimination of group transactions in preparing consolidated accounts (para. 6). FRS 2 and IAS 27 also contain rules on this.

Associates and joint ventures

Definitions of associate and joint ventures

Associates and JVs are defined by both FRS 9 and the Act. FRS 9 defines an associate as 'an entity (other than a subsidiary) in which another entity (the investor) has a participating interest and over whose operating and financial policies the investor exercises a significant influence' (para. 4). Participating interest is discussed above.

FRS 9 defines a joint venture as: 'an entity in which the reporting entity holds an interest on a long-term basis and is jointly controlled by the reporting entity and one or more other venturers under a contractual arrangement' (para. 4). The Act's definition (Schedule 4A, para. 19) is similar.

Associates and JVs are therefore quite different from each other. For example, a typical JV might involve three parties with 33.3% of the JV each. An associate, on the other hand, may involve an investment in the range 20% to 50% but the other shareholdings would typically be diverse or, at least, not held by other JV parties.

Accounting treatment of associates in consolidated accounts

Despite these differences in nature, the accounting for associates and JVs is very similar in UK GAAP. The basic method is 'equity accounting'. That is, in the consolidated profit and loss account, after the operating profit of the group (that is, the parent and its subsidiary undertakings), there is added the group's share of the operating profit of the associates. Because the associates' profit added in is operating profit, it follows that any subsequent line items such as interest and tax need to include the relevant share of the associates' interest and tax. The overall effect is rather like proportional consolidation (that is, including the relevant proportion in each line item), but only from the operating profit line downwards.

Whilst the term 'equity accounting' describes the overall approach to associates, it specifically refers to the practice of including a figure for the investors' share of profits of the associate, as opposed to including only any dividends received from the associate.

On the balance sheet, the group's interest in associates is shown as a single line item among fixed asset investments. This too is an 'equity accounting number', in that, as a result of recognising share of profit in the profit and loss account, it grows to reflect the investing group's share of profits retained in the associate itself. This is in contrast to accounting for a trade investment at cost or valuation with only dividend income being received.

The treatment in international accounting standards (IAS 28) is similar, though, in the profit and loss account, the share of profit of the associates is the share of post-tax profit, and it is presented lower down the group profit and loss account, that is, after interest and before profit before tax.

Accounting treatment of JVs in consolidated accounts

In UK GAAP the accounting treatment of JVs is similar to that of associates. The basic equity accounting as described above is augmented by additional disclosure, and the result is called the 'gross equity method'. In the profit and loss account, FRS 9 requires that 'in the consolidated profit and loss account the investor's share of its joint ventures' turnover should also be shown – but not as part of group turnover . . . [and] in the consolidated balance sheet the investor's share of the gross assets and liabilities underlying the net equity amount included for joint ventures should be shown in amplification of that net amount' (para. 21).

The additional disclosures are required because the view is that joint ventures are more important than associates, and hence the figures for turnover, gross assets and gross liabilities need emphasis. Nevertheless this does not amount to full consolidation; neither, technically, does it amount to proportional consolidation, though it edges close to it.

In international accounting standards, accounting for JVs depends on the nature of the JV, but for the mainstream case of a jointly controlled entity, the choice is between equity accounting and proportional consolidation.

9

Mergers and acquisitions

Introduction

Accounting for acquisitions and mergers has long been a controversial area of accounting. In particular there have been disputes about whether the technique of merger accounting should be permitted, and about the nature and accounting treatment of goodwill. The current UK rules are found in FRS 6 'Accounting for acquisitions and mergers', FRS 7 'Fair values in acquisition accounting' and FRS 10 'Accounting for goodwill and intangibles'. Recent changes in US accounting rules in this area have led to changes to IFRS (IFRS 3 'Business combinations' was published in March 2004). Equivalent changes are likely to be made to UK standards, though the timescale for this is not clear. UK law sets out some details about acquisition and merger accounting.

Companies Act 1985 requirements

The detailed legal rules relating to accounting for acquisitions and mergers are set out in Schedule 4A to the Act. These apply to groups preparing accounts under UK GAAP but not to those preparing accounts under IFRS.

In particular, the Act requires that 'An acquisition shall be accounted for by the acquisition method of accounting unless the conditions for accounting for it as a merger are met and the merger method of accounting is adopted.' (Schedule 4A, para. 8). This is consistent with the requirements of FRS 6. If, in the future, merger accounting is banned, this legal requirement will be superfluous, though not wrong, as the conditions for merger accounting would never be met (see below).

The acquisition method

The Act describes the acquisition method of accounting and provides that: 'The identifiable assets and liabilities of the undertaking acquired shall be included in the consolidated balance sheet at their fair values as at the date of acquisition.' (Schedule 4A, para. 9). The 'identifiable' assets or liabilities of the undertaking acquired means the assets or liabilities which are capable of being disposed of or discharged separately, without disposing of a business of the undertaking.

The key point here is that in acquisition accounting, the assets and liabilities of the target are brought into the consolidated accounts of the acquirer at their *fair values*. More guidance on what this means is found in FRS 7. As to which assets and liabilities are to be recognised, and brought into the accounts at fair value, the legal principle is those that are 'identifiable', which, as described above, is close in meaning to separable. In practice, this legal description is far from definitive, as accounting standards can and do interpret this in a number of different ways, as described below.

The Act provides that the income and expenditure of the undertaking acquired shall be brought into the group accounts only as from the date of the acquisition (Schedule 4A, para. 9(3)). This again sets out a key principle of acquisition accounting, and a key distinction from merger accounting. In acquisition accounting, an acquired entity is brought in to the group accounts of the acquirer from the date of acquisition. Hence, even if all the companies concerned are in a stable state, the group will appear, in the accounts for the year of acquisition, to grow as a result of the acquisition.

The Act requires the acquisition cost of the interest in the shares of the undertaking held by the parent company and its subsidiary undertakings to be set off against the interest of the parent company and its subsidiary undertakings in the adjusted capital and reserves of the undertaking acquired (Schedule 4A, para. 9(4)). For this purpose 'the acquisition cost' means the amount of any cash consideration and the fair value of any other consideration, together with such amount (if any) in respect of fees and other expenses of the acquisition as the company may determine. 'The adjusted capital and reserves' of the undertaking acquired means its capital and reserves at the date of the acquisition after adjusting the identifiable assets and liabilities of the undertaking to fair values as at that date. The resulting amount if positive shall be treated as goodwill, and if negative as a negative consolidation difference (Schedule 4A, para. 9(5)).

A simpler explanation of the accounting adjustments described in the previous paragraph is this. A fair value is established for the consideration given by the acquirer. This is any cash paid plus the fair value of any shares (or other non-cash consideration) issued to the vendors, plus any related expenses. This is compared with the percentage acquired of the fair value of the assets and liabilities of the target. The difference is goodwill – positive or negative. (Accountants use the term 'negative goodwill' rather than negative consolidation difference.)

So, for example, assume that:

- A acquires 80% of B
- B's net assets at book value are 70 but when stated at fair value are 90
- A pays 90 in shares plus 10 in cash; total consideration 100.

The (positive) goodwill is $100 - (90 \times 80\%) = 28$.

The merger accounting criteria

Paragraph 10(1) of Schedule 4A to the CA 1985 sets out what it confusingly calls 'the conditions for accounting for an acquisition as a merger', in other words the conditions for deciding which business combinations should be accounted for as mergers. These are as follows:

'(a) that at least 90 per cent. of the nominal value of the relevant shares in the undertaking acquired is held by or on behalf of the parent company and its subsidiary undertakings,

(b) that the proportion referred to in paragraph (a) was attained pursuant to an arrangement providing for the issue of equity shares by the parent company or one or more of its subsidiary undertakings,

(c) that the fair value of any consideration other than the issue of equity shares given pursuant to the arrangement by the parent company and its subsidiary undertakings did not exceed 10 per cent. of the nominal value of the equity shares issued, and

(d) that adoption of the merger method of accounting accords with generally accepted accounting principles or practice.'

Condition (a) says that at least a 90% holding in the target must be achieved before merger accounting can be considered. However, this does not mean that the whole 90% must have been acquired in one tranche. There could have been a prior holding. However, the nature of the consideration given for that prior holding is important. For example if a prior holding of 20% was acquired for cash in previous years, that would breach the non-equity criterion (condition (c)). But if the 20% had been acquired for shares, then the criteria may well be satisfied.

Condition (b) is broadly stated and seems in line with the conditions in FRS 6 that a merger for accounting purposes must, among other things, involve substantially a share for share exchange.

Condition (c) is, like the rest of the Act, a matter of law, though it is regarded by most accountants as being a misunderstanding on the part of the legislators. The accounting standards in force at the time the EU seventh directive (Council Directive 83/349/EEC on consolidated accounts, OJ 1983 No. L193/1) (the directive that harmonises group accounting, on which the Act is based) was being negotiated allowed that a company could use merger accounting if it was substantially a share for share exchange, but that up to 10% of the consideration, in *fair value* terms, could be in cash or some other form of non-equity consideration. Somehow this became para. 10(1)(c) of Schedule 4A to the Act which refers to 10% of the *nominal value* of the equity shares. Of course, the nominal value of a share is often substantially below its fair value, and so this provision can sometimes stand in the way of accounting for a combination as a merger, even though the cash element might be very small in economic terms.

Condition (d) essentially means that, as well as complying with the rest of Schedule 4A, a combination must comply with relevant accounting standards if merger accounting is to be used. As already noted, it is likely that merger accounting will be banned by future accounting standards. If so, condition (d) will be failed, and hence merger accounting will not be permitted by the Act either.

The merger method

The merger method of accounting is described in Schedule 4A, para. (11) to the Act as follows:

'(2) The assets and liabilities of the undertaking acquired shall be brought into the group accounts at the figures at which they stand in the undertaking's accounts, subject to any adjustment authorised or required by this Schedule.

(3) The income and expenditure of the undertaking acquired shall be included in the group accounts for the entire financial year, including the period before the acquisition.

(4) The group accounts shall show corresponding amounts relating to the previous financial year as if the undertaking acquired had been included in the consolidation throughout that year.

(5) There shall be set off against the aggregate of—
  (a) the appropriate amount in respect of qualifying shares issued by the parent company or its subsidiary undertakings in consideration for the acquisition of shares in the undertaking acquired, and
  (b) the fair value of any other consideration for the acquisition of shares in the undertaking acquired, determined as at the date when those shares were acquired,
  the nominal value of the issued share capital of the undertaking acquired held by the parent company and its subsidiary undertakings.

(6) The resulting amount shall be shown as an adjustment to the consolidated reserves.

(7) In sub-paragraph (5)(a) "qualifying shares" means—
  (a) shares in relation to which section 131 (merger relief) applies, in respect of which the appropriate amount is the nominal value; or
  (b) shares in relation to which section 132 (relief in respect of group reconstructions) applies, in respect of which the appropriate amount is the nominal value together with any minimum premium value within the meaning of that section.'

This description is similar to that in FRS 6, as discussed under the heading 'Merger accounting in the UK', p. 98.

Paragraph 11(2) of Schedule 4A to the Act notes that in merger accounting the existing book values, rather than fair values, are used. This is because the merger accounting presentation involves no notion of one company acquiring another, and no notion of a price being paid. The reference to 'adjustments' is generally taken to mean adjustments to harmonise the accounting policies of the company being acquired with those of the acquirer. Paragraph 11(3) and (4) of Schedule 4A to the Act set out further key features of merger accounting. The date of combination is more or less ignored (save in relation to some footnote disclosures), and the accounts of the merged group are presented as if the companies had always been combined. Similarly the comparative figures are presented using the same assumption.

Paragraph 11(5) of Schedule 4A to the Act appears at first sight similar to the set off used in acquisition accounting that gives rise to goodwill. However it is quite different. In merger accounting, there is no notion of one company acquiring another, hence no notion of a price being paid, nor of goodwill arising. Instead, para. 11(5) of Schedule 4A to the Act for practical purposes describes the set off of the nominal value of the shares issued by the acquirer against the nominal value of the shares of the company being acquired. The difference is put to consolidated reserves; it is purely an accounting adjustment, and not a number that has any meaning.

Share premium, merger relief and group reconstruction relief

The requirements relating to share premiums, merger relief (and group reconstruction relief) are set out in sections 130 to 133 of the Act. These are reproduced and discussed selectively below, insofar as is necessary to understand the related accounting rules. However, it is important to stress that the rules operate independently of the accounting method adopted in the consolidated accounts. Similarly they will apply irrespective of whether the accounts are prepared in accordance with UK GAAP or IFRS.

The rules that follow apply to the issuing company's single entity accounts.

The basic rule relating to setting up a share premium account is set out in section 130(1) of the Act: 'If a company issues shares at a premium, whether for cash or otherwise, a sum equal to the aggregate amount or value of the premiums on those shares shall be transferred to an account called "the share premium account".' So for example, if a company issues shares for cash for above the nominal value of the shares, the excess is credited to a share premium account. A share premium account is not distributable and there are restrictions on what it may be used for.

'Merger relief', as set out in section 131 of the Act, is something of a misnomer. It might better be called relief from the need to set up a share premium account – which is exactly what it is. Merger relief arises in an entity's accounts; it is not a consolidation issue. Moreover, it does not arise only when merger accounting is used in the related consolidated accounts. In other words, it can be used in conjunction with using acquisition accounting on consolidation. Indeed if merger accounting is banned by future accounting standards, merger relief in the entity accounts is likely to survive unchanged and to be available in connection with accounting for some acquisitions.

The key elements of section 131 of the Act for our purposes are the following:

'(1) With the exception made by section 132(8) (group reconstruction) this section applies where the issuing company has secured at least a 90 per cent. equity holding in another company in pursuance of an arrangement providing for the allotment of equity shares in the issuing company on terms that the consideration for the shares allotted is to be provided—
 (a) by the issue or transfer to the issuing company of equity shares in the other company, or
 (b) by the cancellation of any such shares not held by the issuing company.
(2) If the equity shares in the issuing company allotted in pursuance of the arrangement in consideration for the acquisition or cancellation of equity shares in the other company are issued at a premium, section 130 does not apply to the premiums on those shares.'

Thus if A by issuing its equity shares acquires 90% or more of the equity share capital of B, and A's shares are issued at a premium, the general requirement of section 130 of the Act to set up a share premium account does not apply.

Note also that there is nothing that says that the whole of the 90% should be acquired in one tranche. For example, A might already hold 70% of B as a result of an earlier (cash or shares) transaction. But if A then issues equity to acquire the next 20% of B's equity, relief under section 131 arises and applies to the shares issued by A to acquire that 20%. Section 131 states that section 130 does not apply – in other words that no share premium account should be set up (that is, there is no choice). It does not specify what should be done instead. There are two possibilities. One is that the shares issued are still accounted for at fair value; but the amount that would have been credited to the share premium account is instead credited to another reserve, generally called a 'merger reserve'. The other possibility is that under section 133 the premium is disregarded completely, and the shares issued are recorded at their nominal value.

In addition to merger relief, the Act also provides, in section 132, 'group reconstruction relief'. This is similar to merger relief in that it is a relief from the need to set up a share premium account, but the details are different and more complex; in particular a share premium account can still be required under this section. The overall effect of group reconstruction relief is that the operation of section 132 does not generally give rise to a lower carrying value for an asset than it had in its previous place in the group structure. However, the wording of section 132 differs from that of section 131. In particular, it uses the words 'is not required' rather than section 131's 'does not apply'. Hence the generally accepted view is that relief under section 132 is optional.

The final piece of the jigsaw is section 133 of the Act. The key part of this reads as follows:

'(1) An amount corresponding to one representing the premiums or part of the premiums on shares issued by a company which by virtue of sections 131 or 132 of this Act, or section 12 of the Consequential Provisions Act, is not included in the company's share premium account may also be disregarded in determining the amount at which any shares or other consideration provided for the shares issued is to be included in the company's balance sheet.'

This means that, if share premium relief or group reconstruction relief applies, and as a result an amount is not credited to the share premium account, it may be disregarded for the purposes of determining the carrying value of the investment in the acquired company. This relates only to the entity accounts.

For example, assume that shares are issued to acquire another company and merger relief under section 131 is available. The nominal value of the shares issued is £10 and the fair value is £80. The £70 is not credited to the share premium account. Neither does it need to be taken into account for determining the carrying value of the investment. But note the word 'may' in section 133(1): this relief is optional. Hence a company has the choice of recording the transaction either as shown in Box 9.1.

Dr Investment in new subsidiary	£80
Cr Shares issued	£10
Cr Merger reserve	£70

Box 9.1

Or, using section 133 relief, as shown in Box 9.2.

Dr Investment in new subsidiary	£10
Cr Shares issued	£10

Box 9.2

Whilst this is a matter of choice, most practitioners would take the approach in Box 9.2. A lower carrying value for the investment is helpful in that it gives the company less exposure to impairments. That is, without section 133 relief the investment would be recorded initially at its full cost of £80. If it lost say £20 in value, it would need to be written down to a revised carrying value of £60. But with the benefit of section 133 relief, the investment could lose up to £70 of its value before it became necessary to make an impairment write-down.

The accounting treatment in the consolidated accounts follows the acquisition accounting or merger accounting rules of the Act and FRS 6, irrespective of whether section 133 relief is taken in the parent's entity accounts.

97

The current UK standards in overview

The extant accounting standards dealing with accounting for acquisitions and mergers in the UK are FRS 6 'Accounting for acquisitions and mergers', FRS 7 'Fair values in acquisition accounting' and FRS 10 'Accounting for goodwill and intangibles'. The first two standards have been in place since 1994 and FRS 10 has been in place since 1998. However, at the time of writing (March 2005) it appears unlikely that they will survive for more than one to two years. The reason is international harmonisation. Details of the reform of UK and international standards are given at p. 109 below.

The discussion that follows applies to business combinations other than group reconstructions.

Under FRS 6, nearly all business combinations fall to be accounted for as acquisitions. Only a few meet the tests for merger accounting, though if the tests are met, merger accounting is mandatory (unlike under the Act where it is optional). The two methods are based on an entirely different view of a business combination. In an acquisition, the financial statements reflect one company acquiring another. Hence the price paid is reflected. This is allocated among the separable net assets acquired, based on their fair values at the time of acquisition, so as to reflect the cost to the group. The residue is allocated to goodwill, which is generally positive but can be negative. In a merger, on the other hand, there is no notion of one company acquiring another, merely a notion of two companies coming together. Hence the accounting numbers of the two are aggregated, and presented as if the two had always been combined. There is no reflection of the economic price paid by one for the other, and goodwill does not arise.

Merger accounting in the UK

Introduction

FRS 6 describes a merger as:

> 'A business combination that results in the creation of a new reporting entity formed from the combining parties, in which the shareholders of the combining entities come together in a partnership for the mutual sharing of the risks and benefits of the combined entity, and in which no party to the combination in substance obtains control over any other, or is otherwise seen to be dominant, whether by virtue of the proportion of its share-holders' rights in the combined entity, the influence of its directors or otherwise.' [FSA 6, para. 2]

Merger accounting reflects the idea that two companies have come together without either party being dominant – it should not be possible to determine who has acquired whom. Hence neither company is seen as acquiring, or buying, the other. As a result, there is no restatement of the previous carrying values of assets and liabilities of either of the combining companies to fair value; they continue to report their pre-merger carrying values. The one exception to this is that if the accounting policies of the two companies are not the same, they need to be harmonised, and this leads to a restatement of the numbers of one, or possibly both companies. But this is quite different from carrying out a fair value exercise: a fair value exercise is done in an acquisition to allocate the total price paid among the individual assets and liabilities acquired.

It is sometimes argued that financial statements presented using merger accounting are fictitious and cannot present a true and fair view. It is true that the financial statements present the situation 'as if' the two companies had always been combined, when in fact this is simply not the case. However, the view has been taken that this better reflects the substance of the transaction. The alternative would be to show one company as continuing, with the results and net assets of the other being added to it. But this would reflect a primacy to one company which is not (intended to be) present in a merger. Hence the merger accounting presentation is regarded as compliant with GAAP and as giving a true and fair view if used when the criteria are met.

The merger accounting criteria

The criteria in the Act have been described above. FRS 6 also sets out some criteria that have to be met. If the criteria in the Act are met, merger accounting is optional; but if FRS 6's criteria are met, merger accounting is mandatory. The effect of this is that if the criteria in the Act are met but FRS 6's criteria are not, merger accounting may not be used; but if the criteria in both the Act and FRS 6 are met, merger accounting must be used. FRS 6's criteria may be summarised as follows:

'**Criterion 1** – No party to the combination is portrayed as either acquirer or acquired, either by its own board or management or by that of another party to the combination.' Thus if one party's board announces that it is acquiring the other, that becomes self-fulfilling, in accounting terms. In practice, a lot of attention is given to names, logos, and the wording in, for example, press releases and shareholders' circulars if merger accounting is desired.

'**Criterion 2** – All parties to the combination, as represented by the boards of directors or their appointees, participate in establishing the management structure for the combined entity and in selecting the management personnel, and such decisions are made on the basis of a consensus between the parties to the combination rather than purely by exercise of voting rights.' The key word here is 'participate'. In principle, it will be possible for both boards to participate in a decision that the new, combined board should be made up entirely of the board of one of the parties to the exclusion of the other. In practice, auditors, in interpreting this criterion, will look for a reasonable split of board appointments from both parties; otherwise they are likely to take the view that one party has acquired the other.

'**Criterion 3** – The relative sizes of the combining entities are not so disparate that one party dominates the combined entity by virtue of its relative size.' The Explanation part of FRS 6 adds that 'A party would be presumed to dominate if it is more than 50% larger than each of the other parties to the combination, judged by reference to the ownership interests' (para. 68). This presumption can be rebutted but in practice auditors regard this explanation as more or less a rule – it has become known as 'the 60/40 threshold'. The general view is that a 'merger' among parties that are more disparate in size – for example 65/35 – is unconvincing.

'**Criterion 4** – Under the terms of the combination or related arrangements, the consideration received by equity shareholders of each party to the combination, in relation to their equity shareholding, comprises primarily equity shares in the combined entity; and any non-equity consideration, or equity shares carrying substantially reduced voting or distribution rights, represents an immaterial proportion of the fair value of the consideration received by the equity shareholders of that party. Where one of the combining entities has, within the period of two years before the combination, acquired equity shares in another of the combining entities, the consideration for this acquisition should be taken into account in determining whether this criterion has been met.' For accounting purposes, up to 10% of the consideration could be in cash or some other form of non-equity, and this would be regarded as immaterial. However, as noted above, the legal criteria include a restriction that the non-equity should not exceed 10% of the nominal value of the shares, and this is often more restrictive than the equivalent FRS 6 criterion. (It should be noted that the definitions of 'equity' in FRS 6 and the Act are not quite the same.)

'**Criterion 5** – No equity shareholders of any of the combining entities retain any material interest in the future performance of only part of the combined entity.' That is, there must be a complete uniting of interests. It undermines the idea of a merger if one party retains or is granted, for example, special shares that pay dividends according to the performance of a particular subsidiary.

Whilst these are set out as the formal criteria in the standard – and a breach of any of them would preclude merger accounting – in practice they are merely criteria to help determine whether the definition of a merger is met. This definition is quoted above; the key words are 'no party to the combination in substance obtains control over any other, or is otherwise seen to be dominant'. If, despite appearing to meet the above criteria, in practice it is clear that one party is dominant, then that party should be treated as the acquirer.

FRS 6 also refers to a further consideration; though not set out as a formal criterion, its effect is similar. Paragraph 58 of FRS 6 says that merger accounting is not appropriate for a combination where one of the parties results from a recent divestment by a larger entity, because the divested business will not have been independent for a sufficient period to establish itself as being a party separate from its previous owner. Only once the divested business has established a track record of its own can it be considered as a party to a merger.

Merger accounting has gradually become discredited. This is largely because it is almost impossible to develop criteria that effectively distinguish genuine mergers. The FRS 6 criteria are discussed above, but the view has become widely held that even when such restrictive criteria are used, nevertheless some combinations that meet the criteria are in fact acquisitions in substance. Perhaps there are genuine mergers, but they are so rare in the business environment, and so difficult to identify, that it is not worth having a different method of accounting just to get the accounting right for those few, if the result is getting the accounting wrong for some of the combinations that should properly be presented as acquisitions.

Key features of merger accounting

Some of the features of merger accounting have been alluded to already, but they are presented here for completeness:

- Neither company is treated as the acquirer for accounting purposes.
- The economic price paid is not reflected in the balance sheet, though it is disclosed in the notes to the accounts.
- There is no restatement of the carrying values of the assets of either merging company to reflect fair values.
- No goodwill arises. (However, any goodwill already in the balance sheet of either party to the merger as a result of previous acquisitions remains there.)
- The profit and loss account is presented on an aggregated basis, as if the two companies had always been merged. The same principle is used for the cash flow statement.
- The expenses of the transaction are charged to the profit and loss account.
- The balance sheets are aggregated in a similar way, as if the two companies had always been combined.
- The numbers of one or both of the combining companies are restated, where necessary, to harmonise accounting policies for the enlarged group.
- As part of the aggregation of the balance sheets, the reserves of the two companies are combined to form the group reserves (subject to the adjustment described in the next bullet).
- Despite the notions of equality, as a practical matter one company – either one of the two merging companies, or a new holding company superimposed – becomes the top company in the group's legal structure, and is the one that issues shares to the former shareholders of the other company(ies). In the consolidation exercise, it is necessary to set off (a) the investment in the new subsidiary, in the books of the parent, against (b) the share capital, share premium and capital redemption reserve of the

new subsidiary. A difference generally emerges between these numbers and this is added to or deducted from group reserves. It is important to note that this number is not goodwill, as it does not result from comparing fair values. It is simply a consolidation adjustment that has little or no economic significance. Also, as it arises on consolidation only, it has no significance from the perspective of distributable profits, as these are determined at the entity level.

From a practical point of view, the key advantage of merger accounting is that the fair value of the transaction is not accounted for. Hence there is no step up in asset values, and thus no increased charges for depreciation or greater risk of impairments. More importantly, there is no goodwill. Goodwill, especially in service and technology company acquisitions, can be a very large component of the overall value, and to avoid having to account for it is seen as a substantial advantage, for two reasons. First, any amortisation or impairment of goodwill hits reported profits. Second, goodwill on the balance sheet increases the reported capital employed, which worsens the return on capital employed ratio; on the other hand, it improves gearing.

It will be noted that, in the financial statements of the year of a merger, the merger accounting presentation shows no growth as a result of the combination. This is because comparative figures are restated as if the two companies had always been merged. Any growth in the numbers would reflect growth in the underlying businesses.

Acquisition accounting in the UK

Introduction

Acquisition accounting is the mainstream method of accounting for business combinations. It is currently used for more than 95% of UK combinations. This is not to say that it is popular. Acquisitive companies sometimes argue that the accounting effects of the acquisition method are harsh, as it brings with it goodwill and higher depreciation charges. Goodwill is currently, under UK GAAP, subject to amortisation through the profit and loss account, though there is an exception to this which may soon become the mainstream rule if and when IFRS 3 is introduced into UK GAAP. Moreover, since the rules were tightened in 1994 by the introduction of FRS 7, it is no longer possible to provide for the costs of reorganisation or integration of the acquired company into the acquiring group. These costs are now regarded as post-acquisition operating costs and as a result depress the apparent profitability of the transaction, at least in the short term.

Key features of acquisition accounting

Some of the features of acquisition accounting have been alluded to already, but they are presented here for completeness:

- One of the companies is treated as the acquirer for accounting purposes.
- The economic price paid (the fair value of the consideration given, which equates to the cost of acquisition) is recognised in the balance sheet.
- The assets and liabilities of the acquired company are restated to reflect fair values at the date of acquisition.
- The numbers of one or both of the combining companies (but typically those of the acquired company) are restated, where necessary, to harmonise accounting policies for the enlarged group.
- The profit and loss account for the year of acquisition comprises the results for the whole of the current year for the acquiring company together with the results for the post-acquisition period only of the acquired company. The comparative figures are those of the acquiring company only. The same principle is used for the cash flow statement.
- The expenses of the acquisition are treated as part of the cost of acquisition.
- The balance sheet at the start of the year of acquisition is that of the acquiring company only. The balance sheet for any date after the acquisition includes also the net assets of the acquired company.
- As part of the consolidation exercise, the cost of acquisition (that is, the fair value of the consideration given, plus expenses) is set off against the fair value of the net assets acquired. Goodwill emerges as the difference arising from this set off. Goodwill is generally positive but can be negative. The fair value of the net assets acquired is brought into the consolidated balance sheet in place of the capital and reserves of the acquired company at the date of the acquisition. It follows from this that the pre-acquisition reserves of the acquired company are eliminated on consolidation and hence the group reserves at any year end after acquisition comprise the reserves of the acquiring company and its share of the post-acquisition reserves of the acquired company. The pre-acquisition reserves of the acquired company remain in that entity but do not form part of the consolidated reserves of the enlarged group.

It will be noted that the acquisition accounting presentation shows growth as a result of the combination. Thus an acquisitive group can, in its headline figures, give the appearance of growth even though the underlying businesses may be stagnant. However, various required disclosures show whether growth is organic or bought-in.

Fair value of the consideration given

The cost of acquisition of the shares in the new subsidiary is measured at fair value. It is relevant in two contexts. First it is relevant in the entity accounts of the holding company for (a) the valuation of the share premium account or merger reserve and (b) the carrying value of the investment in the new subsidiary (but not, in each case, if relief under section 133 of the Act is taken). Second,

103

in the consolidated balance sheet, the fair value of the consideration given is presented as part of the share capital and share premium or merger reserve. Also, when preparing the consolidated balance sheet, the carrying value of the investment (as shown in the acquiring entity's balance sheet) is disaggregated into the fair value of the separable net assets (see under the heading 'Fair value of the net assets acquired' below) and the residue, which is goodwill. That is, it is the separable net assets and goodwill that are shown in the consolidated balance sheet; whereas the investment in the subsidiary is shown in the balance sheet of the acquiring entity.

Most commonly, the consideration given for the acquisition of a new subsidiary will include cash paid or securities issued by the acquiring company, such as its equity or loan stock. When securities are issued, their fair value needs to be established. If they are quoted securities, this is given by their market value. If they are not quoted, a range of valuation techniques is available. The question arises as to what date should be used. In principle, this should be the price on the date of acquisition. Where control is passed by way of a public offer, the relevant date is the date on which the offer becomes unconditional, usually as a result of sufficient acceptances being received. However, this is not a hard and fast rule. If the price on one date is an unreliable measure of fair value, it is possible to consider the average of market prices over a reasonable period.

Detailed rules relating to fair value of the consideration given are set out in FRS 7 'Fair values in acquisition accounting'.

Fair value of the net assets acquired

In preparing the consolidated accounts, the cost of investment, which is itself given by the fair value of the consideration given, is disaggregated into the fair value of the separable net assets acquired, with the residue being goodwill. This is sometimes called the 'fair value exercise' or 'purchase price allocation'. Detailed rules relating to the fair value of the net assets acquired are set out in FRS 7 'Fair values in acquisition accounting'.

Fair value is defined by FRS 7 as 'The amount at which an asset or liability could be exchanged in an arm's length transaction between informed and willing parties, other than in a forced or liquidation sale'. It follows that market values, such as quoted prices, should be used if available. If not, depreciated replacement cost is helpful. However, it is important that fair values are not overstated. The standard says that the fair value should not exceed the recoverable amount of the asset. The recoverable amount is the higher of the net realisable value – what the company would get from sale of the asset, net of expenses – and the 'value in use'. Value in use is an economic measure, namely the present (that is, discounted) value of the estimated future cash flows that the asset will generate for the company, from continued use (including from its eventual sale).

How these measures of cost and recoverable amount interrelate can be shown by an example. Assume that among the assets being fair valued is some specialised plant. It is currently carried in the target's balance sheet at depreciated historical cost of £5m. The depreciated replacement cost is determined to be £12m. However, it is not being used fully nor very profitably. The net realisable value is found to be only £2m. A value in use calculation is done, based on assumptions about the revenues and margins that are likely to be earned from its most profitable use; the result shows that the value in use is £8m. Hence, the recoverable amount (the higher of net realisable value and value in use) is £8m., reflecting the fact that it is more worthwhile to keep the plant and use it than to sell it. But the recoverable amount of £8m. is less than the depreciated replacement cost of £12m. Hence in this instance the plant's fair value is £8m., and it is at this value that it is included in the consolidated balance sheet.

Two important practical questions are which assets and liabilities should be recognised, and from what perspective should they be fair valued. The key principles are set out in FRS 7 as follows: 'The identifiable assets and liabilities to be recognised should be those of the acquired entity that existed at the date of acquisition' (para. 5); and 'The recognised assets and liabilities should be measured at fair values that reflect the conditions at the date of the acquisition' (para. 6). The implication of these rules is that an acquiring company must account for solely what it acquired, and in the condition it was in on the last day of the target's independent existence before it was acquired. Thus if the acquirer has plans for what it will do with the acquired business post-acquisition, those plans do not affect the fair value exercise; rather they affect the accounting for the post-acquisition period.

The major example of this is that often an acquirer will wish to reorganise the target after acquisition, frequently involving redundancies and integration of the target into the acquirer's group. Under previous accounting practice, pre-FRS 7, it used to be possible to provide for the costs of such reorganisations as part of the fair value exercise. This had a beneficial effect on the post-acquisition results, as the reorganisation cost, when incurred, could be charged against the provision that had been established, and hence did not appear as a charge to the profit and loss account. However, under FRS 7, this is not possible. Planned expenditure on reorganisation cannot be provided for, as it is not a liability of the target. It has to be charged to the profit and loss account of the enlarged group when incurred. There is however a minor exception namely that a provision should be made where the target company was itself committed to a restructuring before the acquirer intervened.

Another example is that a fixed asset may have a particular use in the context of the target, and that use supports, let us say, a fair value, based on value in use, of £100. The acquirer may plan to change the use of the asset. In the new use, the value may be only £70. The loss has to be charged to the profit and loss account of the enlarged group.

Goodwill and other intangibles under UK GAAP

Goodwill and other intangibles are quite similar to each other in many respects. At the margin, it is hard to distinguish one from the other. Indeed they are covered by the same UK accounting standard, FRS 10 'Goodwill and intangible assets'. Nevertheless, in one sense, they are treated very differently, namely that in acquisition accounting, separate intangibles, to which a fair value is ascribed, are accounted for much like any other separable asset such as stock or plant. In contrast, goodwill is the residue that remains: the difference between the cost of acquisition (measured by the fair value of the consideration given) and the aggregate of the fair values ascribed to the separable tangible and intangible assets and liabilities.

A difficult question in many fair value exercises is to what extent to identify amounts as relating to separate intangibles, and to what extent they should be subsumed within goodwill. FRS 10 says that identifiable assets or liabilities are those that are capable of being disposed of or settled separately, without disposing of a business of the entity. It also notes that an intangible should be capitalised separately from goodwill if its value can be measured reliably on initial recognition. If it cannot be measured reliably, it should be subsumed into goodwill. The reference to reliable measurement does not mean that there needs to be a market value. Indeed there are not many examples of intangibles with a market value. But there are techniques by which, for example, brands and licences can be valued. In practice, a degree of professional judgement is applied in deciding whether in a particular instance an intangible should be recognised separately from goodwill or subsumed within goodwill.

There has been considerable controversy among accountants over the decades as to what goodwill is and how it should be accounted for. For many years, in the UK and elsewhere, it was common practice to write off goodwill to reserves. As a result it did not feature on the balance sheet, neither did the profit and loss account reflect any charges in respect of its amortisation or impairment. However, since the introduction of FRS 10 in 1998, it has been necessary to treat goodwill as an asset and, with exceptions, to amortise it against earnings. Goodwill arising pre-FRS 10 was permitted to remain written off to reserves, except that it has to be resurrected on disposal of the business to which it relates, and charged in arriving at the gain or loss on sale, giving the same effect as if the goodwill had been carried as an asset on the balance sheet. FRS 10 is not the end of the debate, as a further change in approach is likely.

While the distinction between goodwill and other intangibles is important from a balance sheet perspective, the distinction matters less to the profit and loss account, as similar rules apply in connection with amortisation and impairment testing. The basic rule is that, where goodwill and intangibles are regarded as having limited useful economic lives, they should be amortised through the profit and loss account systematically over those lives. Where, on the other hand, they are regarded as having indefinite useful economic lives, they should not be amortised.

FRS 10 sets out a rebuttable presumption that goodwill and intangible assets have useful economic lives of twenty years or less. Hence goodwill and intangibles are generally amortised over periods from say five years to twenty years. Judgement is applied in determining the useful economic life, and guidance is given in the standard. In the context of amortisation over periods of twenty years or less, an impairment test is required to be carried out at the end of the first full year following the acquisition and otherwise only where, as for a tangible fixed asset, there is an 'indicator of impairment', such as a current year loss or a low utilisation of the asset.

In contrast, if goodwill or intangibles are amortised over a period exceeding twenty years, or are not amortised at all, it is necessary to carry out an impairment review annually (FRS 10, para. 37; see also FRS 11 for details of impairment reviews).

An impairment review is an onerous exercise, and it carries the risk that it will identify that a significant impairment write down is necessary. Whilst it is also true that the need for a significant write down may be identified when goodwill is being amortised over a shorter period, it is less likely. Moreover, amortisation over no more than twenty years is the norm, and to depart from that makes a company appear unusual. In any case, many companies believe that analysts add back any goodwill amortisation when analysing results. These factors have led to it being relatively rare for companies not to amortise goodwill or indeed to amortise it over a period in excess of twenty years.

Goodwill is usually positive (i.e. an asset), but it can be negative. This is where the aggregate of the fair values of the net assets exceeds the cost of acquisition. This is sometimes described as a bargain purchase – though it is not necessarily a bargain as the low acquisition price might reflect losses in the acquired company. The accounting treatment for negative goodwill is to show it in the balance sheet as a negative item under the goodwill caption within intangible fixed assets. It is then amortised into the profit and loss account but, unlike positive goodwill, it gives rise to an income item. The period of amortisation is generally determined by reference to the depreciation periods of relevant non-monetary assets.

Application of IFRS 3

The current international standard on business combinations is IFRS 3. For UK listed groups and other companies reporting under the EU Regulation (Council Regulation 1606/2002/EC on the application of international accounting standards, OJ No. L243/1) the first time IFRS 3 applies to accounts is for accounting periods starting on or after 1 January 2005 or later; but in those accounts, IFRS 3 applies to acquisitions for which the agreement date is on or after its date of transition (which is 1 January 2004 for a company with a 31 December year end; 1 April 2004 for a company with a March year end and so on). What this means in practice (assuming calendar year reporting) is that a business combination occurring in 2004 would be accounted for under UK GAAP rules in the company's 2004 accounts. But if the EU Regulation (Council Regulation 1606/2002/EC) applies to the company in question, the company will use IFRS for its 2005 accounts, and these will include comparative figures for 2004 restated on an IFRS basis. In those 2005 accounts, a business combination occurring on or after 1 January 2004 would fall under IFRS 3, while a business combination occurring prior to 1 January 2004 would not be required to be restated in accordance with IFRS 3.

Merger accounting banned

Unlike the predecessor standard (IAS 22), IFRS 3 bans the use of merger accounting: all business combinations (excluding group reconstructions, which are outside the scope of IFRS 3) should be accounted for as acquisitions. That is, an acquirer should be identified for accounting purposes even if the two parties are of similar size and describe the combination as a merger.

As noted above, merger accounting has, except in the context of group reconstructions, been quite rare in recent years. However, the standard-setters' view is that, even on this restricted basis, it has been used too widely, that is, used in connection with transactions where an acquirer is identifiable. However, it is likely that merger accounting principles will be retained for use in intra-group transactions.

Acquisition accounting under IFRS 3

In an acquisition, one party gains control over the other. Control is a question of fact – does one party have the power to govern the financial and operating policies of the other? There is a presumption that acquisition of more than one half of the voting rights of another entity confers control.

The key features of acquisition accounting under IFRS 3 are similar to those of FRS 6, as set out above under the heading 'Key features of acquisition accounting'. However, there are two key differences and these are principally in the area of goodwill and intangibles.

The first is that IFRS 3 requires that more separate intangibles be identified than previous standards and this has the effect of reducing the residual amount attributed to goodwill. The intangibles to be identified are: marketing-related intangibles (including newspaper mastheads, non-competition agreements); customer-related intangibles (including customer lists, non-contractual customer relationships); artistic-related intangible assets (including plays, operas and ballets, musical works such as compositions); contract-based intangibles (including franchise agreements, servicing contracts); and technology-based intangibles (such as databases, trade secrets). The full list of separable intangibles may be found in the illustrative examples at the back of IFRS 3. The IASB's principle is sound, namely that the more a company can identify exactly what it has bought, the more informative the financial statements will be. However, judging by recent US experience, there are likely to be practical implementation issues, as the valuation of such intangibles is problematical.

Second, there is a different approach to amortisation of goodwill and intangibles. Goodwill is not amortised at all under IFRS 3. It is tested for impairment annually. This means that, if the goodwill is shown to have at least retained its value, there is no charge to the profit and loss account. But, if there is shown to have been an impairment, there is an immediate charge to write down the goodwill to its recoverable amount. In the case of separate intangibles, they are amortised over their useful economic lives, although in certain cases this may be indefinite, thus leading to nil amortisation. Impairment testing rules apply also to separate intangibles.

Reform of IFRS and UK GAAP

The IASB continues to work on developing more detailed rules for accounting for business combinations, and will bring out proposals for a more detailed standard ('Business combinations Phase II', provisionally called 'Application of the purchase method') in due course.

In the UK, the ASB is considering when to change UK GAAP to incorporate IFRS 3 and Phase II. Its technical plan dated 16 March 2005 indicates that it plans to retain FRSs 6, 7 and 10 until the IASB has finalised a revised IFRS 3, incorporating its Phase II proposals. At that stage, it will withdraw those FRSs and replace them with the newly-revised IFRS 3.

However, irrespective of the ASB's timetable, IFRS 3 will apply, as part of the general application of international accounting standards under the EU Regulation (Council Regulation 1606/2002/EC) from 2005. As noted above, IFRS will apply to the group accounts of listed companies and to any other entities that opt into IFRS.

10
Interaction of accounting with tax

Introduction

Company accounts and corporate tax are closely related in a number of ways. First, assessment of corporation tax is based on complex rules of tax law and practice, but the starting point is the pre-tax profit shown in the company's annual statutory accounts. The context here is the entity accounts of individual companies, as tax is levied at the entity level, not at the consolidated level. Second, accounts need to reflect a company's obligations to pay tax. The most obvious example of this is the tax payable in respect of each year. However, in addition, accountants have developed accounting for 'deferred tax'. Third, there is the question of how the move to IFRS affects tax assessment. These issues are discussed in turn. This chapter seeks to give an introductory guide to accounting aspects of the issues; it is not a guide to tax law or practice.

Accounting profit and its adjustment

Accounting profit – specifically, the profit before tax figure in the profit and loss account – is the starting point for assessment of corporation tax. However, a number of adjustments are made. Examples of adjustments are:

- Depreciation of fixed assets that is charged in arriving at profit is added back, as it is not allowable for tax purposes. In its place there is a system of capital allowances, designed to give tax relief for certain types of capital expenditure. The amount and timing of capital allowances is based on tax law, which reflects the government's desire to give companies incentives to invest. Except by coincidence, capital allowances do not equate to accounting depreciation. An example of the relationship between capital allowances and accounting depreciation is shown below, under the heading 'Deferred tax'.
- Certain types of expenditure are disallowable for tax purposes, for example, fines and some types of entertaining expenses. Where such costs are charged in arriving at accounting profit, they are added back for tax purposes.

- Some items of income, such as certain government grants, may not be taxable.
- Some items of expenditure that are charged in arriving at accounting profit are allowable for tax but in different periods. For example, pension costs are charged in arriving at accounting profit on an accruals basis, but are allowed for tax purposes when paid. This gives rise to a timing difference, which again is reflected in deferred tax.

Hence an adjustment of accounting profit for tax purposes might look as that shown in Box 10.1.

	£
Profit before tax per the statutory accounts	1,000
Add: depreciation	200
Add: entertaining expenses	30
Less: tax-free grants	(60)
Less: capital allowances	(250)
Profit for tax purposes	920

Box 10.1

If the accounting profit were the exact basis for tax purposes, one would expect tax payable of 30% × £1,000 = £300. However, tax payable in fact would be 30% × £920 = £276. The reduction of £24 is a mixture of items that are permanently different for accounting and tax purposes, such as entertaining and grants, and items that feature for both accounting and tax purposes, but whose timing is different, such as depreciation and capital allowances. Note that 30% is the full rate of corporation tax. A starting rate, currently 0%, and a small companies rate, currently 19%, are payable on low profits.

Accounting for current and deferred tax

Current tax

In UK GAAP there is an accounting standard, FRS 16 'Current tax', that sets out a limited number of rules, though in general these are uncontroversial. Current tax is charged in the profit and loss account as an expense, unless the tax in question relates to a gain or loss that is reported in the statement of total recognised gains and losses, in which case the relevant amount of tax is also shown in that statement. In IFRS, some similar rules are set out in IAS 12, though the main focus of that standard is on deferred tax.

Deferred tax

Accounting for deferred tax is a much more complex issue than accounting for current tax. The basic premise is that accounting only for current tax understates a company's liabilities (or assets), as there may be additional liabilities (or assets) that crystallise in future years yet that originate from the profits of the earlier year. An example may clarify.

A company buys a new machine for £1,000 in year 1. For accounting purposes, the machine is assessed as having a useful life of five years, with no scrap value. Hence it is depreciated straight line over five years. For tax purposes, we assume it will attract capital allowances at 25% on a reducing balance basis. So, the pattern of book depreciation and capital allowances over the five years' life is as shown in Box 10.2.

Year	Accounting		Tax	
1	Cost	1,000	Cost	1,000
	Depreciation	(200)	Cap allowances	(250)
		800		750
2	Depreciation	(200)	Cap allowances	(187)
		600		563
3	Depreciation	(200)	Cap allowances	(141)
		400		422
4	Depreciation	(200)	Cap allowances	(105)
		200		317
5	Depreciation	(200)	Cap allowances	(317)*
		NIL		NIL

*Whether capital allowances in year 5 are the remaining £317 in the form of a balancing allowance or are 25% of £317, with the remainder to be allowed over future years, depends on a number of factors. We assume £317 for ease of illustration.

Box 10.2

At the end of year 1, book depreciation has taken the carrying value of the asset down to £800. However, capital allowances of 25% have taken the tax written down value to £750. In year 1, the company has benefited from the capital allowances being higher than book depreciation by £50. However, that is not a permanent benefit but merely a timing benefit, as the £50 benefit will reverse over the remaining life of the asset. That is, over years 2 to 5, the book depreciation will total £800, but the capital allowances will total only £750. If in years 2 to 5, the company made no accounting profits, it would still have to pay tax of £15 (30% of £50), as £800 would be added back to profits in respect of depreciation but only £750 would be deducted for captial allowances.

Accounting rules require companies to provide for deferred tax liabilities such as this £15. The UK GAAP rules are found in FRS 19 'Deferred tax'. FRS 19 defines deferred tax as: 'estimated future tax consequences of transactions and events recognised in the financial statements of the current and previous periods'. At the end of year 1, £15 is the amount of future tax consequences of transactions already undertaken. The £15 will automatically emerge over the next four years as an obligation, even if there are no further profits and no further capital expenditure. That is, the £15 deferred tax is an obligation or liability.

By the end of the second year, the situation is similar to the end of the first year, but by the end of the third year, it has changed in that the tax written down value of £422 is *higher* than the book value of £400. Hence there are tax allowances of £422 to receive in future, whereas there is only book depreciation of £400 to charge. There is therefore a benefit of £22 × 30% = £6.60. At this point, the deferred tax of £6.60 is an asset, as it is a future benefit. It is a benefit because the company will receive over the next two years, in respect of a transaction that has already happened, tax allowances of £422, but incur book depreciation of only £400.

Deferred tax, then, is a liability or asset arising in future in respect of automatic consequences of transactions or events that have already occurred. The example just given involved timing differences. Other sources of timing differences are the different tax treatment of pension costs and share-based payment. In each case, they are accounted for in one period but the tax consequences arise, to some degree at least, in other periods.

In contrast, if an asset is revalued to its market value, the UK GAAP view is that the revaluation of itself does not cause any future tax liabilities to arise. Hence no deferred tax liability is provided. It is the sale of the asset at its revalued amount, or the entering into a binding agreement to sell the revalued asset, that gives rise to a tax liability.

Deferred tax is not provided for in relation to permanent differences. The table in Box 10.2, in which the accounting profit was adjusted for tax purposes, included the adjustments shown in Box 10.3:

Add: entertaining expenses	30
Less: tax-free grants	(60)

Box 10.3

The first item in Box 10.3 is non-deductible for tax purposes; the second is non-taxable. They are called 'permanent differences'; they will never be taxable or deductible, and they cause the company's effective tax rate (the tax charge expressed as a percentage of profit before tax) to be different from the standard rate of 30%. Deferred tax accounting has no role here: there is no liability or asset; the effective tax rate will correctly be less than the standard tax rate.

(That is, in this example it will be less, as the tax-free income exceeds the disallowable expenses. In a different example, the effect could be the other way round.)

Deferred tax is accounted for under IFRS also. The relevant standard is IAS 12 'Taxation'. However, its approach is somewhat different from that of FRS 19. It takes a balance sheet approach and compares the book value of assets and liabilities with their 'tax base'. The tax base of an asset or liability is defined as 'the amount attributed to that asset or liability for tax purposes' (IAS 12, para. 5). Hence the tax base of an asset is defined as 'the amount that will be deductible for tax purposes against any taxable economic benefits that will flow to an enterprise when it recovers the carrying amount of the asset' (IAS 12, para. 7); although the underlying thinking is different, this gives the same answer in practice as the tax written down value explained in the example above of the machine that cost £1,000. Whether this different approach makes a difference in practice depends on the circumstances. It makes no difference to matters such as depreciation and capital allowances. However, it does have the effect that companies that revalue assets should provide deferred tax at the time of revaluation, not at the time of sale or commitment to sell. Hence, in this respect, IAS 12 will give rise to higher tax liabilities than FRS 19.

HM Revenue and Customs and the move to IFRS

As noted above, the starting point for tax assessment is the profit shown in the company's annual statutory accounts. Until now, for UK companies, this has been the profit as calculated under UK GAAP. From 2005, listed companies will have to move to IFRS for their consolidated accounts; and they, along with other entities, will have the choice to move to IFRS at the entity accounts level. One of the big factors for a company, in deciding whether to move to IFRS at the entity level, is the effect that such a move might have on tax assessments.

The Revenue's policy is summarised in its Budget Note 'REV BN 25: tax and accounting (IAS and UK GAAP)', which includes the following:

'WHO IS LIKELY TO BE AFFECTED?

1. Listed companies [note: this means literally companies (i.e. entities) that are listed; it does not refer to groups], other companies and non-corporate entities that choose to adopt International Accounting Standards (IAS).

GENERAL DESCRIPTION OF THE MEASURE

2. The measures are to ensure that companies choosing to adopt IAS to draw up their accounts receive broadly equivalent tax treatment to companies that continue to use UK Generally Accepted Accounting Practice (UK GAAP).

Operative date

3. Periods of account beginning on or after 1 January 2005.

Current law and proposed revisions

4. UK tax law requires the use of accounts drawn up under recognised accounting principles as the starting point for tax returns of trading profits. Since 1998 this requirement has been included in statute law, and provides that the computation of the taxable profits of a trade, a profession or a property business must be based on accounts drawn up under UK GAAP. This applies to individuals as well as companies. UK GAAP is also used to determine the profits in some other areas, especially loan relationships (debt and securities), derivative contracts and intangibles outside the trading context.

5. The revisions will:
- ensure that IAS accounts are valid for UK tax purposes; and
- amend the legislation on loan relationships, derivative contracts, intangibles and R & D [research and development] to accommodate accounting changes, both under IAS and UK GAAP.

DETAIL OF THE CHANGES

Intangible fixed assets

6. Legislation will ensure that where tax relief for amortisation of goodwill has been claimed, relief will not be allowed again if the goodwill is written up to original cost when a company adopts IAS.

Research & Development

7. The benefits of the R & D deductions and credits will be maintained by allowing a claim for revenue expenditure treated as added to the cost of an asset when it is incurred, instead of when it is amortised in the profit and loss account over later periods.'

Further details are set out regarding financial assets and liabilities (loan relationships), derivative contracts and currency accounting, but these are not reproduced here.

This policy is already reflected in legislation: section 50 of the Finance Act 2004 redefines 'generally accepted accounting practice' to include both EU adopted IAS and UK GAAP for periods beginning on or after 1 January 2005. Section 51 deals with the situation where a company is permitted to use IAS and has a transaction with another group company which uses UK GAAP. If the transaction has as a main benefit the conferring of a tax advantage as a result of different accounting treatments, the IAS company will have to use UK GAAP for the transaction for tax purposes.

Indeed the DTI has legislated to make it rare for some companies in a group to use UK GAAP and others to use IFRS. The Companies Act 1985 (International Accounting Standards and Other Accounting Amendments) Regulations 2004 (SI 2004 No. 2947) provides, in the new section 227C to the Act, that all UK subsidiaries within a group should use the same accounting standards – either IFRS or UK GAAP – unless there is a 'good reason' for a group company to use a different basis. The DTI has given some examples of genuine cases where mixed GAAP within a group would be acceptable. An example of an acceptable use is where a group using IAS acquired a subsidiary that had not been using IFRS; in the first year of acquisition, it might not be practical for the newly acquired company to switch to IAS straight away. But tax is not among the examples given.

The practical effect

There are likely to be a variety of practical tax effects arising from a change to IFRS. Some of these may be very specific, either because of an unusual effect of the change in accounting rules, or because of a complexity in the rules on, say, the taxation of derivatives.

But there is a much more straightforward point of general application. Simply put: if profits under IFRS are higher (or lower) than under UK GAAP, the tax payable is likely to be higher (or lower). This could arise either (a) in terms of timing: where revenue or expenses are recognised earlier (or later) than under UK GAAP; or (b) it might arise in terms of permanent differences: where an item is recognised as income (or expense) under IFRS whereas it is not so recognised, or not recognised at the same amount, under UK GAAP.

For example, if a receipt of £300 is recognised in the profit and loss account over a three-year period under UK GAAP but under IFRS is recognised as revenue immediately, then on a move to IFRS the tax treatment would in a simple case follow the accounting, and the tax payable of £90 (£300 × 30%) would be accelerated into year 1, rather than spread over the three years.

So the Revenue statement (quoted above) that 'companies choosing to adopt IAS to draw up their accounts receive *broadly equivalent tax treatment* to companies that continue to use . . . UK GAAP' [emphasis added] is, at best, an oversimplification. What it seems to mean in practice is that (a) where there is a specific tax rule affecting an item, that rule continues to apply; but (b) where tax follows GAAP, and profits under IFRS are higher (or lower) than under UK GAAP, tax assessments will also be higher (or lower) in an equivalent manner.

11

Assets

Introduction

The key questions that arise in relation to assets are: what is the definition of assets; which assets are recognised on balance sheet, and when are they first recognised; and how are the assets that are recognised on balance sheet measured. There are also questions of how assets should be classified and presented on balance sheets; and questions of depreciation. These issues are considered in turn.

In a formal sense, the UK Statement of principles (para. 4.6) defines assets as: 'rights or other access to future economic benefits controlled by an entity as a result of past transactions or events'. Less formally, an asset is something of value that a company has.

Recognition of assets

From the definition, it might appear that all a company's assets are recognised on the balance sheet. In fact, they are recognised only if they pass certain recognition criteria, for example that they can be measured with sufficient reliability. For this reason, and in some cases because the asset in question is not controlled by the company, assets such as a company's reputation, its skilled workforce and its self-developed brands – valuable though they may be – are not recognised on balance sheet.

Measurement of assets

Traditionally, accounting has been strongly based on historical cost. As noted in chapter 7 at p. 72, one of the recent developments in accounting is the increased use of fair value or a similar valuation basis, resulting in a mixed measurement model. The use of fair value rather than cost varies depending on the type of asset, and also varies to some degree as between UK GAAP and IFRS. For example, property, plant and equipment may be measured in both UK GAAP and IFRS at either cost or valuation (FRS 15; IAS 16). For investment properties, however, there is the same choice in IFRS (IAS 40) but valuation is compulsory under UK GAAP (SSAP 19). For investments and other financial assets the picture is more complex as it depends (a) in IFRS, into which of the four categories of financial asset the item is classified under IAS 39, and (b) whether, in UK GAAP, FRS 26 applies to the company and to the year in question. Goodwill is accounted for at cost under both IFRS and UK GAAP. In slight contrast, other intangibles are nearly always carried on a cost basis; they can in principle be carried on a valuation basis, but the criteria are strict and as a result that treatment is rare. Under IAS 41, biological assets are carried at an amount based on fair value. In general, current assets are carried at the lower of cost and net realisable value, though some financial assets, for example those held for trading, and derivatives, are carried at fair value (see chapter 15 at pp. 157–9).

Impairment of assets

Whether an asset's carrying value is based on cost or fair value, there is an underlying principle that it should not be carried on a balance sheet at more than its recoverable amount. That is, in stating an asset on a balance sheet at a particular amount, there is an implication that it is worth that amount, or more. In this context, 'worth' could mean that the asset could be sold for at least that amount, or it could refer to the fact that it will generate cash flows over a period of at least that amount, in present value terms (see below).

More formally expressed, recoverable amount is the higher of:

- net realisable value (NRV) (IFRS term: fair value less costs to sell); and
- value in use.

The NRV, or fair value less costs to sell, is 'the amount obtainable from the sale of an asset . . . in an arm's length transaction between knowledgeable, willing parties, less the costs of disposal' (IAS 36, para. 6).

Value in use is 'the present value of the future cash flows expected to be derived from an asset' (IAS 36, para 6). 'Present value' refers to the time value of money. For example, if an asset will generate £105 in one year's time and interest rates are 5%, the present value of that cash flow is £100. This process is also called 'discounting'.

The notion of recoverable amount being the higher of two measures as set out above reflects commercial reality. That is, if an asset has an NRV of £80 but a value in use of £100, a rational management would keep the asset rather than sell it. Hence the recoverable amount is £100. Thus if the asset's carrying value is less than £100 no impairment write down is required; but if the carrying value is above £100 the asset has to be written down to £100.

The rules on impairment of assets – both as to when they should be carried out and as to the methodology – are complex. It should be recognised, however, that impairment testing is an imprecise art. An asset's NRV might be easily established, though that will depend on the type of asset. But an asset's value in use is at best an estimate and is only as good as the forecast of future cash flows that the asset will generate – such a forecast is necessarily uncertain, especially when the time horizon extends to a long period. Having said that, it is important for companies to test assets for impairment at appropriate times, as otherwise they risk being carried on balance sheets at unjustifiable amounts. This is one of those occasions when accountants speak of the numbers being 'roughly right rather than exactly wrong'.

Impairment, as discussed above, applies to fixed assets, though the same underlying principle – that an asset should not be carried at above its recoverable amount – applies also to current assets. In the case of current assets, the principle is generally achieved by using as the measurement basis the lower of cost and net realisable value.

Classification and presentation of assets

Assets are classified as either current assets or fixed assets in UK GAAP. In IFRS, the terms current and non-current are used. With minor differences, the effect is similar. The presentation of different types of assets on a UK GAAP balance sheet in summary form is:

- Fixed assets
  - Intangible assets
  - Tangible assets
  - Investments
- Current assets
  - Stocks
  - Debtors
  - Investments
  - Cash

This follows directly from the Companies Act and a more detailed version of this is shown in chapter 3 at p. 30. Fixed assets are defined as those 'which are intended for use on a continuing basis in the company's activities' and current assets are defined as 'assets not intended for such use' (CA 1985, section 262). Hence there is no time limit for realisation which determines in which category the asset is included.

Under IFRS, the Companies Act formats do not apply but classification as between current and non-current is determined by IAS 1 (para. 57), which states that:

> 'An asset shall be classified as current when it satisfies any of the following criteria:
> (a) it is expected to be realised in, or is intended for sale or consumption in, the entity's normal operating cycle;
> (b) it is held primarily for the purpose of being traded;
> (c) it is expected to be realised within twelve months after the balance sheet date; or

(d) it is cash or a cash equivalent (as defined in IAS 7 Cash Flow State-ments) unless it is restricted from being exchanged or used to settle a liability for at least twelve months after the balance sheet date.
All other assets shall be classified as non-current.'

Depreciation

Some fixed (or non-current) assets last for a long period of time and maintain their value, whereas others lose value as time passes. For example, a fixed asset investment may, if well selected, hold or increase its value over a long period. The same applies, generally, to land. Whereas a building, or a piece of plant or IT equipment may lose its value over a period. For this latter category of assets, depreciation is relevant. The term 'depreciation' is used in connection with tangible fixed assets. Depreciation is a common phenomenon in everyday life: many non-accountants are expert at the depreciation of cars, for example. Depreciation, for accounting purposes, is defined as: 'the systematic allocation of the depreciable amount of an asset over its useful life', where depreciable amount is 'the cost of an asset, or other amount substituted for cost, less its residual value' (IAS 16, para. 6). The UK definition is similar. Depreciation is:

> 'The measure of the cost or revalued amount of the economic benefits of the tangible fixed asset that have been consumed during the period. Consumption includes the wearing out, using up or other reduction in the useful economic life of a tangible fixed asset whether arising from use, effluxion of time or obsolescence through either changes in technology or demand for the goods and services produced by the asset.' [FRS 15, para. 2].

The key point that these definitions make clear is that depreciation is an exercise in allocation of cost (less residual value) over accounting periods. It does not seek to reflect interim valuations of assets. For example, a company might own a car costing £10,000, and expect to keep it for four years, at the end of which period its expected residual value will be £4,000. The depreciable amount is £6,000 and the annual depreciation, on a straight line basis, is £1,500. Thus at the end of the first year, the car is carried in the balance sheet at a net book value of £8,500. This is so, even though the second-hand value of the car is very likely to be less than £8,500. The car is not impaired (see above) as the company expects to carry on using it profitably over the next three years, at the end of which it will be sold for an estimated £4,000.

Like many aspects of accounting, depreciation involves estimates. The use-ful life of the asset and its residual value at the end of that life can only be estimates. For that reason, FRS 15 and IAS 16 require companies to keep under review their estimates; for example if an asset looks likely to last longer than originally expected, the depreciation profile should be slowed down. Despite such adjustments, it is quite common for an asset, when sold, to realise an amount more or less than its residual value. Any such difference is reported in the profit and loss account as a profit or loss on sale.

Amortisation

Goodwill and other intangibles are covered by their own accounting standards: FRS 10 in UK GAAP and IAS 38 and IFRS 3 in IFRS. Accountants, perhaps to confuse the public, use the term 'amortisation' for intangibles, rather than depreciation, though the meaning is the same. While in principle intangibles are, under UK GAAP, subject to amortisation, there are exceptions. FRS 10 envisages a minority practice under which goodwill and intangibles need not be amortised if the facts of the case demonstrate an indefinite life. This requires a true and fair override of the CA 1985 in the case of goodwill; and for both good-will and intangibles the amortisation is replaced by annual impairment testing. Under IFRS, goodwill is now not amortised but is tested annually for impairment. Intangibles are amortised in general but non-amortisation (replaced with annual impairment testing) is possible if an indefinite life can be demonstrated.

Disclosure

Various details of assets have to be given in the notes to the accounts, but for the most part these merely provide additional details about items that are recognised on balance sheet. Examples include movements on tangible and intangible fixed assets, and details about investments. There is also a requirement (FRS 12, para. 94; IAS 37, para. 89) to disclose certain contingent assets.

12
Liabilities

Introduction

As noted in chapter 1, a balance sheet can be considered, in summary form, as follows:

Assets *less* liabilities = Shareholders' funds

Shareholders' funds is called 'Capital and reserves' in the Companies Act format, and is called 'equity' in IAS.

Hence liabilities are one of the major components of a balance sheet. The key questions that arise in relation to liabilities are: what is the definition of liabilities, and how they are distinguished from shareholders' funds; which liabilities are recognised on the balance sheet, and when they are recognised; and how are the liabilities that are recognised on the balance sheet measured. There are also questions of how liabilities should be presented on balance sheets, and questions of disclosure, including disclosure of contingent liabilities. These issues are considered in turn.

Definition of liabilities

Liabilities are defined in the ASB's Statement of principles as 'obligations of an entity to transfer economic benefits as a result of past transactions or events' (SoP 4.23). A similar definition is found in the IASB's Framework.

This definition was developed as part of the ASB's reform of accounting in the early 1990s. During the 1980s, some companies had sought to distort their accounting by setting up liabilities – in particular provisions for items such as restructuring costs – on a large scale but a discretionary basis. For example, a company might have had a more profitable year than expected, but would know that it was likely to incur costs in future years in restructuring its business. It would therefore set up, at the end of the profitable year, a provision for these future costs, thereby reducing the profits of that year. However, this technique fell into disrepute as it amounted to little more than profit smoothing, and failed to represent the results of the year in question.

The ASB's definition takes a much more precise and restrictive approach to what can be regarded as a liability. The definition starts by saying that, in order for there to be a liability, there must already be an *obligation*. This means that the entity is not free to avoid the outflow of resources. If a company merely had an idea that it might undertake a restructuring in a year's time, that would not count as a liability, as the company could abort or change its plans – it is not committed to that course of action and can avoid the costs involved if it so chooses. The ASB's SoP adds that, for a liability to exist at the balance sheet date, the obligation to transfer economic benefits must have resulted from a past transaction or event. So for example, an obligation under a warranty would be recognised only to the extent of goods actually sold at the end of the accounting year.

The definition of a liability applies in a number of contexts. In this chapter, we consider the general case of creditors and provisions. In chapter 15, we consider capital instruments such as various types of debt instruments, preference shares and equity shares. Careful analysis is sometimes needed to establish which of those should be accounted for as liabilities and which are shareholders' funds.

Recognition of liabilities

A liability might appear to exist in terms of the definition (see above) but that does not automatically mean that it should be recognised on balance sheet. This point is well explained in the accounting standard on provisions (FRS 12 'Provisions, contingent liabilities and contingent assets'). This deals with provisions which are, as the balance sheet formats show (see chapter 3 at p. 31), a subset of liabilities, namely those that are liabilities 'of uncertain timing or amount'. However, much of its thinking applies to all liabilities. FRS 12 states that:

> 'A provision should be recognised when:
> (a) an entity has a present obligation (legal or constructive) as a result of a past event;
> (b) it is probable that a transfer of economic benefits will be required to settle the obligation; and
> (c) a reliable estimate can be made of the amount of the obligation.
> If these conditions are not met, no provision should be recognised.'
> [FRS 12, para. 14]

From this quotation, it is clear that where an obligation exists, it is recognised only if there is a probable transfer to another party of economic benefits. For example, a company might guarantee the borrowings of a second company. A guarantee is a legal obligation. But if the second company is financially sound, it is unlikely that the first company will have to pay up under its guarantee. Hence no liability is recognised by the first company.

Also obligations are recognised only if a reliable estimate can be made of the amount of the liability. For example, a company might have potential obligations in relation to claims from customers or employees in respect of damage of some kind. It may be that a payment is considered 'probable', but in the early stages of the case, it may be very difficult to estimate the liability with sufficient reliability for inclusion in the balance sheet. In these circumstances, it is appropriate to give footnote disclosure (see below).

Liabilities are recognised not only in respect of legal obligations but also in respect of constructive obligations. These are obligations that derive:

> 'from an entity's actions where:
> (a) by an established pattern of past practice, published policies or a sufficiently specific current statement, the entity has indicated to other parties that it will accept certain responsibilities; and
> (b) as a result, the entity has created a valid expectation on the part of those other parties that it will discharge those responsibilities.'
>
> [FRS 12, para. 2]

Examples of constructive obligations include those arising as a result of environmental damage and reorganisations. In the former case, whilst the law requires some environmental damage to be rectified, there may be other examples where there is no legal requirement to rectify but the company has an announced policy, and an established practice of rectifying damage of that kind. This creates an expectation among third parties that the company will continue to follow its policy and practice, and this gives rise to the need to record a constructive obligation on the balance sheet. In the case of restructuring or reorganisation of a business, similar principles apply. But here, because restructuring is a common example, and perhaps because of earlier abuses in this area, FRS 12 is more specific:

> 'A constructive obligation to restructure arises only when an entity:
> (a) has a detailed formal plan for the restructuring identifying at least:
>   (i) the business or part of a business concerned;
>   (ii) the principal locations affected;
>   (iii) the location, function, and approximate number of employees who will be compensated for terminating their services;
>   (iv) the expenditures that will be undertaken; and
>   (v) when the plan will be implemented; and
> (b) has raised a valid expectation in those affected that it will carry out the restructuring by starting to implement that plan or announcing its main features to those affected by it.'
>
> [FRS 12, para. 77]

The aim, in connection with constructive obligations, is that a company should record a liability where it is for all practical purposes obliged to incur the expenditure in question. Perhaps it is not legally committed to incur the expenditure; but if it did not incur it, it would be damaged from a reputational point of view. For example, if a company announced a restructuring in sufficiently specific terms to meet para. 77 (quoted above), it could in theory revoke its decision and say to employees that it had changed its mind, and their jobs are to be maintained after all. But this is not the situation in which most companies would wish to find themselves.

Measurement of liabilities

Accounting has largely moved away from prudence towards neutrality of measurement. Hence liabilities should be measured at the best estimate of the amount that will be required to settle them. A provision for restructuring should be recognised at the best estimate of the amount to be incurred, without adding a further amount (sometimes called a 'cushion'). The equivalent applies in the context of normal creditors – that is, those where, unlike provisions, the amount and timing are known. If a creditor that does not bear interest is not payable for say two years, it should be recorded at its 'present value', that is, reflecting the time value of money. This is known as discounting. For example, if interest rates were 10%, £110 payable in one year or £121 payable in two years would be equivalent to £100 payable today. Discounting would be done where the effect is material. In general, discounting starts to become material if the period involved is more than one year, although this also depends on the absolute amount. Discounting applies to provisions as well as to creditors.

Presentation of liabilities on balance sheets

Chapter 3 reproduced the whole of the Companies Act Schedule 4 balance sheet format 1. From that format, we may note that the sections dealing with liabilities are:

- E: Creditors: amounts falling due within one year
- H: Creditors: amounts falling due after more than one year
- I: Provisions for liabilities and charges
- J: Accruals and deferred income.

A key point in format 1 is that liabilities falling due within one year ('current liabilities') are presented separately from those falling due after more than one year. The balance sheet presentation as a whole has the current liabilities deducted from current assets, to show net current assets. Current assets and liabilities are generally regarded as being involved in the operating cycle of a business. Long-term liabilities, on the other hand, are viewed as part of a business's longer-term financing. A business needs a certain amount of long-term finance; part of this is provided in the form of shareholders' funds, and often part in the form of long-term liabilities. The relationship between these is known as 'gearing'. Consider the summarised balance sheet in Box 12.1.

Fixed assets		100
Current assets	70	
Less current liabilities	50	
Net current assets		20
Net assets		120
Long-term debt		40
Shareholders' funds		80
Total capital		120

Box 12.1

Gearing for this company can be expressed in a number of ways: there is no single agreed definition. A popular measure is long-term debt (40) to share-holders' funds (80), i.e. 50%. An alternative is to express the extent to which total long-term capital is provided by debt, i.e. $40/120 = 33.3\%$.

As may also be noted from the four headings above (E, H, I, J), provisions are shown separately from short and long-term creditors. This is because provisions are, relative to creditors, uncertain as to timing or amount. Accruals and deferred income is also shown separately; however, there are also format headings for accruals and deferred income within short and long-term creditors (E and H), and it is more common to show them there.

Balance sheet format 2 does not make the distinction between short and long-term creditors, although it requires the analysis to be given in the notes. Format 2 is used infrequently and is not considered further here.

Disclosure, including contingent liabilities

Various details of liabilities have to be given in the notes to the accounts, but for the most part these merely provide additional details about items that are recognised on balance sheet, such as bank loans. In this respect, no further comment is needed. However, there is a further class of disclosures that warrant comment, namely those in relation to contingent liabilities.

A contingent liability is defined as:

'(a) A possible obligation that arises from past events and whose existence will be confirmed only by the occurrence of one or more uncertain future events not wholly within the entity's control; or

(b) a present obligation that arises from past events but is not recognised because:

(i) it is not probable that a transfer of economic benefits will be required to settle the obligation; or

(ii) the amount of the obligation cannot be measured with sufficient reliability.'

Part (a) of the definition deals with those liabilities that are genuinely contingent, that is, whether the liability arises depends on whether an uncertain future event occurs. Part (b) deals with matters that are not contingent in the same way. Rather they are actual liabilities (such as an existing guarantee) where an outflow of resources is not likely; or they are those rare cases where there is an actual liability but it is not recognised on the balance sheet because it is not possible to measure it with sufficient reliability. Despite these differences, the accounting implications are the same, namely that contingent liabilities should not be recognised on balance sheet. However certain details should be given about contingent liabilities in the notes to the accounts:

> 'Unless the possibility of any transfer in settlement is remote, an entity should disclose for each class of contingent liability at the balance sheet date a brief description of the nature of the contingent liability and, where practicable:
> (a) an estimate of its financial effect, measured in accordance with paragraphs 36–55;
> (b) an indication of the uncertainties relating to the amount or timing of any outflow; and
> (c) the possibility of any reimbursement.'
> [FRS 12, para. 91; IAS 37, para. 86 is similar.]

Liabilities under IFRS

The accounting rules in IFRS are very similar to those in UK GAAP. IAS 37 'Provisions, contingent liabilities and contingent assets' is very similar to the UK's FRS 12 of the same name. Hence the above comments about definition, recognition, measurement and disclosure apply in a similar way in IFRS. A difference, however, is that the Act's formats, discussed under the above heading of presentation, do not apply to companies adopting IFRS, as they are part of Schedule 4 to the Act, which is disapplied to IFRS companies.

13

Leases

Introduction

The current UK accounting standard dealing with this topic, SSAP 21 'Accounting for leases and hire purchase contracts', was issued in 1984 and was the first UK accounting standard to require the substance, rather than the legal form, of a transaction to be reflected in the accounting treatment, predating FRS 5 by ten years. When issued, it was sufficiently controversial that Ian Hay Davison, the then Chairman of the ASC, wrote a Foreword to accompany the standard justifying its issue.

SSAP 21 deals with the accounting for operating leases, finance leases and hire purchase contracts. Prior to the issue of SSAP 21, although assets acquired under hire purchase agreements, and the associated obligation to pay, were capitalised on the hirer's balance sheet, the accounting treatment for leases was very different. Leases were simply accounted for as the payments were made, thus no asset or obligation appeared on the lessee's balance sheet.

In a nutshell, SSAP 21 sets out different accounting treatments according to whether the lease is a finance lease or an operating lease. In a finance lease, a lessee is in substance buying the asset and paying on deferred terms in the same way as it would if it took out a loan to buy the asset and was then repaying the loan. Accordingly, SSAP 21 requires the asset to be capitalised by the lessee (and depreciated over its useful economic life or, if shorter, the lease term) and the related obligation to be recognised on balance sheet as equivalent to a loan. For other leases (operating leases), SSAP 21 argues that the asset has not in substance been purchased by the lessee and thus the asset and related financing obligation are not recognised on its balance sheet. Instead the lease payments are charged in its profit and loss account, generally on a straight-line basis, over the lease term. Lessor accounting mirrors that of the lessee.

Accompanying SSAP 21 are lengthy Guidance Notes dealing with some of the practical issues and problem areas arising. For lessors, the Finance and Leasing Association (FLA) SORP 'Accounting issues in the asset finance and leasing industry' provides additional guidance and recommendations.

UITF 28 'Operating lease incentives' contains rules on accounting for operating leases when incentives, such as upfront cash payments, reimbursement of expenses or rent-free periods, are provided to induce a lessee to enter into a lease. In essence the incentives are amortised over the lease term or, if shorter, the period to the rent review where the rent reverts to market rent.

The accounting treatment under IFRS is similar. However, both the UK and IFRS accounting treatments are set to change as there is a project under way to radically alter the accounting treatment for operating leases.

This chapter will run through the accounting treatment (including disclosure) under current UK GAAP, then current IFRS and will finish by looking at future developments.

Leases under UK GAAP

Definitions

Finance lease and operating lease are defined in SSAP 21 as follows:

> 'A *finance lease* is a lease that transfers substantially all the risks and rewards of ownership of an asset to the lessee. It should be presumed that such a transfer of risks and rewards occurs if at the inception of a lease the present value of the minimum lease payments including any initial payment, amounts to substantially all (normally 90 per cent or more) of the fair value of the leased asset. The present value should be calculated by using the interest rate implicit in the lease (as defined in paragraph 24 [of SSAP 21]). If the fair value of the asset is not determinable, an estimate thereof should be used.
>
> Notwithstanding the fact that a lease meets the conditions in paragraph 15 [the paragraph above], the presumption that it should be classified as a finance lease may in exceptional circumstances be rebutted if it can be clearly demonstrated that the lease in question does not transfer substantially all the risks and rewards of ownership (other than legal title) to the lessee. Correspondingly, the presumption that a lease which fails to meet the conditions in paragraph 15 is not a finance lease may in exceptional circumstances be rebutted.'
>
> 'An *operating lease* is a lease other than a finance lease.'
>
> [SSAP 21, paras. 15–17.]

The distinction between finance lease and operating lease is important because the accounting treatment for the two is very different.

SSAP 21 defines a *hire purchase contract* as 'a contract for the hire of an asset which contains a provision giving the hirer an option to acquire legal title to the asset upon the fulfilment of certain conditions stated in the contract'. SSAP 21 requires each hire purchase contract to be accounted for as a finance lease or as an operating lease depending on which definition is met (usually finance lease).

129

Treatment of operating leases

The analysis of the transaction here is that the lessor not only retains legal ownership of the asset but also beneficial ownership. Accordingly the lessor continues to recognise (or, in the case of an asset specially purchased for the transaction, starts to recognise) the asset on its balance sheet and recognises rental income. The lessee does not recognise the asset on its balance sheet but simply records a rental expense over the lease period. For both the lessee and lessor, the accounting treatment is to recognise the rentals in the profit and loss account on a straight line basis over the lease term, even if the payments are not made on such a basis, unless another systematic and rational basis is, for a lessee, more appropriate, and for a lessor, more representative of the time pattern in which the benefit from the leased asset is receivable. This is illustrated in the following example.

E Limited leases a piece of equipment from O Limited for two years starting 1 September in year 1. Rentals of £12,000 are payable quarterly in advance. E has a calendar accounting period. At the end of the first accounting period E will have paid £24,000. However the amount charged in the accounting periods is as shown in Box 13.1.

Year 1	£16,000
Year 2	£48,000
Year 3	£32,000

Box 13.1

These figures reflect the normal principles of accruals accounting. For example, in year 1 the lessee has had the benefit of the equipment for four months, and so charges to its profit and loss account four months' rentals ($£12,000 \times 4/3 = £16,000$).

UITF 28 'Operating lease incentives' clarifies that the above rule about straight-line charging (subject to another systematic and rational basis not being more appropriate) applies even where the lessor pays a large up-front incentive to the lessee or there is an initial rent-free period, although the UITF Abstract modifies the rule slightly and requires the incentive/absence of rent to be spread over the shorter of the lease term and the period to when it is expected that the rentals will be revised to a market rent. Generally this arises on property leases and UITF 28 confirms that its principle applies to any form of incentive given by the lessor to the lessee to induce the lessee to enter into the lease other than expenditure incurred that enhances the property to the extent that the lessor benefits. For example, if the lessor pays for part of the lessee's fitting out costs, but the expenditure is incurred solely on items specific to the lessee such as a shop front bearing the lessee's name, the expenditure has to be treated as a deduction from rental income (lessor)/payments (lessee) and spread over the period to the rent review when rentals revert to market rental (or, if shorter, the lease term). However, if the lessor pays for an extension to the property, this has enduring benefit to the lessor as he has a larger property to rent out, both to the current lessee and to future lessees and so such expenditure would be capitalised on the lessor's balance sheet and depreciated rather than being treated as a reduction from the rental income. Similarly, in this latter case the lessee would not make any adjustment when expensing the lease rentals over the period of the lease.

Treatment of finance leases

A lease meets the definition of a finance lease if it transfers substantially all the risks and rewards of ownership of the asset to the lessee and if the present value of the minimum lease payments that will be made amounts to substantially all of the fair value of the asset. This sets the tone for the accounting. Although the lessor retains legal title to the asset (except possibly at the end of the lease when a purchase option may be exercised by the lessee), beneficial ownership has transferred to the lessee on inception of the lease, and both lessee and lessor account as though the lessor has sold the asset to the lessee and the lessee has a loan from the lessor for the capital sum. Thus the lessee recognises in its balance sheet both the asset and a liability for the same amount. The excess of the rental

On day 1	Debit Fixed assets		£100,000			
	Credit Liabilities					£100,000
In years 1 to 5						
	Year 1	Year 2	Year 3	Year 4	Year 5	Total
Dr P&L account – interest expense	£5,604	£4,519	£3,367	£2,144	£846	£16,480
Dr Finance lease obligation – reduction of liability	£17,692	£18,777	£19,929	£21,152	£22,450	£100,000
Cr Cash – payment of cash	£23,296	£23,296	£23,296	£23,296	£23,296	£116,480
Dr P&L account – depreciation expense	£20,000	£20,000	£20,000	£20,000	£20,000	£100,000
Cr Fixed assets – provision for depreciation	£20,000	£20,000	£20,000	£20,000	£20,000	£100,000

Box 13.2

payments over the capital sum recognised on day 1 is recorded as interest through the profit and loss account. The total amount recognised as interest is allocated to each accounting period at a constant rate on the outstanding balance. The asset is accounted for as any other asset, thus it is depreciated over its useful economic life (or, if shorter, the lease term) and is reviewed for impairment if there is an indicator of impairment.

Consider the following example. On 1 January, X Limited entered into a lease with Y Limited under which X leases a machine from Y for five years at a quarterly rental of £5,824. The machine's expected residual value at the end of the five years is nil and its fair value on day 1 is £100,000. The lease is a finance lease and the lessee will account for it as shown in Box 13.2.

The table in Box 13.2, shows that the lessee records as expenses in its profit and loss account both (a) interest on the liability to pay rentals; the interest is higher in early years ('front loaded') as it is a constant percentage on the amount of principal outstanding; and (b) depreciation on the asset, as if it were owned; we assume straight-line depreciation for this purpose. Hence the total charge is front loaded (£25,604 in year one reducing to £20,846 in year 5).

The lessor's accounting mirrors the above in aggregate, although there are differences in the allocation of interest to the accounting periods (see Boxes 13.3 and 13.4).

On day 1	Debit Receivable	£100,000	
	Credit Asset		£100,000

Box 13.3

The day 1 accounting entries in Box 13.3 reflect the lessor no longer having the original asset, but disposing of that in favour of an amount receivable from the lessee. Then, during years 1 to 5, the lessor receives cash which he allocates to interest income and collection of principal, as illustrated here. Lessors are required under SSAP 21 to allocate the interest income to the different accounting periods so as to give a constant periodic rate of return on the 'net cash investment' in the lease. The net cash investment in the lease represents the total cash invested after taking account of all the cash flows associated with the lease.

In years 1 to 5						
	Year 1	Year 2	Year 3	Year 4	Year 5	Total
Dr Cash – received from lessee	£23,296	£23,296	£23,296	£23,296	£23,296	£116,480
Cr P&L account – interest income	£5,749	£4,558	£3,321	£2,065	£787	£16,480
Cr Receivable – collection of principal	£17,547	£18,738	£19,975	£21,231	£22,509	£100,000

Box 13.4

Consider now a lessor that manufactures assets at a cost of £800 each and either sells them for £1,000 (immediate payment) or leases them out. Where the lease is a finance lease the accounting logic is that the lessor has sold the asset to the lessee. Accordingly, under SSAP 21 the lessor can book the gross selling profit of £200 at the start of the lease period and allocate the lease interest income over the remainder of the lease period as above. If, on the other hand, the lease is an operating lease no gross selling profit can be recognised as the accounting reflects the view that the lessor still owns the asset.

Classification of leases into finance or operating

One of the most critical questions in lease accounting presently is whether the lease is an operating lease or a finance lease. For lessees, classification as an operating lease is normally favoured as the accounting for this does not give rise to a liability on the balance sheet thus not adversely affecting the gearing ratio. On the other hand, lessors generally favour classification as finance leases. From an accounting perspective, this gives rise to a current, rather than fixed, asset. More fundamentally, however, the risk profile of a finance lease is different for the lessor than that for an operating lease and this is the real reason why many lessors prefer the lease to be structured as a finance lease.

Included in the definition of a finance lease is the following sentence 'It should be presumed that such a transfer of risks and rewards occurs if at the inception of a lease the present value of the minimum lease payments including any initial payment, amounts to substantially all (normally 90 per cent or more) of the fair value of the leased asset' (SSAP 21, para. 15). This reference to 90% has given rise to what is often referred to as 'the 90% test' or 'the 90% rule' under which it is argued that if the present value of the minimum lease payments is less than 90% the lease is an operating lease. SSAP 21 does not express this as a rule, however, and it is important to look at wider issues when classifying leases. Support for this wider consideration (rather than simply applying a 90% test) is given by FRS 5, which requires that 'the specific provisions of any standard or statute should be applied to the substance of the transaction and not merely to its legal form and, for this purpose, the general principles set out in FRS 5 will be relevant'. For example, the present value of the minimum lease payments for a lessee may total 88% of the asset's fair value but the minimum lease period may be equal to the asset's useful economic life. In this instance the substance is that the lessee has the use of the asset for its entire useful economic life and thus should treat the lease as a finance lease and account as though it had purchased the asset; in effect it is simply a bargain purchase. Nevertheless, it may be that different indicators point in different directions and there is no clear view, or that there is no overriding factor that swings the balance in classifying the lease. In these situations emphasis does tend to get put on the numerical analysis.

Fundamental to the numerical analysis are the 'minimum lease payments'. These are defined as shown in Box 13.5.

	Lessee	Lessor
Rentals over the 'lease term'	✓	✓
Residual amounts guaranteed by lessee	✓	✓
Residual amounts guaranteed by a party related to lessee, e.g., by parent or fellow subsidiary of lessee	✓	✓
Residual amounts guaranteed by party NOT related to lessee	✗	✓

Box 13.5

This difference in definition can lead to different classification. Consider an asset with a useful economic life of six years. A lessor enters into a lease under which a lessee will lease it for three years, the present value of the lease payments being, say, 65% of the asset's fair value on day 1. The lease will probably be classified as an operating lease by the lessee. If, however, the lessor also enters into an agreement with a third party (unrelated to both lessee and lessor) under which the third party agrees to purchase the asset from the lessor at the end of the three years for a fixed sum if the lessor chooses to offer it to the third party, the present value of the fixed sum being 35% of the asset's fair value on day 1, the lessor would classify the lease as a finance lease.

'Lease term' can also be critical to the classification of a lease. The 'lease term is the period for which the lessee has contracted to lease the asset and any further terms for which the lessee has the option to continue to lease the asset, with or without further payments, which option it is reasonably certain at the inception of the lease that the lessee will exercise' (SSAP 21, para. 19).

The interest rate used in the numerical calculation should be the 'interest rate implicit in the lease'. This is defined in para. 24 as being the interest rate which, when applied to the amounts the lessor expects to receive in respect of the asset, including any unguaranteed residual value, gives a present value equal to the fair value of the asset. It is, in other words, the total estimated yield that the lessor expects to earn over the course of the lease.

The lease agreement may cover more than simply the lease of an asset. For example, it may also provide for maintenance of the asset over the lease period. In analysing a lease to determine its classification it is only the payments relating to the use of the asset that are taken into account. Other payments, such as for maintenance, are excluded from the numerical calculation and are accounted for separately.

Sale and leaseback transactions

SSAP 21 specifically addresses sale and leaseback transactions. Broadly, its approach is that if an entity sells an asset and the leaseback is an operating lease, that transaction is accounted for as a disposal of the asset; hence a gain or loss on disposal is reported.

If the leaseback is a finance lease, the entity (the seller/lessee) has not in substance disposed of the asset at all; it has merely disposed of legal title. Hence, under a sale and finance leaseback, the cash received is treated as financing, rather than disposal proceeds; and any apparent profit or loss is deferred and amortised over the shorter of the lease term and the useful economic life of the asset.

Where an asset is sold and leased back under an operating lease, the appropriate accounting treatment under SSAP 21 is to record the sale of the asset and then separately to account for the operating lease. Hence the asset no longer appears on the selling company's balance sheet; beneficial, as well as legal, title having now passed to the lessor. SSAP 21 specifies that the profit/loss arising on sale is to be recognised immediately providing the sale price was fair value.

Disclosures

SSAP 21 requires various disclosures to be made in the accounts. In the main, for lessees, these call for disclosure of how the leases entered into by the lessee have impacted on the accounts. Two disclosures that relate to future expenditure are:

- The amount of any commitments existing at the balance sheet date in respect of finance leases entered into but whose inception (the earlier of bringing the asset into use and the date from which rentals first accrue) occurs after the year end (SSAP 21, para. 54).
- The amount of the payments (subdivided into those in respect of land and buildings and those in respect of other leases) the lessee is committed to make during the following year in respect of operating leases, analysed into the amounts in respect of leases expiring in the following year, in the second to fifth years inclusive and over five years from the balance sheet date (SSAP 21, para. 56).

These two disclosures correspond to the disclosures required by Schedule 4, para. 50(3) and (5) respectively.

For lessors the disclosures generally amplify how the leases have affected the amounts in the accounts. Two disclosures that might give an indication of future potential are:

- The cost of assets acquired in the period for the purpose of letting under finance leases (SSAP 21, para. 60(c)).

- The gross amount of assets held for use in operating leases together with the related accumulated depreciation (SSAP 21, para. 59).

In addition, a number of disclosures are recommended by the SORP issued by the FLA.

Leases under IFRS

The relevant standard is IAS 17 'Leases'. It is very similar to SSAP 21, classifying leases into finance leases (those that transfer substantially all the risks and rewards incident to ownership of an asset) and operating leases (leases other than finance leases), with the resulting accounting treatment also being very similar. There are, nevertheless, a number of key differences as follows:

- Under IAS 17 a lessor recognises interest income in respect of a finance lease so as to give a constant periodic rate of return on the lessor's *net investment* in the lease whereas under SSAP 21 the requirement is to allocate the interest income so as to give a constant periodic rate of return on the lessor's *net **cash** investment* in the lease (or using an alternative method that is partly based on the *net cash investment* in the lease). Although the total income recognised over the lease term is unaffected this can lead to large differences in individual years where the tax allowances and incentives relating to leases are substantial.
- Leases of land and buildings have to be separated under IAS 17 into two components: a lease of the land and a lease of the buildings, with each component being accounted for separately. Because land lasts forever, any lease term (say ninety-nine years) is generally regarded as not being a significant part of the life of the land. Hence, the land element will generally be classified as an operating lease. The buildings element will be classified as either a finance lease or an operating lease in the normal way. The two components need not be separated out under SSAP 21 and are generally considered jointly. It is therefore more likely that finance leases will arise (in respect of the buildings) under IAS 17 than under SSAP 21.
- There is no reference to 90%, or any other percentage, that gives rise to a presumption of a finance lease in IAS 17 whereas SSAP 21's reference to 90% can sometimes be seen as an indicator of a finance lease in the absence of other indicators.

SIC 27 'Evaluating the substance of transactions involving the legal form of a lease' sets out guidance on when IAS 17 should determine the accounting treatment of a lease and when, instead, a series of transactions, involving one or more leases, should be viewed as a whole. Although FRS 5 'Reporting the substance of transactions' does not directly address when SSAP 21 applies and when a series of transactions should be considered as a whole, its principles are consistent with SIC 27.

IFRIC 4 'Determining whether an arrangement contains a lease' sets out guidance for determining when IAS 17 should be applied to a transaction involving the right to use an asset in return for a series of payments even though there is no lease in legal terms. There is no direct equivalent in UK GAAP, although FRS 5 may lead to similar results.

The way forward

The IASB and ASB have a joint project to develop new guidance on lease accounting. At its heart is the premise that all lease obligations should be recognised on balance sheet. In essence, if it goes ahead all leases will be accounted for in a way similar to the way in which finance leases are currently accounted for. The devil is, however, in the detail and a number of practical issues are giving rise to considerable problems as the standard-setters try to take this project forward.

14
Pensions

Introduction

Pensions have become a considerable economic and political problem. Deficits have risen due to increased longevity, lower interest rates and poor investment performance. Pensions accounting questions arise in two contexts: in relation to the accounts of pension schemes themselves and in relation to the treatment of the cost of pensions in the accounts of the sponsoring companies. It is with the latter question that this chapter is concerned. The current accounting rules are set out in FRS 17 'Retirement benefits' and IAS 19 'Employee benefits'.

Defined contribution and defined benefit

Fundamentally, pension schemes take one of two forms.

Defined contribution schemes

A defined contribution (DC) scheme is defined as one 'into which an employer pays regular contributions fixed as an amount or as a percentage of pay and will have no legal or constructive obligation to pay further contributions if the scheme does not have sufficient assets to pay all employee benefits relating to employee service in the current and prior periods' (FRS 17, para. 2). So, for example, the employee might pay 5% of pensionable pay into the fund and the employer might pay 8% of pensionable pay. The pension paid to the employee is based solely on the size of the fund into which those contributions have grown. If, say, the investment performance has been poor, and as a result the pension is lower than expected, that is that: there is no obligation on the company to pay additional amounts.

The accounting treatment of a defined contribution scheme is straightforward. The contributions payable to the fund in respect of a year should be charged to the profit and loss account as an expense in that year. Note the word 'payable', not paid. This is an accruals basis, not simply a cash basis. For example, taking a December year-end company, if the contributions in respect of December salaries are not paid over to the fund until January, that amount should nonetheless be charged as an expense in the year to December.

Defined benefit schemes

A defined benefit (DB) scheme is 'a pension or other retirement benefit scheme other than a defined contribution scheme' (FRS 17, para. 2). That is, if the obligation of the company is anything other than limited to the contributions that are defined (for example 8% of salary, as above), the scheme is DB. The most common example of a DB scheme is a 'final salary' scheme. Typically, an employee is promised a pension based on his or her final salary. For example, based on forty years' employment, the pension might be 40/60ths of final salary, or of the average salary in the last three years' service immediately prior to retiring.

The obligations of an employer in respect of a DB scheme are complex and open-ended. The scheme ideally needs to be fully funded by the date of the employee's retirement, meaning that it contains a fund sufficient to pay, say, 40/60ths of salary. But whether it will have a fund of sufficient size depends on investment performance, interest rates, mortality, employee behaviour (the extent to which people leave or stay until retirement, for example) and other variables. Actuaries are employed to make estimates periodically of the progress of a fund and to recommend what level of future contributions is necessary.

As is well known, many DB schemes have in recent years swung from surplus into significant deficit, even to the extent that these deficits have in some cases overshadowed the fortunes of the company itself. This is especially so in some traditional industries (e.g. engineering, steel) where the scheme reflects the former size of the company. Scheme deficits have also become significant barriers to company takeovers.

It will not be surprising that accounting for DB schemes is complex and controversial.

Accounting for defined benefit schemes

To reflect, in the accounts of the sponsoring company, only the contribution payable in respect of the year to the fund in the case of a DB scheme would not properly reflect the uncertainties and obligations to which the employer is subject. For example, in previous years some schemes found they were in significant surplus and the actuary was able to recommend a 'contribution holiday', that is, that the company did not need to pay any contributions to the fund for say three years. But to charge nil to the profit and loss account as pensions expense would not reflect the underlying expense and obligation to which the company was subject.

The initial way of dealing with this in UK GAAP was set out in SSAP 24 'Pension costs'. This applied from 1988 until 2004. SSAP 24 was a pragmatic standard that sought to reflect in the profit and loss account a reasonably smooth pensions charge – typically a roughly constant percentage of payroll. Hence if the company benefited in cash terms from a contribution holiday, there was nonetheless a charge made to the profit and loss account to reflect the continuing underlying trend of cost. Any difference between the contribution paid and the charge to the profit and loss account was treated as a provision or, if an asset, as a prepayment. Whilst this was initially thought to be an appropriate treatment, it gradually became clear that it had two related weaknesses: (a) a broadly smooth trend of cost in the profit and loss account was comforting but not realistic; and (b) the provisions and prepayments that arose on the balance sheet were not real assets and liabilities but were rather meaningless figures left over from the smoothing process. This focus on the profit and loss account at the expense of the balance sheet gradually fell out of favour. Hence a method of accounting for pension costs was needed that focused on reflecting on the balance sheet meaningful assets and liabilities.

When DB pensions are looked at from the perspective of the balance sheet, the question is: what assets and liabilities does the sponsoring company have at the end of the year? To answer this, we have to look at the fund itself. If the fund has a deficit, it is argued that the company has an obligation to fund that deficit. If the fund has a surplus, the company can, to an extent, benefit from that surplus. Hence, in simple terms, a deficit on the fund is shown as a liability of the company; and a surplus in the fund is shown as an asset of the company (though this is restricted to the extent that the company is able to recover the surplus either through reduced contributions in the future or through refunds from the scheme).

FRS 17

FRS 17 'Retirement benefits', published in 2000, takes a balance sheet approach. When it was originally introduced, reflecting surpluses and deficits on the company's balance sheet was very controversial and so initially it was permitted – and most companies took the permission – to continue with SSAP 24 accounting in the balance sheet and profit and loss account, whilst giving the FRS 17 information in the notes to the accounts. FRS 17 came fully into force, replacing SSAP 24 only in 2005.

FRS 17 has been welcomed by users of accounts as giving rise to more transparency in company accounts to pensions. By the time it was fully introduced in 2005, it was reasonably well accepted by companies also. Nonetheless it can be very dramatic in its effect, in particular the way in which the swings from opening surplus/deficit to closing surplus/deficit are handled. This varies as between FRS 17 and its international equivalent, IAS 19. IAS 19 is discussed below.

Under FRS 17, the difference between the opening and closing surplus/deficit is analysed into a number of components which are reported in different places in the profit and loss account and statement of total recognised gains and losses (STRGL). This can best be explained by use of a simplified example, the assumptions for which are set out in Box 14.1.

Scheme assets, 1 January 2004	3,000
Scheme obligations, 1 January 2004	(4,000)
Deficit, 1 January 2004	(1,000)
Deficit, 31 December 2004	(1,500)
Movement (deterioration) in year	(500)
Contribution to scheme during year	100

Box 14.1

For this purpose, FRS 17 requires the scheme assets to be stated at fair value (i.e. market value where there is a market). Scheme liabilities are measured on the actuarial basis known as the projected unit method, and are then discounted to present value using a current rate of interest on a high quality corporate bond.

We see from the above that the deficit has increased during the year. This may be due to a fall in the value of investments and/or an increase in the value of the scheme's liabilities to pay pensions. The true deterioration or loss is 600, as the deficit increased by 500 despite 100 of cash being put into the scheme. Hence the overall loss of 600 needs to be reported as part of performance for the year. Under FRS 17 it would be reported as shown in Box 14.2; the figures are purely illustrative but are typical.

Profit and loss account	
Current service cost (1)	(50)
Interest cost (2)	(160)
Expected return on assets (3)	150
	(60)
Statement of total recognised gains and losses	
Actuarial gains and losses (4)	(540)
Total impact on performance statements	(600)

Notes
1. This represents what, at the start of the year, is the expected cost of the additional pension benefit to be earned by the employee (which is the additional obligation incurred by the scheme) in the year, without reference to whether the scheme is in surplus or deficit or indeed whether it is funded at all. This is shown as an expense within operating profit.
2. Say 4% interest on liabilities of 4,000.
3. Say 5% return on assets of 3,000. Items (2) and (3) are shown in the interest area of the profit and loss account.
4. This actuarial loss is the remainder of the cost, which typically comprises a loss in value of the investments and/or a loss due to an increase in the value of the scheme liabilities. Other factors such as changes in mortality and other assumptions also affect this number.

Box 14.2

FRS 17 also requires extensive footnote disclosures, primarily about DB schemes.

IAS 19

IAS 19 is the international standard on pension costs. In fact it is called 'Employee benefits' and deals with a wider range of benefits than just pensions. For example, it also deals with short-term benefits such as holiday pay and bonuses, and with long-term benefits payable during employment. However, its principal focus is pensions and other retirement benefits. In these terms, it is the equivalent of FRS 17 rather than SSAP 24, in the sense that it is balance sheet oriented and involves stating the scheme assets in the fund at fair value and scheme obligations measured using current interest rates.

However, the reporting of financial performance in IFRS is not the same as in UK GAAP. The requirement is to present a profit and loss account and, since 2004, a statement of changes in equity showing either (a) all change in equity, or (b) changes in equity other than those arising from transactions with equity holders acting in their capacity as equity holders. Option (b) can be viewed as a further performance statement equivalent to the UK STRGL, but it is not compulsory in this form and it is not at this stage so widely recognised as a performance statement as in UK GAAP. Hence, referring back to the worked example above, all the 600 has, on the face of it, to be recognised in the profit and loss account for the year, and this is indeed one of the options under IAS 19. Because of its potentially dramatic effect on the profit and loss account, it is hardly ever used.

However a more popular choice on the part of companies that have adopted IFRS already is to use a pragmatic technique that IAS 19 calls the 'corridor method' (IAS 19, paras. 92–5). This allows a company to carry forward on the balance sheet, rather than recognise in income, an element of the actuarial gains and losses. Basically, the first chunk of actuarial gains and losses can be ignored for accounting purposes and the remainder may be spread over a period, being the expected average remaining working lives of the employees. It is widely accepted that this 'corridor' method has no conceptual basis, and indeed it takes accounting back to the rather meaningless SSAP 24-type spreading discussed above.

In 2004, the IASB, being uncomfortable with the corridor method, made a limited revision to IAS 19 and added a third option, namely to allow companies to recognise the actuarial gain or loss outside the profit and loss account; but, where this is done, the actuarial gain or loss must be recognised in full. This has the effect of introducing into IAS 19 a treatment broadly equivalent to UK-style FRS 17 accounting and hence it is likely that, in applying IFRS, UK companies will adopt this third optional treatment.

The effect of pensions on realised profits

The calculation of realised profits is discussed more generally in chapter 16. Questions about realised profits arise only in the accounts of individual entities; they do not apply to group accounts as it is companies, not groups, that make distributions.

Here we consider the effect of accounting for pension costs on realised profits. The ICAEW, together with the ICAS, published in December 2004 'Tech 50/04 – Guidance on the effect of FRS 17 "Retirement benefits" and IAS 19 "Employee benefits" on realised profits and losses'.

The key points of Tech 50/04 may be summarised as follows. In order to establish the impact that a surplus or deficit under FRS 17 has on a company's realised profits, it is necessary to:

- identify the cumulative net gain or loss taken to reserves in respect of the pension surplus or deficit; and
- establish the extent to which that gain or loss is realised.

In this context, it does not matter whether the amounts that have ended up in reserves went through the profit and loss account or the STRGL.

The basic guidance (para. 3.1) is that a cumulative loss taken to reserves is a realised loss. This is because it results from the creation of, or an increase in, a provision for a liability or loss resulting in an overall reduction in net assets. Similarly, a cumulative net credit in reserves constitutes a realised profit; but this is only to the extent that it is represented by an asset to be recovered by agreed refunds, and the refunds will take the form of qualifying consideration (para. 3.2). See chapter 16 at p. 168 for the meaning of 'Qualifying consideration'.

In a simple case, the impact on reserves is the same as the pensions asset or liability recognised on the balance sheet. But as the Tech points out (para. 2.3), this is not necessarily the case, as differences may arise from (a) net contributions paid to the scheme or (b) any asset or liability introduced as a result of a business combination.

15

Financial instruments, including capital instruments

Introduction

'Financial instruments' is a broad term, encompassing a wide range of financial assets and financial liabilities. These terms are defined below. A subset is 'capital instruments', that is all instruments issued by an entity as a means of raising finance, comprising the entity's equity instruments, together with debt instruments such as loans and debentures.

The term 'capital instruments' is not generally used in IFRS and US GAAP, but has been used in UK literature and accounting standards in the context of the company that issues the instruments. By contrast, the broader term 'financial instruments' is internationally recognised and is used in the context of the investor as well as the issuer of the instrument; for example, it includes ordinary shares in the accounts of the investing company as well as the issuing company, and encompasses a number of additional contracts that are not regarded as capital instruments, for example, trade debtors and creditors, and derivatives.

Historically, in UK GAAP, there have been accounting standards dealing with capital instruments (FRS 4) and disclosures about financial instruments (FRS 13). These have now largely been superseded by FRS 25 'Financial instruments: disclosure and presentation' and FRS 26 'Financial instruments: measurement', which are based very closely on IASs 32 and 39. FRSs 25 and 26 replace FRS 13 and most of FRS 4 as well as amending a number of other standards. The scope and effective date of FRSs 25 and 26 are highly complex and interrelate to the adoption of a number of other recently issued standards such as FRS 23 'The effects of changes in foreign exchange rates' and FRS 24 'Financial reporting in hyperinflationary economies'.

This chapter will address financial instruments as a whole but will concentrate on capital instruments as they tend to have a greater effect on the work of lawyers.

Background

At its most basic, capital instruments issued by a company are either shares or debt (shares include share options and warrants, which are invitations to subscribe for, or acquire, shares at a later date). Traditionally, this legal analysis dictated the accounting treatment under FRS 4, with shares being recognised in shareholders' funds and debt in the liabilities section of the balance sheet.

However, for accounting periods beginning on or after 1 January 2005 companies are required, by FRS 25 and the Companies Act (following changes introduced to it by the Companies Act 1985 (International Accounting Standards and Other Accounting Amendments) Regulations 2005 (SI 2004 No. 2947)), to classify their capital instruments as debt or equity in accordance with the substance of the instrument. Accordingly some preference shares are now classified as debt in the balance sheet.

Another new standard, FRS 26, is mandatory for listed entities (entities with securities traded on a regulated market of an EU Member State) for accounting periods beginning on or after 1 January 2005; for some other entities for accounting periods beginning on or after 1 January 2006; and is not mandatory for some entities at all. It sets out the rules on measurement of financial instruments and is based on the measurement section of IAS 39. Both FRS 26 and IAS 39 adopt a mixed model with some instruments being measured at fair value and others at historical cost.

Financial assets are divided into four categories, and financial liabilities are divided into two categories. Details of these, and of the accounting treatments applicable to each, are set out under the heading 'Financial instruments other than capital instruments', p. 157 below.

FRSs 25 and 26 contain a large number of other rules, for example, on hedge accounting, embedded derivatives, and offsetting financial assets and financial liabilities to name but a few.

The accounting treatments that follow are based on the rules issued in December 2004 in FRSs 25 and 26.

Definitions

The following definitions apply in FRSs 25 and 26, although it should be noted that because these definitions are so widely drawn there are a large number of exclusions from the standards themselves. The rules contained in the standards are to be applied to financial assets, financial liabilities and capital instruments, rather than to financial instruments.

A *financial instrument* is any contract that gives rise to a financial asset of one entity and a financial liability or equity instrument of another entity (FRS 25, para. 11).

A *financial asset* is any asset that is:

  (a) cash;
  (b) an equity instrument of another entity;
  (c) a contractual right:
      (i) to receive cash or another financial asset from another entity; or
      (ii) to exchange financial assets or financial liabilities with another entity under conditions that are potentially favourable to the entity; or

(d) a contract that will or may be settled in the entity's own equity instruments and is:
   (i) a non-derivative for which the entity is or may be obliged to receive a variable number of the entity's own equity instruments; or
   (ii) a derivative that will or may be settled other than by the exchange of a fixed amount of cash or another financial asset for a fixed number of the entity's own equity instruments. For this purpose the entity's own equity instruments do not include instruments that are themselves contracts for the future receipt or delivery of the entity's own equity instruments (FRS 25, para. 11).

A *financial liability* is any liability that is:

(a) a contractual obligation:
   (i) to deliver cash or another financial asset to another entity; or
   (ii) to exchange financial assets or financial liabilities with another entity under conditions that are potentially unfavourable to the entity; or
(b) a contract that will or may be settled in the entity's own equity instruments and is:
   (i) a non-derivative for which the entity is or may be obliged to deliver a variable number of the entity's own equity instruments; or
   (ii) a derivative that will or may be settled other than by the exchange of a fixed amount of cash or another financial asset for a fixed number of the entity's own equity instruments. For this purpose the entity's own equity instruments do not include instruments that are themselves contracts for the future receipt or delivery of the entity's own equity instruments (FRS 25, para. 11).

An *equity instrument* is any contract that evidences a residual interest in the assets of an entity after deducting all of its liabilities (FRS 25, para. 11).

Basic classification rule

Paragraph 15 of FRS 25 sets out the basic rule, applying to all issuers of financial instruments, in respect of classification of financial instruments in the financial statements, which is that a financial instrument, or its component parts, shall be classified as a financial asset, financial liability or equity instrument in accordance with its substance. Where an entity issues a compound instrument, such as convertible debt, it is separated into its component parts; in the case of convertible debt this would be a debt component together with an equity component, being an option over shares, with each being presented separately on the balance sheet.

The critical element in determining whether there is a financial liability is whether there is an obligation to deliver cash, other financial assets or to exchange financial assets or liabilities on terms that are potentially unfavourable to the issuer.

Shares

Types of shares and balance sheet classification

There are many different forms of shares; the most common examples are ordinary shares, preference shares, redeemable preference shares and participating preference shares. Under FRS 4, these would always have been accounted for by the issuing company within shareholders' funds, but now they are classified as either financial liabilities or as equity instruments in accordance with their substance.

The Application Guidance to FRS 25, for example, explains that preference shares that are redeemable on a fixed date or at the option of the holder contain a financial liability as the issuer has an obligation to transfer a financial asset. The Guidance explains that the issuer's potential inability to satisfy the obligation, say, because of insufficient distributable profits or funds, does not negate the obligation and it is the obligation that determines the classification.

The table in Box 15.1 sets out the balance sheet classification of the common types of shares.

Type of share	Balance sheet classification
Preference shares redeemable for a fixed amount and paying a fixed annual dividend	Financial liability
Preference shares redeemable for a fixed amount but with a discretionary dividend	The capital element would be classified as a financial liability and the dividend element would be classified as an equity instrument
A preference share paying fixed annual dividends but with no redemption option	Financial liability
Participating preference shares where the annual dividend comprises a fixed amount plus an additional amount equal to a proportion of the dividend payable on the ordinary shares	The fixed dividend element would be classified as a financial liability and the participating dividend component would be classified as equity
Ordinary shares	Equity instruments

Box 15.1

A preference share paying fixed annual dividends but with no redemption option will still be classified as a financial liability as the present value of the dividend payments, which form the issuer's obligation, will equal the capital value of the shares.

Equity shares and relevant shares

FRS 4 divided shares into two categories: equity shares and non-equity shares. The Companies Act 1985 also uses the term equity shares but its definition is different, generally being wider, to that used in FRS 4 and it is therefore important to clarify which definition applies if these terms are used in documents.

Under the Act (section 744) a share is an equity share unless both its rights to dividends *and* capital are restricted and thus if its rights to either dividends or capital, but not both, are restricted the share is still an equity share under the Act, whereas such a share would be a non-equity share under FRS 4.

FRS 4 defined equity shares as all shares other than non-equity shares. Non-equity shares were shares possessing any of the following characteristics:

(a) any of the rights of the shares to receive payments, whether in respect of dividends, redemption or otherwise, are for a limited amount that is not calculated by reference to the company's assets or profits or the dividend on any class of equity share;

(b) any of their rights to participate in a surplus on a winding-up are limited to a specific amount that is not calculated by reference to the company's assets or profits and such limitation had a commercial effect in practice at the time the shares were issued or, if later, at the time the limitation was introduced;

(c) the shares are redeemable either according to their terms or because any party other than the issuer can require their redemption (FRS 4, para. 12).

If a preference share were issued that had a fixed right to annual dividends, say, equal to 6% of nominal share capital, but had unrestricted liquidation rights then it would be a non-equity share for the purposes of FRS 4 but would be an equity share under the Act.

Another defined term in the Act is 'relevant shares'. These are referred to in Schedule 4A in the conditions that must be complied with if merger accounting is to be permitted under the Act. Relevant shares are those shares carrying unrestricted rights to participate both in distributions and in the capital on a liquidation. Thus the preference share referred to in the paragraph immediately above would not be a relevant share. With the demise of merger accounting under accounting standards (see chapter 9) the importance of the term 'relevant share' will fall away.

Issue of shares

Where shares are issued for more than their nominal value, the amount equal to their nominal value is recorded in share capital and the balance of consideration is recorded in share premium under section 130 of CA 1985. (There are exceptions to the recording of share premium in the form of merger relief and group reconstruction relief – see chapter 9, p. 95.) For example, if a company issued 100,000 £1 ordinary shares each for £2.50 cash, the entries in the accounting records would be as shown in Box 15.2.

Dr	Cash	£250,000	
Cr	Share capital account		£100,000
Cr	Share premium account		£150,000

Box 15.2

It is important to stress that these would be the legal entries in the accounting records irrespective of the balance sheet classification of the shares as financial liabilities or equity instruments.

Any expenses incurred in issuing the shares may be deducted from the share premium account, providing the balance on the share premium account is at least equal to the amount of the expenses. In the above example if share issue expenses of £3,000 had been incurred, the relevant entry would be as in Box 15.3.

Dr	Share premium account	£3,000	
Cr	Cash		£3,000

Box 15.3

Deducting share issue expenses from share premium account applies irrespective of whether the shares being issued (and thus in respect of which the expenses are incurred) are issued at a premium. For example, if a company issued 100,000 £1 ordinary shares at par and incurred expenses of £1,500 in doing so, the entire £1,500 may be deducted from the share premium account balance, even though no premium arose on the share issue, providing the balance on the share premium account is at least £1,500. To the extent that there is insufficient in the share premium account – say the share premium account stood at £700 before the issue expenses were deducted – the balance of issue costs, £800 in this example, would have to be deducted from another reserve, most probably the profit and loss account reserve. The entries for this last scenario are shown in Box 15.4.

Dr	Cash	£100,000	
Cr	Share capital account		£100,000
Dr	Share premium account	£700	
Dr	Profit and loss account reserve	£800	
Cr	Cash		£1,500

Box 15.4

FRS 4 introduced the following definition of issue costs, applying to both shares and debt: issue costs are 'the costs that are incurred directly in connection with the issue of a capital instrument, that is, those costs that would not have been incurred had the specific instrument in question not been issued' (para. 10). Although the applicable part of the standard has been drastically shortened by FRS 25, the definition remains as it is still relevant for debt issues. The definition in FRS 4 became generally regarded as also applying for the purposes of the Companies Act. FRS 26 uses the term 'transaction costs', which are defined as those 'incremental costs that are directly attributable to the acquisition, issue or disposal of a financial asset or financial liability. An incremental cost is one that would not have been incurred if the entity had not acquired, issued or disposed of the financial instrument' (para. 9). The FRS 26 definition of transaction costs is consistent with the FRS 4 definition of issue costs, save that transaction costs is a broader term that applies to financial assets as well as to an issuer's financial liabilities and equity instruments.

Deducting issue costs is one of very few permitted uses of the balance on the share premium account. Moreover, if the costs are deducted from share premium rather than from the profit and loss account reserve they do not reduce distributable profits. These factors sometimes cause considerable attention to be paid to what can and cannot be regarded as an issue cost. It is only costs that are directly incurred in the issue of the particular instrument that meet the definition, for example, stamp duty payable on the issue, lawyers' fees incurred for drawing up the necessary documentation and underwriting fees. Costs such as management remuneration that would have been incurred regardless of the issue, researching alternative forms of finance, negotiating sources of finance and assessing the feasibility of particular instruments, fall outside the defini tion of issue costs. In the case of a stand-alone issue of shares what can and cannot be regarded as an issue cost is generally uncontroversial. Debate often arises where an issue of shares is part of a larger transaction, such as an acqui- sition of a business, a listing or a financial restructuring. In these cases care is needed to ensure an appropriate allocation of the total costs of the combined transaction. For example, where shares are issued as part of an acquisition of a business, the costs incurred in having accountants or lawyers undertake due diligence work in respect of the potential acquisition are unlikely to satisfy the definition of share issue costs whereas the lawyers' fees for drawing up the necessary documentation for the share issue would be included in share issue costs.

Accounting treatment post-issue

From a legal perspective, the issue of shares causes share capital and poten- tially share premium to arise. However, as described above, for accounting purposes the net proceeds of the issue must be classified as financial liabilities or equity instruments, or a mixture of the two, according to the substance of the instrument's terms, and accounted for as set out in the following sections.

Equity instruments – accounting treatment

In accordance with the above accounting entries, the net proceeds of an issue of equity are credited to share capital and share premium account and this forms the carrying amount in the shareholders' funds part of the balance sheet. On presen- tation of a balance sheet this will be disclosed as share capital and as share pre- mium as required by the formats in Schedule 4 to the Act (detailed in chapter 3 at p. 30). It is important to note that for 2005 onwards, unlike in previous years, the amount disclosed in the balance sheet in respect of share capital and share premium will not necessarily equal the total balance in these two accounts in an entity's legal accounting records. Instead the amount disclosed on the balance sheet will be the share capital and share premium only in respect of shares that are classified as equity instruments (plus share premium that arose on shares that have since been redeemed – see later). Where an entity has issued shares that are classified as financial liabilities the amount that in legal terms is share capital and share premium will not be presented as such in the balance sheet but will instead form part of the liabilities.

Prior to 2005, dividends paid and/or proposed in respect of shares were recognised in the profit and loss account. Practice was to recognise dividends that had been declared in respect of a year in that year's profit and loss account with the accrual sitting in balance sheet liabilities, even if the dividend was proposed after the end of that year. However, with effect for accounting periods beginning on or after 1 January 2005, FRS 21 'Post-balance sheet events' mandates that only dividends proposed by the balance sheet date can be recognised in the balance sheet as a liability. Dividends declared in respect of a year but proposed after the end of that year must now be excluded from balance sheet liabilities.

Financial liabilities – accounting treatment

The accounting rules for measuring financial liabilities are now contained in FRS 26 for listed and certain other entities and in FRS 4 for all other entities (including, for 2005, those non-listed entities that will be required to follow FRS 26 for 2006 onwards unless they choose to adopt FRS 26 early).

Regardless of which accounting standard applies, an instrument that is in substance debt will be presented in the liabilities section of the balance sheet irrespective of the legal form of the instrument. Traditionally, loans have been presented in the liabilities section and this remains unchanged, although convertible debt will now be analysed into a debt component and an option to acquire shares with only the former being presented in the liabilities section of the balance sheet. Certain shares, for example, preference shares paying a fixed annual dividend and redeemable for a fixed amount, will now also be presented in the liabilities section of the balance sheet. For such shares, the accounting records will record an amount in share capital and share premium, but on the balance sheet, although there will be a category for share capital and for share premium there will be nothing presented under those headings in respect of shares whose substance is debt; instead these amounts will be presented within liabilities on the balance sheet.

For example, consider a company which, upon its formation, issues 1,000,000 £1 ordinary shares for £1.50 per share and 400,000 £1 preference shares for £1.50 per share paying an annual dividend of 6% and redeemable at £1.50 per share in five years' time. The legal entries in its accounting records are shown in Box 15.5.

Dr	Cash	£2,100,000	
Cr	Share capital account		£1,400,000
Cr	Share premium account		£700,000
	Box 15.5		

However, assuming the substance of the preference shares is that they are classified as liabilities, the company's balance sheet immediately after its formation will be as shown in Box 15.6.

Assets – cash	£2,100,000
Liabilities – loan	(600,000)
Net assets	£1,500,000
Share capital	£1,000,000
Share premium	500,000
Total equity	£1,500,000

Box 15.6

Accounting treatment under FRS 26

Under FRS 26, financial liabilities are subclassified into the following two categories:

(a) financial liabilities at fair value through the profit and loss account; and

(b) all other financial liabilities.

Any financial liability held for trading must be classified as a financial liability at fair value through the profit and loss account. The same applies to derivatives that have a negative value, unless they are used in hedge accounting. In addition, any other financial liability can be designated as held at fair value through the profit and loss account providing the designation is made when the liability is issued or assumed; this is the so-called 'fair value option'. (Note that in connection with the version of IAS 39 endorsed for use in the EU, there are certain restrictions on the use of the fair value option; but this is a complex and fast-moving area of financial instrument accounting and it is important to obtain up-to-date professional advice.)

The initial carrying amount on issue of the instrument for both categories of financial liability should be the instrument's fair value. The initial proceeds received will often be equal to fair value. However, if the 'interest' payments are not at a market rate, fair value will be derived as the net present value of the payments to be made over the life of the instrument.

Financial liabilities in category (a) are carried in each subsequent set of financial statements at fair value with the change from the previous fair value being recognised in the profit and loss account for the period.

The majority of financial liabilities, however, will be within category (b). These are carried in subsequent balance sheets at 'amortised cost' using the effective interest method. ('Amortised cost' is a phrase that applies more naturally to assets; it may be easier to think of amortised proceeds in the case of liabilities.) This operates as follows. The difference between the initial carrying amount and the total amount of payments that the issuer may be required to make in respect of interest or dividend payments and redemption payments represents the total finance cost. Because transaction costs are deducted when calculating the initial carrying amount this has the effect that the transaction costs are included in the total finance cost. The total finance cost is allocated over the term of the instrument at a constant rate on the carrying amount and, in accordance with FRS 26, is recognised as an interest expense in the profit and loss account. Consider the following example. X Limited issued 100,000 10 pence redeemable preference shares on 1 January 2005 for £1 each. Issue expenses totalled £10,000. The shares pay an annual dividend of 2 pence per share on 1 January every year and are to be redeemed for £1.10 each on 1 January 2010.

On issue, the company receives £100,000 in proceeds from issuing shares. In the accounting records, £10,000, the nominal value, is recognised in share capital and the balance of £90,000 is recognised in share premium. The issue expenses of £10,000 are deducted from share premium. The shares are to be classified as financial liabilities in the financial statements. The initial carrying value of the liability will be £90,000 (£100,000 − issue expenses of £10,000). Assuming the company has a 31 December year end, the amount charged as interest to the profit and loss account and the balance sheet carrying amount is as shown in Box 15.7.

Year	P&L	Balance sheet
2005	£5,538	£95,538
2006	£5,755	£99,293
2007	£5,986	£103,279
2008	£6,230	£107,509
2009	£6,491	£112,000
Total	£30,000	

Box 15.7

The amount charged in the profit and loss account each year is greater than the dividend payable for each year. This excess represents an accrual of the redemption premium together with the spreading of the issue expenses. The total charge over the five years of £30,000 comprises the £10,000 issue expenses, £10,000 aggregate dividend payments and £10,000 redemption premium. The amounts are recognised in the interest line in the profit and loss account. In each case, the balance sheet figures assume that the interest for the year just ended has not yet been paid. So, for example, the balance sheet liability at 31 December 2009 represents principal of £110,000 and interest payable on 1 January 2010 of £2,000.

Disclosures

Accounting standards

Within accounting standards the intention is for all the disclosure requirements eventually to be contained in one standard and to apply to all entities. However, this has not yet been achieved.

Previously disclosures on capital instruments for all companies were mandated by FRS 4 (these expanded upon the amounts included in the accounts together with requiring details about holders' rights to payments, conversion, etc.) and disclosures on the wider financial instruments were mandated for listed and other public interest entities by FRS 13 (the requirements included narrative, as well as numerical, disclosures and were generally more exacting requiring, inter alia, the fair value of each category of financial instruments to be disclosed).

FRS 25's disclosure requirements are grouped under the following headings:

- risk management policies and hedging activities
- terms, conditions and accounting policies
- interest rate risk
- credit risk
- fair value
- collateral
- reclassification
- income statement and equity
- impairment
- defaults and breaches.

Quite when these disclosures must be given and by which entities is a complex matter. The disclosure requirements of FRS 25 are mandatory in the accounting period in which FRS 26 is applied except that certain parent companies and subsidiary undertakings are exempt from the disclosure requirements even if FRS 26 is applied by them. FRS 13's disclosures remain in force for those entities within its scope that do not give the FRS 25 disclosures.

An exposure draft of a new standard intended to replace the disclosure requirements of FRS 25 has been issued. The intention is for the new standard to apply to all entities (other than FRSSE entities) and be effective for accounting periods beginning on or after 1 January 2007. The disclosures proposed are even more extensive than those contained in FRS 25. As with FRS 25 the disclosures will be based on the accounting classification of the instrument. Thus if a share is classified as a financial liability, the disclosures given about it will be whatever is required to be given about financial liabilities.

155

Companies Act 1985

Traditionally the Companies Act 1985 has required disclosures about a company's share capital and debentures. These remain in force. It is important to note, however, that the disclosures required about the authorised and the issued shares must continue to be given for any instruments that legally are shares whether these are accounted for as equity instruments or financial liabilities.

New disclosures have been introduced into the Companies Act regarding fair values. All companies other than small companies will now have to disclose the fair value of derivatives. In addition, a number of other disclosures are required if a company either chooses to value its financial instruments or carries financial instruments at an amount greater than fair value. Whether these disclosures will be required is dependent on the accounting classification rather than on the legal form of the instrument.

Treasury shares

From 1 December 2003 certain companies have been able to purchase up to 10% of their issued share capital and hold them in treasury for subsequent sale, transfer in connection with an employee share scheme or cancellation. Prior to this date, any shares purchased had to be cancelled. The Companies Act rules governing treasury shares (or 'own shares') are to be found in sections 162 to 162G of the Companies Act 1985.

The accounting treatment for treasury shares is to deduct them from shareholders' funds ('equity' in IFRS terms). They are in effect treated as though they had been cancelled and, for example, disregarded when calculating earnings per share. While they are deducted from shareholders' funds as a whole, they are not deducted from share capital as such, as the balance sheet figure for share capital represents the nominal value of the shares legally in issue (which, of course, includes the treasury shares held by the issuing company). In law, treasury shares must be purchased out of distributable profits. It is therefore helpful if the presentation on the balance sheet and/or the note disclosures reflect the using up of distributable profits.

There has developed a common practice of listed groups setting up Employee Share Ownership Plan (ESOP) trusts to purchase and hold shares in the listed company for use in ESOPs and Long-Term Incentive Plans (LTIPs), although this practice became prevalent primarily because until December 2003 a company could not purchase and hold shares in itself or its parent. The accounting treatment for such shares in the group accounts of the listed company is the same as for treasury shares, i.e. deduct from shareholders' funds, although previously such shares were recognised as assets on the group balance sheet as well as on the company balance sheet of whichever company was regarded as the sponsoring company of the ESOP trust. Where the sponsoring company is not the listed company whose shares are held by the trust the accounting in its single entity accounts continues to be recognition as an asset, being an investment in shares in a group undertaking. Where the sponsoring company is the listed company whose shares are held by the trust the accounting in its single entity accounts now is also the same as for treasury shares, i.e. deduct from shareholders' funds.

Repurchase and cancellation of shares

Under the CA 1985, a company can redeem or cancel shares providing the rules in Chapter VII (sections 159 to 181) are followed.

Until 1 December 2003, if a company purchased its own shares it had to cancel them. Since 1 December 2003 companies have been able to purchase up to 10% of their issued share capital and hold them in treasury. All other shares, if purchased by the company, must be cancelled.

Where the shares had been accounted for as equity instruments, the amounts paid on the redemption or cancellation of the shares, together with directly incurred expenses, and the proceeds of any fresh issues of shares, net of directly incurred expenses, are reported in the reconciliation of shareholders' funds in the financial statements.

Where the shares had been accounted for as financial liabilities in the financial statements, any difference between the carrying value in the balance sheet and the amount paid on redemption, inclusive of transaction costs, will be recognised in the profit and loss account.

Financial instruments other than capital instruments

As stated earlier, FRS 26 lays down rules on measurement of all financial instruments, not just capital instruments, although, because the definitions are so widely drawn, as with FRS 25, there are a large number of exclusions from the standard itself. The standard stipulates the accounting treatment of financial assets and financial liabilities, but not equity instruments.

Financial assets include: cash, debtors, a holding of shares of another company (although an interest in a subsidiary, associate or joint venture will often be excluded) and derivatives with a positive value. Financial liabilities include, in addition to capital instruments, creditors, financial guarantees and derivatives with a negative value.

Financial assets and liabilities are initially measured at fair value plus or minus, other than for those assets and liabilities subsequently measured at fair value through the profit and loss account, directly incurred transaction/issue costs. This means that any long-term debtors and creditors not subject to a market rate of interest will need to be discounted and the net present value recognised initially. For example, if a company sells goods to a third party for £150,000 payable in two years' time, the selling company must record turnover and a debtor for £136,054 (assuming market rates of interest of 5%) on sale and interest income of £6,803 and £7,143 in years 1 and 2 respectively.

In order to determine the subsequent accounting, the financial assets and liabilities are divided into subcategories as follows. Financial assets are divided into:

(a) financial assets at fair value through profit or loss;
(b) held-to-maturity investments;
(c) loans and receivables; and
(d) available-for-sale financial assets.

Category (d) is the residual category, for all financial assets that do not meet the definitions of the first three categories.

Categories (b) and (c) are accounted for at amortised cost using the effective interest method while categories (a) and (d) are accounted for at fair value. The amortised cost method operates as described above for financial liabilities. Changes in fair value of assets in category (a) are recognised in the profit and loss account whereas changes of fair value for available-for-sale assets, other than where these are in respect of foreign exchange movements or impairments, are taken initially to reserves (and reported in the STRGL) but the cumulative amount of such gains and losses is subsequently recognised in the profit and loss account on the sale ('derecognition') of the asset.

As outlined above, financial liabilities are divided into:

(a) financial liabilities at fair value through profit or loss; and
(b) all other financial liabilities.

Those in category (b) are measured at amortised cost using the effective interest method and those in category (a) are measured at fair value. These are discussed above.

Any financial asset or liability held for trading must be classified as at fair value through the profit and loss account. In addition, any other financial asset or liability can be designated as held at fair value through profit and loss provided the designation is made on issue or acquisition. A financial asset or liability must be classified as held for trading if it is:

'(i) acquired or incurred principally for the purpose of selling or repurchasing it in the near term;
(ii) part of a portfolio of identified financial instruments that are managed together and for which there is evidence of a recent actual pattern of short-term profittaking; or
(iii) a derivative (except for a derivative that is a designated and effective hedging instrument).'

[FRS 26, para. 9]

FRS 26 has a number of other rules, primarily dealing with hedge accounting and embedded derivatives.

The scope and effective date of the standard are highly complex. However, for any listed entity (securities traded on a regulated market of an EU Member State) the standard is effective for accounting periods beginning on or after 1 January 2005.

Accounting under IFRS

FRSs 25 and 26 are based very closely on IASs 32 and 39. Accordingly, for most companies there is now a large degree of conformity between UK GAAP and accounting under IFRS. There are very few differences between FRS 25 and IAS 32 and thus the presentation and disclosure rules are almost identical. The main difference is in the scope of the disclosure requirements; not all entities preparing accounts under UK GAAP have to give the disclosures whereas under IFRS they apply to all entities.

More differences exist between FRS 26 and IAS 39. The issue is further complicated by the fact that there are two versions of IAS 39. As explained in chapter 2, EU companies whose securities (shares, debt etc) are traded on a regulated market in the EU have to prepare their consolidated accounts from 2005 onwards in accordance with IFRSs *that have been adopted by the EU*. The version of IAS 39 that has been adopted by the EU is not the extant version that is applicable to any entity directly applying IFRSs (rather than applying them by virtue of the EU regulation).

The main differences between FRS 26 and the version of IAS 39 that UK listed companies will be required to follow from 2005 are as follows:

(a) the scope is different; IAS 39 applies to all entities whereas FRS 26 is only mandatory for listed entities (periods beginning on or after 1 January 2005) and other entities, excluding FRSSE entities, that recognise financial instruments in their accounts at fair value (periods beginning on or after 1 January 2006) as permitted by the new rules introduced in to the Companies Act by the Companies Act 1985 (International Accounting Standards and Other Accounting Amendments) Regulations 2004 (SI 2004 No. 2947);

(b) the provisions of IAS 39 dealing with recognition and derecognition of financial instruments have been omitted from FRS 26 (with FRS 5 remaining in force);

(c) certain of the rules on hedge accounting are less restrictive in the EU version of IAS 39 than in FRS 26; and

(d) the EU version of IAS 39 requires liabilities held for trading (and derivatives at a loss) to be fair valued through profit and loss, but removes the option to fair value other liabilities; however, other liabilities can be treated as fair value through profit and loss under FRS 26.

16

Realised and distributable profits

Introduction

The questions of which profits are realised and which are distributable are important for both accountants and lawyers. The questions arise for an individual company, not for a group: it is companies that make distributions, not groups. Thus, for example, in a simple group comprising a parent and its subsidiary, the subsidiary may make a distribution to its parent out of profits available for that purpose. The parent may then, if it has profits available for distribution, make a distribution to its shareholders. But to speak of the group having distributable profits or having made a distribution is not valid.

Accordingly, the matters discussed in this chapter relate to individual companies; and, as the focus is on UK law, the discussion concerns what amounts are realised and distributable for UK companies. For companies registered in other countries, the rules may be different from those in the UK, though the rules for companies registered in other EU Member States are likely to be broadly similar, as the national laws of all Member States are based on the second EU company law directive of 1976.

'Realised' and 'distributable'

The two terms 'realised' and 'distributable' are related but separate and it is important to distinguish them.

It is appropriate to speak of a specific component of profit or gain as being realised (or not). Taking a very simple example, if a company buys an asset for 100 and sells it for cash of 120, it has made a realised profit of 20. This is because (a) it is clear that the profit has been made (it can be measured reliably) and (b) it has been received in cash. On the other hand, if the company has a building that cost 1,000 and it is now valued at 1,200, it may recognise that revaluation gain of 200 in its accounts, but it has not realised the gain. Hence the gain is regarded as an unrealised profit. A fuller analysis of what is realised and unrealised is given below.

What profits are available for distribution is a matter for a company as a whole, based on the cumulative position at the relevant date. It will include, therefore, the aggregate of its transactions and events in the year (such as the two examples in the previous paragraph) and the company's history, for example, whether it has an accumulation of realised profits from previous years. Again, a fuller analysis of this is given below.

General rules on distributions

Before turning to the Companies Act 1985, we should note that, under common law, a company cannot lawfully make a distribution out of capital. In addition, directors have fiduciary duties in the exercise of the powers conferred on them. Directors must therefore specifically consider, inter alia, whether the company will still be solvent following a proposed distribution. Thus directors should consider both the immediate cash flow implications of a distribution and the continuing ability of the company to pay its debts as they fall due.

Part VIII of the Act sets out rules relating to 'Distribution of profits and assets'. Section 263 defines what may be distributed, starting in the negative: 'A company shall not make a distribution except out of profits available for the purpose' [section 263(1)]. Subsection (2) states that, with some exceptions, '"distribution" means every description of distribution of a company's assets to its members, whether in cash or otherwise'.

The most common type of distribution is a dividend. A dividend is often paid annually, sometimes supplemented by interim dividends, especially in the case of listed companies. In addition, companies sometimes pay one-off so-called 'special' dividends, perhaps to return a lump sum of cash to shareholders beyond the normal pattern of regular distributions. Moreover, a distribution need not be in cash: it can be a transfer of any asset. For example, one way of effecting a demerger is to make a distribution in specie of either (a) the assets of the division that is to be demerged or (b) the shares of the subsidiary that is to be demerged.

Perhaps the key provision is section 263(3), which states that: 'For the purposes of this Part [Part VIII on distributions], a company's profits available for distribution are its accumulated, realised profits, so far as not previously utilised by distribution or capitalisation, less its accumulated, realised losses, so far as not previously written off in a reduction or reorganisation of capital duly made.' Simplifying this somewhat, profits available for distribution can be viewed as accumulated realised profits less realised losses. A definition of realised profits and realised losses is given in section 262(3) – see p. 165 below. As section 263(3) further notes, this is subject to the additional provisions for investment companies and insurance companies, but these are not discussed here.

There is however an important complication that further restricts distributions by public companies. That is that the basic rule in section 263(3) still applies but section 264 adds:

'A public company may only make a distribution at any time—
(a) if at that time the amount of its net assets is not less than the aggregate of its called-up share capital and undistributable reserves, and
(b) if, and to the extent that, the distribution does not reduce the amount of those assets to less than that aggregate'.

Section 264 goes on to specify that 'net assets' has its normal accounting meaning of aggregate assets less aggregate liabilities. It also explains that a company's undistributable reserves are, in simplified form: (a) share premium account; (b) capital redemption reserve; and (c) accumulated unrealised profits less unrealised losses.

The practical effect of these rules can best be seen in the table in Box 16.1.

Examples of distributable profits in private and public companies

	Company 1		Company 2		Company 3		Company 4	
	£	£	£	£	£	£	£	£
A Share capital		1,000		1,000		1,000		1,000
B Unrealised profits	150		150		150		–	
C Unrealised losses	–		(200)		(200)		(200)	
D Net unrealised profits		150		–		–		–
E Net unrealised losses		–		(50)		(50)		(200)
F Realised profits	300		300		300		300	
G Realised losses	–		–		(120)		(120)	
H Net realised profits		300		300		180		180
I Share capital and Reserves		1,450		1,250		1,130		980
Maximum distributable profit:								
Private company (H)		300		300		180		180
Public company (H-E)		300		250		130		Nil

Box 16.1

So, for example, in company 2, the net unrealised loss of £50 is not relevant for a private company but restricts distributions for a public company. In company 4, the same principle applies but the effect is more dramatic: the public company cannot make any distribution at all.

Relevant accounts

The Act states that, in order to determine whether a company has profits available to distribute, and (if it is a public company) whether the additional conditions are satisfied, reference must be made to the '*relevant accounts*' [section 270]. The items to be referred to in the relevant accounts are:

- profits, losses, assets and liabilities
- provisions
- share capital and reserves.

The relevant accounts are normally the company's latest audited financial statements that have been laid before the company in general meeting (section 270(3)). However, where a distribution would exceed the amount that is distributable according to the latest audited financial statements, *interim accounts* must be prepared in addition to the latest financial statements to see whether the intended distribution can be justified. (The term 'interim accounts' as used here has a different meaning from the interim accounts required to be published regularly under the Listing Rules.) Moreover, *initial accounts* must be prepared and used where a company proposes to make a distribution during its first accounting reference period or before the date on which it lays its first audited financial statements before its shareholders.

The requirements relating to interim and initial accounts depend on whether the company in question is private or public. If it is private, management accounts together with appropriate adjustments can be used to support a distribution. However, if it is a public company, the requirements are more onerous. The detailed requirements are set out in sections 272 to 274. The main points are that all relevant accounts, including interim and initial accounts, must be properly prepared and must give a true and fair view, except that any matters that are not material for determining whether the proposed distribution is lawful may be omitted. In addition, with regard to any initial accounts (but not interim accounts) the auditors must have reported whether the accounts have been properly prepared. Annual accounts will, for a public company, be audited in any event. In connection with annual or initial accounts, if the audit opinion is qualified, the auditors must say whether that qualification is material in determining the legality of the proposed distribution.

Relationship with reporting of performance

The Act's rules about which profits are realised and distributable, though based on accounting numbers, are primarily legal rules concerned with regulating company distributions. They do not necessarily equate to the modern accounting notion of profit or performance. This section explores the way in which profits, and the wider notion of 'financial performance', are reported.

The current approach to reporting financial performance under UK GAAP is governed by FRS 3 'Reporting financial performance'. This requires that companies prepare and publish (a) a profit and loss account and (b) a STRGL. Most of the company's transactions are reported in the profit and loss account; but the STRGL extends the notion of financial performance by recording items such as revaluation gains and losses on fixed assets such as land and buildings. The aggregate of the profit recorded in the profit and loss account and the other gains and losses recorded in the STRGL is called 'total recognised gains and losses for the year'.

Total recognised gains and losses for the year is a measure that seeks to record performance in its widest sense. It is important to distinguish from it those other items that affect the company's shareholders' funds (or net assets) but which are not economic performance – that is, items such as new capital raised or redeemed, and dividends and other distributions. The distinction can be shown as illustrated in Box 16.2.

Profit for the year (from the P&L account)	U
Other gains and losses (e.g. property revaluation)	V
Total recognised gains and losses	W
Proceeds of new shares issued	X
Dividends paid	(Y)
Increase in shareholders' funds (net assets) in the year	Z

Box 16.2

The line 'total recognised gains and losses (W)' is the most comprehensive measure of economic performance that accounting can achieve. This is not to say that it is perfect. For example, a company may well develop the value of its brands or other intangibles through advertising but that enhancement in value is not recorded by present-day accounting, largely because the measurement difficulties would render any numbers too unreliable.

Put another way, total recognised gains and losses is the change in reported net assets during the year, excluding contributions from or distributions to shareholders in their capacity as shareholders. It is the change in reported net assets rather than the change in the value of the net assets, as not all assets and liabilities will be recorded at valuation.

The STRGL is a UK innovation and hence in some other parts of the world the prevailing view is that profit is restricted to items recorded in the profit and loss account. An item such as the gain on a property revaluation has generally been regarded as being concerned more with balance sheet valuation than with performance measurement, though a change to IFRS (IAS 40) in 2000 required changes in value of investment properties to be recognised as part of the profit and loss account. The IASB is currently debating whether it should move its standards onto a more comprehensive approach to reporting performance than merely the profit and loss account. For the moment, international standards give limited recognition to the point. IAS 1 requires companies reporting under IFRS to present a 'Statement of changes in equity'. This includes the items shown in the UK STRGL; it allows but does not require the inclusion of increases in equity caused by transactions with shareholders.

In a UK context, what is presented in the profit and loss account and what is presented in the STRGL is determined partly by accounting standards and partly by the law. For companies preparing UK GAAP accounts, para. 12(a) of Schedule 4 to the Act provides that 'only profits realised at the balance sheet date shall be included in the profit and loss account'. (Note that, being part of Schedule 4, this is disapplied to companies that follow IFRS. However the basic rules relating to distributions, from section 263 still apply.)

As to which transactions give rise to realised profits, guidance is given in TECH 7/03, which is discussed in the next section. However, it is possible, despite para. 12(a), to include an unrealised profit in the profit and loss account. This may be done by invoking para. 15 of Schedule 4, which is a type of true and fair override: if there are special reasons for departing from the accounting principles (such as the rule in para. 12(a)), the directors 'may do so, but particulars of the departure, the reasons for it and its effect shall be given in a note to the accounts'. The most established use of this override in recent years has arisen with certain gains and losses on foreign currency translation. These gains and losses are required by SSAP 20 to be included in the profit and loss account even though, in the case of the gains on long-term foreign currency items, they have been regarded as unrealised. However, under Tech 7/03 para. 16(d) (quoted below) and para. 34, such items are now regarded as realised profits, even when the underlying loan is long term. Apart from that example from recent practice, this override is not invoked frequently.

Tech 7/03

Introduction

The 'minor definitions' in Part VII (Accounts and Audit) of the Act (section 262(3)) include the following definition of realised profits and realised losses:

> 'References in this Part to "realised profits" and "realised losses", in relation to a company's accounts, are to such profits or losses of the company as fall to be treated as realised in accordance with principles generally accepted, at the time when the accounts are prepared, with respect to the determination for accounting purposes of realised profits or losses.'

This somewhat circular definition has been taken by accountants to mean that realised profits and losses are whatever accountants think they are at the time. Guidance from the accountancy institutes helps to determine what this is.

Original guidance was issued in 1982 (TR 481 and 482). This was superseded by Tech 7/03, 'Guidance on the determination of realised profits and losses in the context of distributions under the Companies Act 1985', published in March 2003 by the Institute of Chartered Accountants in England and Wales and the Institute of Chartered Accountants of Scotland. Although it is described as 'guidance', it is regarded by accountants as de facto rules as it is the most authoritative statement in the area. It has been confirmed by English and Scottish counsel as being consistent with the law at 31 December 2002. The full text is available on the ICAEW website (icaew.co.uk).

Principles of realisation

As Tech 7/03 notes, the basic accounting guidance in this area is given by FRS 18 'Accounting policies', which states that 'it is generally accepted that profits shall be treated as realised for [the purposes of applying the definition of realised profits in companies legislation] only when realised in the form either of cash or of other assets the ultimate cash realisation of which can be assessed with reasonable certainty' (FRS 18, para. 28).

As well as endorsing FRS 18, Tech 7/03 sets out two further principles of realisation. First, it notes (para. 12) that 'In assessing whether a company has a realised profit, transactions and arrangements should not be looked at in isolation.' This is an important point, as it brings into the analysis the principle of substance over form and, more specifically, the thinking in FRS 5 'Reporting the substance of transactions'. Paragraph 12 adds: 'A realised profit will arise only where the overall commercial effect on the company satisfies the definition of realised profit set out in this guidance. Thus a group or series of transactions or arrangements should be viewed as a whole, particularly if they are artificial, linked (whether legally or otherwise) or circular.' Tech 7/03 includes Appendix A on intra-group transactions, which is discussed below.

Second, it notes (para. 13) that 'a profit previously regarded as unrealised becomes realised when the relevant criteria set out in this guidance are met (for example, a revaluation surplus becomes realised when the related asset is sold for "qualifying consideration"). Similarly, a profit previously regarded as realised becomes unrealised when the criteria set out in this guidance cease to be met.'

Definitions

The definition of profit in Tech 7/03 is:

> '15 "Profit" for the purpose of section 262(3) comprises:
> (a) "gains", as defined in the Accounting Standards Board's "Statement of Principles for Financial Reporting", that is, "increases in ownership interest not resulting from contributions from owners", and

(b) other amounts which are profits as a matter of law, or which are treated as profits, including:
  (i) gratuitous contributions of assets from owners in their capacity as such,
  (ii) an amount taken to a so-called "merger reserve" reflecting the extent that relief is obtained under sections 131 or 132 of the Companies Act 1985 from the requirement to recognise a share premium account, and
  (iii) a reserve arising from a reduction or cancellation of share capital, share premium account or capital redemption reserve'.

This is not an obvious definition of profit to an accountant, but results from discussions with counsel in developing Tech 7/03. An accountant would regard 'profit' as being the result reported in the profit and loss account, and 'total recognised gains and losses' as being a wider measure of performance. The latter measure equates to 'gains' in the above quotation. Accountants would generally not see any of the three items within (b) in the above quotation as being part of profit, but counsel has advised that they should be so regarded for the purposes of analysing what is treated as a realised profit.

Tech 7/03 then defines a realised profit at some length:

'16 A profit is realised where it arises from:
(a) a transaction where the consideration received by the company is "qualifying consideration", or
(b) an event which results in "qualifying consideration" being received by the company in circumstances where no consideration is given by the company, or
(c) the recognition in the profit and loss account of the profit arising from the use of the marking to market method of accounting, in those cases where the method is properly adopted in accordance with law and generally accepted accounting principles (see paragraphs 35 to 40), or
(d) the translation of:
  (i) a monetary asset which comprises qualifying consideration, or
  (ii) a liability
  denominated in a foreign currency, or
(e) the reversal of a loss previously regarded as realised, or
(f) a profit previously regarded as unrealised (such as amounts taken to a revaluation reserve, merger reserve or other similar reserve) becoming realised as a result of:
  (i) consideration previously received by the company becoming "qualifying consideration", or
  (ii) the related asset being disposed of in a transaction where the consideration received by the company is "qualifying consideration", or
  (iii) a realised loss being recognised on the scrapping or disposal of the related asset, or

(iv) a realised loss being recognised on the write-down for depreciation, amortisation, diminution in value or impairment of the related asset, or

(v) the distribution in specie of the asset to which the unrealised profit relates, in which case the appropriate proportion of the related unrealised profit becomes a realised profit, or

(g) a reduction or cancellation of capital (i.e., share capital, share premium account or capital redemption reserve) which results in a credit to reserves where the reduction or cancellation is confirmed by the court, except to the extent that, and for as long as, the company has undertaken that it will not treat the reserve arising as a realised profit, or where the court has directed that it shall not be treated as a realised profit, or

(h) a reduction or cancellation of capital (i.e., share capital, share premium account or capital redemption reserve) which is undertaken by an unlimited company without confirmation by the court and which results in a credit to reserves, in which case the amount so credited represents a realised profit to the extent that the consideration received for the capital:

(i) was qualifying consideration; or

(ii) has subsequently become qualifying consideration; or

(iii) has subsequently been written off (for example, by way of depreciation) and the loss arising has been treated as realised; or

(iv) was originally paid up either by a capitalisation of realised profits or by a capitalisation of unrealised profits or reserves which, had they not been capitalised, would subsequently have become realised.'

The definition of a realised loss is briefer: 'Losses should be regarded as realised losses except to the extent that the law, accounting standards or this guidance provide otherwise. The statutory position is set out in Appendix B.' (para. 17). That is, while not all losses are realised, there is a lack of symmetry in that losses are realised unless there is a specific reason to the contrary, whereas profits are realised only if they meet a complex definition.

A key definition is that of 'qualifying consideration'. This phrase is used extensively in the definition of realised profit, quoted above.

'18 Qualifying consideration comprises:

(a) cash, or

(b) an asset for which there is a liquid market, or

(c) the release, or the settlement or assumption by another party, of all or part of a liability of the company, unless

(i) the liability arose from the purchase of an asset that does not meet the definition of qualifying consideration and has not been disposed of for qualifying consideration, and

(ii) the purchase and release are part of a group or series of transactions or arrangements that fall within paragraph 12 of this guidance; or

(d) an amount receivable in any of the above forms of consideration where:

(i) the debtor is capable of settling the receivable within a reasonable period of time; and

(ii) there is a reasonable certainty that the debtor will be capable of settling when called upon to do so; and

(iii) there is an expectation that the receivable will be settled.'

Completing the definitions is 'asset for which there is a liquid market', which is used in part (b) of the definition of qualifying consideration.

'19 Asset for which there is a liquid market means that:

(a) the asset belongs to a homogeneous population of assets that are equivalent in all material respects; and

(b) an active market, evidenced by frequent transactions, exists for that asset; and

(c) the market has sufficient depth to absorb the asset without a significant effect on the price that underpins the carrying amount; and

(d) the company is capable of readily disposing of the asset, and it can do so without curtailing or disrupting its business; and

(e) the asset is readily convertible into known amounts of cash at or close to its carrying amount.'

Effects of Tech 7/03

Changes in circumstances

Following the principle in para. 13 (quoted above), paras. 20 to 27 of Tech 7/03 elaborate on the fact that treatment as realised (or unrealised) may change over time. First, the principles of realisation may change. Second, and likely to be a more frequent event, a change in law or accounting regulation may affect realised profits. For example, when the current standard on deferred tax (FRS 19) was introduced in 2000, it had the general effect of requiring companies to provide more deferred tax than hitherto. Broadly, this used up accumulated realised profits to the extent of the increased provision. Third, there may be a change in commercial circumstances. For example, a sale of goods or services may have led to the establishment of a debtor (or 'receivable') in the balance sheet. At the time, it was thought that the debtor would pay, and so this represented 'qualifying consideration'. Subsequently, the debtor may get into financial difficulty such that there is then no expectation that the receivable will be settled in cash or any other form of qualifying consideration. At that stage, what was initially regarded as a realised profit would no longer be so regarded. In accounting terms, there would be a provision for bad debts, or a write-off of that particular debt, resulting in an expense in the profit and loss account.

The fact that circumstances may change in one of these ways does not undermine the validity of treating the profit as realised in the first place, or of making a distribution based on it. This is because the Act defines realised

169

profits and losses for determining the lawfulness of a distribution as 'such profits or losses of the company as fall to be treated as realised in accordance with principles generally accepted, *at the time when the accounts are prepared*, with respect to the determination for accounting purposes of realised profits or losses' (section 262(3), emphasis added).

A particular application of this has been important in recent years in relation to pensions. It may continue to be important in future depending on what policy companies adopt under IFRS when accounting for the actuarial gain or loss: that is, whether they opt for full recognition or the corridor approach. In UK GAAP, FRS 17 'Retirement benefits' was introduced in November 2000. Until 2005, it required only footnote disclosures, and permitted a continuation of the old accounting rules (SSAP 24) in the balance sheet and profit and loss account in that period. The result was often that the footnoted FRS 17 information showed a much larger deficit than the SSAP 24 numbers. Hence accumulated realised profits, driven by the SSAP 24 numbers, understated the deficit. Nevertheless, this does not mean that the FRS 17 disclosures should have supplanted the SSAP 24 numbers, nor does it mean that distributable profits should have been withheld beyond the amount implied by the SSAP 24 numbers – as they were the numbers in the 'relevant accounts' (see above). Paragraph 22 of Tech 7/03 describes this situation in the following way: 'for example, where items that will fall to be treated as liabilities or provisions under a new standard have not been recognised as such in those accounts, directors do not have to pay regard to such liabilities or provisions merely because they are disclosed in the notes to the accounts'.

General examples of realised profits

Paragraphs 28 to 31 give a number of examples of realised profits and losses. Most of these require no amplification. However, it is worth noting that 'A gift (such as a "capital contribution") received in the form of qualifying consideration' is a realised profit. A capital contribution would typically be received from a parent company or other shareholder. In accounting terms, a capital contribution would be recorded in reserves and presented in the reconciliation of movements in shareholders' funds. That is, it would not be reported in either the profit and loss account or the statement of total recognised gains and losses. Nevertheless, despite being shown as a transaction with shareholders, it is regarded by Tech 7/03 as a realised profit. A gift from a third party would also be a realised profit but the accounting treatment would differ: it would be recognised in the profit and loss account.

Some other specific examples are discussed in the sections that follow.

Pension deficits

For companies that are complying with FRS 17 (UK GAAP) or IAS 19 (IFRS), questions arise about the impact of pensions deficits on realised profits. For a discussion of this, see the section 'The effect of pensions on realised profits' in chapter 14.

Mark to market gains and losses

The phrase 'marking to market' is generally used to refer to stating marketable securities at market value in the balance sheet and recognising the gains and losses in the profit and loss accounts when they arise, that is, not waiting until the asset is sold and the gain or loss is received in cash. This is a treatment that has been pioneered by banks in respect of certain assets held for trading. This mark to market treatment has been recognised by the banking SORP 'Accounting for securities'.

Tech 7/03 notes that whether a mark to market gain is realised depends on the type of company. For a banking company that prepares its accounts in accordance with Schedule 9 to the Act, the profit is realised. For subsidiaries of banks and other market makers and dealers in investments, any such gain is also realised by virtue of the banking SORP 'Accounting for securities' and by virtue of the practice being sufficiently widespread to have become 'generally accepted'. However, whether the same applies to other types of company is to some degree still an open question.

For companies adopting IFRS, mark to market accounting for certain financial assets is required by IAS 39. Similarly, it is required by FRS 26, the UK version of IAS 39. That is, mark to market accounting is now becoming an accepted part of profit measurement. But, as discussed above, this is not necessarily the same as whether the profit in question is realised.

Share-based payment

This book does not deal in any detail with accounting for share-based payment. Suffice it to say here that there have been UK GAAP rules dealing with employee share schemes for some years (UITF Abstracts 13 and 17) and these were updated in 2003 (UITF Abstracts 38 and 17(revised)). In terms of IFRS, there were virtually no rules until IFRS 2 'Share-based payment' was published in March 2004, as part of the stable platform for application for 2005. IFRS 2 was then issued in the UK as FRS 20 in April 2004. Under IFRS 2/FRS 20, a charge is made to the profit and loss account in respect of an award of shares or share options, for example to employees, based on the fair value of the award at grant date, for example the fair value of options granted. Also, under IAS32/FRS 25, UITF Abstracts 38 and (for treasury shares, i.e. own shares that are held by the company without reference to an employee share scheme) UITF Abstracts 37, any 'own shares' are deducted from shareholders' funds rather than shown as an asset.

Various questions arise in connection with the effect of accounting for such arrangements on realised profits. Guidance is given in Tech 64/04, published in 2004 by the Institutes of Chartered Accountants; this deals with the effect of accounting for share schemes in accordance with UITF Abstracts 38 and 17 (revised). Guidance on the effect of IFRS 2/FRS 20 is still in preparation at the time of writing.

Intra-group transactions

As noted above, Tech 7/03 notes (para. 12) that 'In assessing whether a company has a realised profit, transactions and arrangements should not be looked at in isolation.' This applies in particular in relation to intra-group transactions, because in the past certain transactions have been carried out, involving members of the same group, that have sought to generate realised and distributable profits at the entity level, despite the fact that the transaction is artificial or circular from a wider perspective. Appendix 1 to Tech 7/03 addresses the question of whether, or in what circumstances, such transactions give rise to realised profits. Some of the issues considered in Appendix 1 are discussed below.

In connection with *dividends*, three situations are discussed. The starting point is that, subject to the points made in the following paragraphs, a dividend received or receivable from a subsidiary will be a realised profit if the dividend is in the form of qualifying consideration. Most obviously, therefore, a dividend realised in cash will be a realised profit. In addition, a dividend receivable will be a realised profit if the debtor meets the characteristics described above in part (d) of the definition of qualifying consideration. Put another way, if a subsidiary declared a dividend to its parent but left it outstanding on inter-company account and had no ability or intention of settling it, that would not give rise to a realised profit to the parent. Paragraph A5 of Appendix 1 also makes the point that it is necessary to consider whether a dividend from a subsidiary has given rise to an impairment in the value of the investment in the subsidiary.

The second situation outlined relating to dividends is a circular transaction in which a subsidiary pays a dividend to its parent and the parent uses the proceeds to reinvest in the subsidiary. Here, in general, the dividend received would not give rise to a realised profit to the parent, even if received in cash.

The third point is that, in principle, there is no difference caused by the dividend being paid by the subsidiary out of pre-acquisition profits. As in the general case, it is important to consider whether an investment is impaired following a dividend, especially one of unusual size. However, for companies (in this context, a parent entity) using IFRS, it should be noted that the most recent version of IAS 27 'Consolidated and separate financial statements' (para. 4) requires that a parent should treat a dividend paid by a subsidiary out of pre-acquisition profits as a reduction in the cost of investment.

Further examples relate to sales of assets between group companies. First, if a parent sells an asset to a subsidiary, any profit on the sale will not represent a realised profit for the parent if it does not receive an asset which is in the form of qualifying consideration. In summary, the profit would be unrealised if:

- there is an agreement or understanding regarding the repurchase of the asset by the parent; or
- the parent directly or indirectly provides the funds for the purchase, or reinvests the proceeds in the subsidiary; or
- the subsidiary is unlikely to be able to meet its obligations under any borrowings used to fund the purchase without recourse to the parent.

Similar considerations apply where the subsidiary sells an asset to the parent. For example, if a subsidiary sells an asset to its parent, and makes a profit on the sale, it could, other things being equal, distribute that profit to the parent. However, the profit would not be realised in the hands of the parent. The reason is that the transaction is very similar in its overall effect to a distribution of the asset in specie to the parent – which is not a transaction on which the parent would record a realised profit, unless the asset distributed itself took the form of qualifying consideration.

A third example is given in Appendix 1 to Tech 7/03 concerning a sale of an asset from one subsidiary to a fellow subsidiary, followed by a dividend to the parent of the profit made on the sale. Similar principles arise to those discussed above.

The underlying theme in Appendix 1 to Tech 7/03 is to apply a substance over form approach to intra-group transactions. In the past, some such transactions have, rightly or wrongly, been regarded as giving rise to realised profits. Tech 7/03 has to some extent tightened the rules in this area.

17

Disclosures in published accounts

Introduction

Published financial information in the UK is centred around a company's profit and loss account, statement of total recognised gains and losses, balance sheet and cash flow statement – the four primary statements. Extensive notes to the accounts provide more detailed disclosure in support of the numbers in these primary statements. For example, there are notes to give more detail about the categories of fixed assets (plant, motor vehicles and so on) and to give details of the movements during the year (the amount at the beginning of the year, the additions, disposals, depreciation and so on). Similar details are given about provisions, share capital and reserves and many other items in the primary statements.

In addition, there are disclosures under a number of headings that do not directly amplify the items in the primary statements, but are free-standing. Some apply to all companies; some apply to listed companies only; and some apply to all companies but the amount of disclosures depends on whether the company is listed. This chapter contains a brief discussion of these free-standing disclosures, under the following headings:

- Corporate governance disclosures
- Operating and financial review
- Directors' report
- Directors' emoluments
- Related party relationships and transactions
- Segment disclosure

Corporate governance disclosures

UK listed companies are required by Listing Rule 12.43A to include in their annual report and accounts a two-part disclosure statement in relation to the 2003 FRC Combined Code, which applies to UK listed companies for periods beginning on or after 1 November 2003. The first part is to explain how the company has applied the main and supporting principles of the Code. The second part of the disclosure is a statement as to whether or not the company has complied throughout the accounting period with the provisions set out in Section 1 of the Code. If there are instances of non-compliance the company must specify the Code provisions with which it has not complied, and (where relevant) for what part of the period such non-compliance continued, and give reasons.

From 1 November 2003 a listed company is required to have its auditor review the corporate governance statement disclosures in relation to nine of the forty-eight 2003 FRC Combined Code provisions.

Schedule C of the Code provides a list of the disclosures that a company is required to make in its annual report. This is reproduced below.

'SCHEDULE C: DISCLOSURE OF CORPORATE GOVERNANCE ARRANGEMENTS

The Listing Rules require a statement to be included in the annual report relating to compliance with the Code, as described in the preamble. For ease of reference, the specific requirements in the Code for disclosure are set out below:

The annual report should record:

- a statement of how the board operates, including a high level statement of which types of decisions are to be taken by the board and which are to be delegated to management (A.1.1);
- the names of the chairman, the deputy chairman (where there is one), the chief executive, the senior independent director and the chairmen and members of the nomination, audit and remuneration committees (A.1.2);
- the number of meetings of the board and those committees and individual attendance by directors (A.1.2);
- the names of the non-executive directors whom the board determines to be independent, with reasons where necessary (A.3.1);
- the other significant commitments of the chairman and any changes to them during the year (A.4.3);
- how performance evaluation of the board, its committees and its directors has been conducted (A.6.1);
- the steps the board has taken to ensure that members of the board, and in particular the non-executive directors, develop an understanding of the views of major shareholders about their company (D.1.2).

The report should also include:

- a separate section describing the work of the nomination committee, including the process it has used in relation to board appointments and an explanation if neither external search consultancy nor open advertising has been used in the appointment of a chairman or a non-executive director (A.4.6);
- a description of the work of the remuneration committee as required under the Directors' Remuneration Reporting Regulations 2002, and including, where an executive director serves as a non-executive

director elsewhere, whether or not the director will retain such earnings and, if so, what the remuneration is (B.1.4);

- an explanation from the directors of their responsibility for preparing the accounts and a statement by the auditors about their reporting responsibilities (C.1.1);
- a statement from the directors that the business is a going concern, with supporting assumptions or qualifications as necessary (C.1.2);
- a report that the board has conducted a review of the effectiveness of the group's system of internal controls (C.2.1);
- a separate section describing the work of the audit committee in discharging its responsibilities (C.3.3);
- where there is no internal audit function, the reasons for the absence of such a function (C.3.5);
- where the board does not accept the audit committee's recommendation on the appointment, reappointment or removal of an external auditor, a statement from the audit committee explaining the recommendation and the reasons why the board has taken a different position (C.3.6); and
- an explanation of how, if the auditor provides non-audit services, auditor objectivity and independence is safeguarded (C.3.7).

The following information should be made available (which may be met by making it available on request and placing the information available on the company's website):

- the terms of reference of the nomination, remuneration and audit committees, explaining their role and the authority delegated to them by the board (A.4.1, B.2.1 and C.3.3);
- the terms and conditions of appointment of non-executive directors (A.4.4) . . . ; and
- the terms of reference of any remuneration consultants, together with a statement of whether they have any other connection with the company (B.2.1).

The board should set out to shareholders in the papers accompanying a resolution to elect or re-elect:

- sufficient biographical details to enable shareholders to take an informed decision on their election or re-election (A.7.1).
- why they believe an individual should be elected to a non-executive role (A.7.2).
- on re-election of a non-executive director, confirmation from the chairman that, following formal performance evaluation, the individual's performance continues to be effective and to demonstrate commitment to the role, including commitment of time for board and committee meetings and any other duties (A.7.2).

The board should set out to shareholders in the papers recommending appointment or reappointment of an external auditor:

- if the board does not accept the audit committee's recommendation, a statement from the audit committee explaining the recommendation and from the board setting out reasons why they have taken a different position (C.3.6).'

Operating and financial review

The OFR has for some years been a voluntary statement published by most listed companies and some other public interest companies. It is primarily a narrative statement, outside the audited accounts but part of the annual report. It is similar to the US 'Management discussion and analysis'. The content of OFRs has generally followed the non-mandatory guidance issued by the ASB in 1993 (updated 2003).

Government proposals

Whilst this non-mandatory approach has been reasonably successful, the DTI took the view that narrative reporting across a wider range of issues than just financial performance was increasingly important. Hence they brought forward proposals for legislation in May 2004 to require listed companies to prepare a statutory OFR. The main proposals were as follows:

An OFR should be a balanced and comprehensive analysis of:

(a) The development and performance of the business of the company and its subsidiary undertakings during the financial year.
(b) The position of the company and its subsidiary undertakings at the end of the year.
(c) The main trends and factors underlying the development, performance and position of the business of the company and its subsidiary undertakings during the financial year.
(d) The main trends and factors that are likely to affect their future development, performance and position, prepared so as to enable the members of the company to assess the strategies adopted by the company and its subsidiary undertakings and the potential for those strategies to succeed.

The review should include:

(a) A statement of the business, objectives and strategies of the company and its subsidiary undertakings.
(b) A description of the resources available to the company and its subsidiary undertakings.
(c) A description of the principal risks and uncertainties facing the company and its subsidiary undertakings.
(d) A description of the capital structure, treasury policies and objectives and liquidity of the company and its subsidiary undertakings.

Also, to the extent necessary to comply with the review objective and other general requirements above, the review should include information about:

177

- the employees of the company and its subsidiary undertakings;
- environmental matters; and
- social and community issues.

The legislation has not been finalised at the time of writing but in November 2004, the government announced its conclusions in response to the consultation process. It indicated that:

- The OFR will apply to all quoted companies. This means those admitted to the Official List; or officially listed in the European Economic Area; or admitted to either the New York Stock Exchange or NASDAQ.
- In order to allow companies adequate time to prepare for implementation, the regulations will come into effect for financial years beginning on or after 1 April 2005.
- The substance of the proposals that were published for consultation in May (see above) will not be changed as the government believes that the objectives and content of the OFR are appropriate.
- Directors will be expected to apply 'due care, skill and diligence' in preparation of the OFR. They must firstly meet the review objective and provide necessary information to satisfy the general requirements to be set out in the regulations. They should also ensure that they consider and include information relating to their environmental, employment and social and community policies to the extent necessary for shareholders to understand how these are impacting the business and wider community.
- Guidance notes will provide clarity to companies about advising share-holders of the need to treat directors' judgements (particularly about future events or prospects) with caution. Specific disclosures about impending developments or matters in the course of negotiation will not be required.
- Auditors should consider whether the OFR is consistent with the company's accounts and whether it contains any inconsistencies based on any matters that have come to their attention during the audit.
- The FRRP will review the OFR in response to third party enquiries and in relation to possible omissions or misstatements. In order to allow the new regime time to settle, the FRRP's enforcement role in reviewing OFRs will be delayed until financial years starting on or after 1 April 2006.

ASB Reporting Standard

The statutory requirements relating to the OFR will not be detailed and the ASB is developing a new style of document, a 'Reporting Standard', on the OFR to complement the legislation. The ASB published its proposals as 'RED 1' in November 2004.

The proposals are principles-based and require that the OFR:

- reflects the directors' view of the business;
- focuses on matters that are relevant to investors;
- has a forward-looking orientation;
- complements as well as supplements the financial statements;
- is comprehensive and understandable;
- is balanced and neutral; and
- is comparable over time.

The OFR should provide a balanced and comprehensive analysis of:

- the development and performance of the business during the year;
- the entity's position at the year end;
- the main trends and factors underlying the development, performance and position of business of the entity during the year; and
- the main trends and factors likely to affect future development, performance and position, to help investors to assess an entity's strategies and the potential for those strategies to succeed.

The proposals provide a basic framework for disclosure but allow directors the flexibility to tailor the OFR to an entity's particular circumstances. The framework covers:

- the nature, objectives and strategies of the business;
- the development and performance of the business (for current and also future periods);
- the resources, risks and uncertainties and relationships that may affect the entity's long-term value; and
- the position of the business (including a description of the capital structure, treasury policies and objectives and liquidity of the entity for current and also future periods).

The exposure draft describes other matters about which information may be relevant for disclosure including: persons with whom the entity has relations (such as customers and suppliers); employees; receipts from, and returns to, shareholders; environmental matters; and social and community issues.

Directors will be required to disclose the key performance indicators (KPIs) judged to be the most effective in measuring delivery of their strategies and in managing their businesses. The exposure draft sets out disclosures that should be made for each key KPI included in the OFR, in order that investors can understand and evaluate each one.

Directors' report

Section 234 of the Act requires the directors of all companies to prepare a directors' report '(a) containing a fair review of the development of the business of the company and its subsidiary undertakings during the financial year and their position at the end of it, and (b) stating the amount (if any) which they recommend should be paid as dividend'. Section 234 then refers to Schedule 7 which sets out more specific requirements. These include:

- directors' interests in shares and debentures of the company
- political donations and expenditure
- charitable donations
- company's acquisition of its own shares
- employment of disabled people
- employee involvement
- policy and practice on payment of creditors.

This list, taken together with the requirement in section 234 for a 'fair review' (see above) have tended to produce a report containing a somewhat random collection of information, much of it introduced as political imperative or fashion of the day. Especially in the case of listed companies, where the disclosure of the 'fair review' is addressed in much more detail in the OFR, the directors' report is left as a rather odd document.

The law relating to the directors' report is about to change. The DTI's proposed legislation that is introducing the statutory OFR for listed companies is also introducing a reform of the directors' report for all companies except small companies. The main intention is to expand the current requirement for a 'fair review', which has typically resulted in minimalist disclosure by many companies. The draft regulations revise the content requirements for the directors' report so that it will in future contain a review of the development and performance of the business and of its position, together with a description of the principal risks and uncertainties that it faces. The review must be a balanced and comprehensive analysis, consistent with the size of the business. All companies, except small companies, will, therefore, be required to produce such a review. However, the government proposes to provide an exemption for medium-sized companies not to provide certain non-financial information.

Directors' emoluments

By historical standards and compared with practice in most other countries, the current UK requirements for the disclosure of directors' emoluments are extremely detailed, onerous and complex, especially in the case of listed companies. It is a tribute to the complexity of the requirements that a comprehensive treatment of the subject (as in PricewaterhouseCoopers LLP, Manual of Accounting – UK GAAP (Kingston upon Thames: CCH, 2005)) takes over a hundred pages. The details of directors' emoluments, taking the form of a report of the remuneration committee in the case of listed companies, is also one of the most widely read parts of a company's annual report.

The requirements in this area are primarily those in the Companies Act 1985. The Listing Rules also include requirements, though for the most part these duplicate those in the Act. There is no role for accounting standards in this area.

Requirements relating to all companies

The basic legal requirements are set out in section 232, which refers to Schedule 6 to the Act, in which the detailed requirements are found. Schedule 6, Part 1 sets out the requirements relating to the emoluments of directors, pensions, compensation for loss of office and sums paid to third parties for directors' services.

The headings under which the Act requires disclosure are:

- Aggregate emoluments. For this purpose, emolument includes fees and bonuses, taxable expense allowances, benefits in kind, and emoluments in respect of accepting office (sometimes called 'golden hellos').
- Gains made by directors on the exercise of share options.
- Amounts receivable in respect of long-term incentive schemes.
- Value of company contributions to pension schemes.
- The number of directors to whom benefits are accruing in respect of (a) money purchase pension schemes and (b) defined benefit pension schemes.

Requirements relating to unquoted companies

In addition to the above, unquoted companies (which include companies listed on AIM) must comply with requirements relating to:

- emoluments and other benefits of the highest paid director
- excess retirement benefits
- compensation for loss of office
- sums paid to third parties in respect of directors' services.

Quoted companies

Section 234B requires quoted companies to prepare a directors' remuneration report, details of which are set out in Schedule 7A. In Schedule 7A, Part 2 relates to information about remuneration committees, performance related remuneration and liabilities in respect of directors' contracts. Part 3 relates to detailed information about directors' remuneration.

The matters that need to be disclosed fall under the following headings:

- Details of the composition of the remuneration committee and details of its advisers
- A statement of policy on directors' remuneration
- Performance graph
- Service contracts
- Compensation for past directors (explanation for awards)
- Individual directors' emoluments and compensation
- Share options
- Long-term incentive schemes
- Pensions
- Excess retirement benefits of directors and past directors
- Compensation for past directors (details of awards)
- Sums paid to third parties in respect of directors' services

The first five of the above are not subject to audit; the last seven are subject to audit.

Related party relationships and transactions

Accounting standards require disclosure by companies of related party relationships and transactions. The UK standard (FRS 8) is broadly similar to the international standard (IAS 24). The underlying reason for the disclosure requirements is that a reader of accounts will assume, unless told otherwise, that the transactions are with third parties and are at arm's length prices. If this is not the case, the reader needs to be put on notice, so that he or she can bear the fact in mind when reading the accounts. For example, a transaction between related parties may be at a non-market price resulting in one party making a loss, or a sub-normal profit, or on the other hand an above market margin on the transaction. Without knowing that some transactions were between related parties, the non-market profit margins shown in the accounts would be perplexing.

It is important to note that there is no requirement to substitute an arm's length price for the actual price charged to the related party. It is merely a matter of factual disclosure of the relationship that subsists and the transactions that have taken place.

A key part of the standards is the definition of who is regarded as a related party. FRS 8 defines related party in terms of control and influence, in the following way. Two or more parties are related when at any time during the financial year:

- one party has direct or indirect control over the other; or
- the parties are subject to common control from the same source; or

- one party has influence over the financial and operating policies of the other to an extent that that other party might be inhibited from pursuing at all times its own separate interests; or
- the parties, in entering a transaction, are subject to influence from the same source.

Hence, for example, a parent and its subsidiaries are related parties, as are associates and joint ventures, and directors. Having said that, there are certain exemptions for intra-group transactions.

The disclosure requirements of FRS 8 may be summarised as follows:

- Disclosure of control – that is, disclosure of the controlling party and, if different, the ultimate controlling party.
- Disclosure of transactions and balances, including:
  - Names of the transacting related parties
  - A description of the relationship between the parties
  - A description of the transactions
  - The amounts involved
  - Any other elements necessary for an understanding of the financial statements
  - Amounts due at the balance sheet date and any doubtful debts
  - Amounts written off in the period.

IAS 24 is a similar standard to FRS 8 except that the exemption relating to subsidiaries is not the same.

Segment disclosure

A further area of disclosure required by accounting standards is segment disclosure. Like related party disclosures, the information required by the relevant standards has no impact on the numbers in the profit and loss account or balance sheet, but it does enable better understanding of the results and assets, and therefore the financial situation of the whole company or group.

Segment disclosures are not required in the same way for all companies. In the UK, certain disclosures (limited to analysis of turnover) are required by para. 55 of Schedule 4 to the Act. SSAP 25 adds further requirements but applies only to public companies, banking or insurance companies or groups, and other companies whose size exceeds ten times the Act's criteria for defining a medium-sized company. SSAP 25 requires, for companies within its scope, analysis of:

- turnover
- profit or loss before tax (before or after interest)
- net assets.

This analysis should be done in two ways: by class of business, and by geographical segment. This analysis is useful to users of accounts to enable them to understand the components of profit and to understand which parts of the overall business are showing growth.

The equivalent international standard, IAS 14, has some similarities; for example, it requires analysis by class of business and by geographical segment. But it is different in two important respects. First, it applies to fewer entities: to those that are publicly traded and to those that are in the process of issuing equity or debt securities in public securities markets. Second, it requires disclosure of significantly more information, in two senses: it will typically require a company to identify more segments than SSAP 25; and for those segments it requires more disclosure than SSAP 25, including analysis of capital expenditure and analysis of gross assets and gross liabilities, rather than net assets. This higher level of disclosure has troubled some companies, and pleased some analysts and other users of accounts in the context of UK companies adopting IFRS.

18
Use of financial information in contracts and agreements

Introduction

Financial statements are used in many ways, most notably to monitor and analyse the profitability of a business both internally by its management and externally by shareholders and other interested parties. But an important specific role of financial statements is that they are used in various contracts and agreements. For example:

- A limit to the amount that a company may borrow may be based on ratios taken from the financial statements, such as gearing, interest cover or other measures. If such limits are breached, various consequences may arise including the debt being immediately repayable.
- In an agreement for the sale or purchase of a subsidiary, the price to be paid may include an initial amount plus a further amount of contingent consideration that may be payable depending on the level of profits in the period (typically one to three years) after the sale.
- Part of the remuneration of a director, manager or group of employees may be based on an accounting measure such as growth in (or absolute amount of) a measure of profit such as operating profit, pre-tax profit, post-tax profit or earnings per share.
- In a regulated industry, the regulator may restrain a company from charging a level of prices that results in the company making more than a given percentage of profit on its capital employed, defined in a certain way, for example with assets measured at current cost.

In this chapter, we explore how accounting measures are applied in situations such as the above. We do so by means of case studies on the first two topics, that is, borrowing covenants and contingent consideration in a sale of a company. The three key points that apply, however, to all such uses of information from financial statements are:

- The agreement or contract must specify exactly what the measure is and how it is calculated. For example, a vague reference to the level of, or increase in, 'profit' is of little value if it does not specify (a) which level of profit (for example, profit before tax); (b) whether it is per the financial statements or whether it is adjusted in some way; (c) to which period it relates.

- The agreement or contract must specify whether the GAAP to be used is that which applied when the agreement was entered into ('frozen GAAP') or whether it is the GAAP that applies from time to time ('rolling GAAP').
- In particular at present, it is important to be clear whether the measure is calculated on the basis of UK GAAP or IFRS, and how the agreement or contract deals with any transition to IFRS that the company might make.

Case study 1 – borrowing covenants

When a company borrows money from a bank, or raises money in a bond issue or similar exercise, there will frequently be controls or restrictions put in place by the lender. These are normally called 'borrowing covenants' and they are often based on ratios taken from the financial statements.

The most common financial statement ratios used in borrowing covenants are those directly relating to the amount, or proportion of debt, that is, gearing (a balance sheet measure), or interest cover, which is its profit and loss account equivalent. So, for example, a borrowing covenant might say that the company's gearing should not exceed X% or that the interest should be at least Y times covered by operating profit. If these ratios are breached, various consequences may arise such as the debt being immediately repayable, or the lender imposing tougher restrictions on expenditure.

Whilst the terms 'gearing' and 'interest cover' are generally understood, there is no standardised definition. Gearing, for example, means broadly the relationship of debt to equity (shareholders' funds) on the balance sheet. But it can be defined in a number of ways, including:

1. Long-term debt compared to equity
2. Long-term debt compared to equity plus long-term debt
3. Long-term and short-term debt compared to equity
4. Long-term and short-term debt net of cash balances compared to equity.

From the balance sheet in Box 18.1 we can see how each of the above measures of gearing is calculated.

This company's gearing is calculated in the following way under the four definitions shown above:

1. $70/55 = 127\%$
2. $70/(70 + 55) = 56\%$
3. $(70 + 15)/55 = 154\%$
4. $(70 + 15–10)/55 = 136\%$

Quite literally, this company's gearing can be viewed as anything in the range 56% to 154%, depending on how one defines gearing. None of these is right or wrong in an absolute sense. The key point is that is it important to define the terms and to apply the definition consistently. It might be best to use a

Fixed assets		100
Current assets		
Stock	30	
Debtors	20	
Cash	10	60
Current liabilities		
Creditors	(20)	
Short-term bank loan	(15)	(35)
Long-term debt		(70)
Net assets		55
Share capital		10
Reserves		45
Equity		55

Box 18.1

definition like the second one, where the denominator includes both debt and equity; in this way the gearing figure cannot exceed 100% (unless there is a deficit of shareholders' funds), and this makes gearing easier to understand. In this example, we can say that 56% of total long-term funding comes from debt and thus 44% comes from equity. The approach can be refined, for example to include short-term debt, as in example 3, or to include short-term debt net of cash as in example 4.

A gearing calculation, being based on balance sheet figures, suffers from the inadequacies of the balance sheet, for example that it does not show a comprehensive picture of all the company's assets. There may be intangible assets that have significant value but which do not meet the criteria for recognition on a balance sheet. Or some of the assets that are recognised, for example property, may be worth significantly more than their carrying value in the balance sheet. These factors make a gearing ratio less than ideal.

An alternative approach is what is sometimes called 'income statement gearing', or 'interest cover'. This considers the extent to which interest is covered by profit before interest. (Another way to look at it is the proportion of profit that is taken up with interest payments.) Consider the following profit and loss account under UK GAAP (see Box 18.2).

On the face of it, interest is twice covered by profit before interest (that is, operating profit), or, arithmetically, interest cover is 2.0. But one could validly express it in different ways:

- If exceptional costs are excluded, so as to give a picture of the ratio in a more typical year, the ratio would be 2.8 (that is, $(10 + 4)/5 = 2.8$). A

Sales	100
Cost of sales	(70)
Gross profit	30
Distribution costs	(10)
Admin costs – normal	(6)
Admin costs – exceptional	(4)
Operating profit	10
Interest payable	(5)
Interest receivable	2
Profit before tax	7
Tax	(2)
Profit after tax	5

Box 18.2

drawback with this is that exceptional costs can be hard to define clearly and some companies are known to argue in nearly every year that they have exceptional costs. A variant is that profit might be calculated after adding back amortisation of goodwill.

• If interest is considered to be interest payable net of interest receivable, the ratio would be 3.33 (that is, $10/(5 - 2) = 3.33$).

At a more detailed level, there is the question of what exactly is to be included in interest payable. At a minimum, one would expect it to be literally the interest payable on loans. But the line 'interest payable' in a profit and loss account would normally include some other related items such as amortisation of any fees relating to the borrowing that meet the accounting definition of 'finance costs' (FRS 4). Under IFRS, as discussed below, there are more items to be potentially included in interest payable. This underlines the need to specify the meaning of terms used in covenants and similar agreements.

Again, none of these definitions of interest cover is right or wrong in an absolute sense. As with gearing, the key point is to define the terms and to apply the definition consistently.

Whilst gearing and interest cover are the most common types of borrowing covenants, there are others. These include:

• Net assets being at least a specified amount.
• EBITDA (see chapter 6, p. 67) being at least a specified amount, or a specified percentage of debt.
• Contingent liabilities (treated as off balance sheet) not exceeding X% of net tangible assets.

- Operating cash flow (from the cash flow statement) exceeding the total of gross financing costs and the principal amount of gross borrowings to be repaid in a specified period.

Impact of IFRS

The move to IFRS introduces further complications into borrowing covenants, though their resolution is not difficult so long as it is clear (a) whether GAAP of the year the covenant was signed applies (frozen GAAP) or whether the GAAP of the year in question applies; and (b) how various key terms are to be defined under each GAAP. In general, especially where large amounts are involved, or where the borrowing is close to the specified limits, it will be worth renegotiating the covenants so that it is clear between the lender and the borrower whether and exactly how IFRS affects the covenants.

The effect of a move to IFRS could be either beneficial or detrimental to a particular company: there is no uniform effect. Among the factors that could affect a company's accounting numbers are the following:

- Adoption of IAS 39 on financial instruments will generally introduce more fair values and therefore more volatility into the numbers. Some of the volatility will affect operating profit; some will affect interest payable and/or interest receivable; and some will affect net assets only (i.e. equity). This point does not apply, however, if FRS 26 applies to the company in question.
- Under UK GAAP (FRS 3), some exceptional items, such as gains/losses on sale of fixed assets, and costs of fundamental reorganisations, are presented after operating profit, but these will be reported as part of operating profit in IFRS.
- Some preference shares that were previously classified as part of equity or, if issued by a subsidiary, part of minority interest, are classified under IAS 32 as debt. This could affect gearing in a major way.

Case study 2 – sale and purchase of a subsidiary

In an agreement for the sale or purchase of a subsidiary, the price to be paid may include an initial amount plus a further amount of contingent consideration that may be payable depending on the level of profits in the period (typically one to three years) after the sale. This is sometimes called an 'earn-out' clause. This often arises because there is genuine uncertainty about the fair value of the operation being sold, and the level of profits achieved after the sale provides further evidence of the fair value.

In these circumstances, the sale and purchase agreement will include a term specifying the additional amounts that will be payable and the basis of their calculation. As with borrowing covenants, it is important to be clear exactly how various terms are defined, whether they will remain on a frozen GAAP basis or whether they will change as GAAP changes, and also how any change to IFRS will affect the calculation.

Assume that group A sells subsidiary S to group B in 2003. Consideration payable is defined as £100m. plus a further amount payable in April 2006 based on the profits of S for the three years 2003, 2004 and 2005. The agreement provides that the additional consideration shall be 20% of the operating profit of each of the three years.

For 2003 and 2004, S prepares its accounts under UK GAAP, though in 2004 it adopts the FRS 17 pension accounting rules on a voluntary basis (it would have to adopt them in 2005 but chooses earlier adoption). In 2005, it changes to IFRS in line with the instructions from the parent company of group B.

The results of S are shown in Box 18.3. For simplicity, we assume that the underlying results are exactly the same for each year. However, because of the accounting changes just described, the accounting numbers are different.

£m.	2003 (UK GAAP pre-FRS 17)	2004 (UK GAAP with FRS 17)	2005 (IRFS)
Sales	100	100	100
Cost of sales	(70)	(70)	(70)
Gross profit	30	30	30
Admin costs	(10)	(9)	(16)
Operating profit	20	21	14
Fundamental re-organisation costs	(7)	(7)	—
Profit before interest	13	14	14
Interest cost	(4)	(3)	(3)
Profit before tax	9	11	11

Box 18.3

The following points and assumptions should be noted in relation to the table in Box 18.3:

- Moving to FRS 17 for pension costs decreases the regular pension cost within admin costs and also affects the interest cost figure. It would in practice also affect the actuarial gain or loss in the statement of total recognised gains and losses, but that is not relevant and is not shown here.

- Costs of a fundamental reorganisation are shown below operating profit in UK GAAP under FRS 3, but there is no equivalent category under IFRS. The costs are shown within operating costs under IFRS.
- In practice there would probably be other changes in accounting arising from the move to IFRS, but in order to simplify the example it is assumed that there are only the two just discussed.

Because the earn-out clause is not sufficiently specific about the basis of profit measurement, there are a number of possible interpretations, and this can sometimes give rise to disputes and litigation, where the effect of different interpretations is material. At least three possible interpretations can be inferred, as follows.

First, if the earn-out clause operated on a frozen GAAP basis, the calculation would be as shown in Box 18.4.

2003 Operating profit £20m. × 20% = £4m.
2004 and 2005: same calculation
Total amount payable: £4m. × 3 years = **£12m.**

Box 18.4

Second, it could be argued that the move to IFRS was not foreseen at the time of the agreement as, although it was known to be optional for an entity to move to IFRS from 2005, it was far from clear whether many entities – and S in particular – would do that. On the other hand, it is accepted that UK GAAP develops from time to time, and it is to be inferred from the absence of a frozen GAAP clause that the figures under UK GAAP for each of the years are to be taken at face value. On this basis the calculation would be as shown in Box 18.5.

2003 Operating profit £20m. × 20% = £4m.
2004 Operating profit £21m. × 20% = £4.2m.
2005: same calculation as 2004 (i.e. as if UK GAAP still applied), that is £4.2m.
Total amount payable: £4m. + £4.2m. + £4.2m. = **£12.4m.**

Box 18.5

Third, it could be argued that the move to IFRS is just part of the continuing development of GAAP, and in that sense is no different from the adoption of FRS 17 in 2004 as part of UK GAAP. On this basis, the calculation would be as shown in Box 18.6.

191

2003 Operating profit £20m. × 20% = £4m.
2004 Operating profit £21m. × 20% = £4.2m.
2005 Operating profit £14m. × 20% = £2.8m.
Total amount payable: £4m. + £4.2m + £2.8m. = **£11m.**

Box 18.6

It is not difficult to see that there is ample scope for disagreement about how the earn-out clause should operate, and therefore merit in making it very clear in the agreement exactly how such clauses should operate. The same applies to other similar uses of information from financial statements.

Appendices

Appendix 1
List of UK accounting standards (SSAPs and FRSs), Statements and UITF Abstracts

Statements of Standard Accounting Practice

SSAP 4   Accounting for government grants
SSAP 5   Accounting for value added tax
SSAP 9   Stocks and long-term contracts
SSAP 13   Accounting for research and development
SSAP 17   Accounting for post balance sheet events
SSAP 19   Accounting for investment properties
SSAP 20   Foreign currency translation
SSAP 21   Accounting for leases and hire purchase contracts
SSAP 24   Accounting for pension costs
SSAP 25   Segmental reporting

Financial Reporting Standards

FRSSE   Financial reporting standard for smaller entities
FRS 1   Cash flow statements
FRS 2   Accounting for subsidiary undertakings
FRS 3   Reporting financial performance
FRS 4   Capital instruments
FRS 5   Reporting the substance of transactions
FRS 6   Acquisitions and mergers
FRS 7   Fair values in acquisition accounting
FRS 8   Related party disclosures
FRS 9   Associates and joint ventures
FRS 10   Goodwill and intangible assets
FRS 11   Impairment of fixed assets and goodwill
FRS 12   Provisions, contingent liabilities and contingent assets
FRS 13   Derivatives and other financial instruments: disclosures
FRS 14   Earnings per share
FRS 15   Tangible fixed assets
FRS 16   Current tax
FRS 17   Retirement benefits
FRS 18   Accounting policies
FRS 19   Deferred tax
FRS 20 (IFRS 2) Accounting for share-based payment

FRS 21 (IAS 10)	Events after the balance sheet date
FRS 22 (IAS 33)	Earnings per share
FRS 23 (IAS 21)	The effects of changes in foreign exchange rates
FRS 24 (IAS 29)	Financial reporting in hyperinflationary economies
FRS 25 (IAS 32)	Financial instruments: disclosure and presentation
FRS 26 (IAS 39)	Financial instruments: measurement
FRS 27	Life assurance

ASB statements

Statement of aims
Foreword to accounting standards
Statement of principles for financial reporting
Foreword to UITF Abstracts
Interim reports
Preliminary announcements
Operating and financial review

UITF Abstracts

UITF Abstract 4	Presentation of long-term debtors in current assets
UITF Abstract 5	Transfers from current assets to fixed assets
UITF Abstract 6	Accounting for post-retirement benefits other than pensions
UITF Abstract 9	Accounting for operations in hyper-inflationary economies
UITF Abstract 11	Capital instruments: issuer call options
UITF Abstract 15	Disclosure of substantial acquisitions
UITF Abstract 17	Employee share schemes
UITF Abstract 18	Pension costs following the 1997 tax changes in respect of dividend income
UITF Abstract 19	Tax on gains and losses on foreign currency borrowings that hedge an investment in a foreign enterprise
UITF Abstract 21	Accounting issues arising from the proposed introduction of the euro
UITF Abstract 22	The acquisition of a Lloyd's business
UITF Abstract 23	Application of the transitional rules in FRS 15
UITF Abstract 24	Accounting for start-up costs
UITF Abstract 25	National insurance contributions on share option gains
UITF Abstract 26	Barter transactions for advertising
UITF Abstract 27	Revision to estimates of the useful economic life of goodwill and intangible assets
UITF Abstract 28	Operating lease incentives
UITF Abstract 29	Website development costs
UITF Abstract 30	Date of award to employees of shares or rights to shares
UITF Abstract 31	Exchanges of businesses or other non-monetary assets for an interest in a subsidiary, joint venture or associate

UITF Abstract 32	Employee benefit trusts and other intermediate payment arrangements
UITF Abstract 33	Obligations in capital instruments
UITF Abstract 34	Pre-contract costs
UITF Abstract 35	Death-in-service and incapacity benefits
UITF Abstract 36	Contracts for sales of capacity
UITF Abstract 37	Purchases and sales of own shares
UITF Abstract 38	Accounting for ESOP trusts
UITF Abstract 39	(IFRIC Interpretation 2) – Members' shares in co-operative entities and similar instruments
UITF Abstract 40	Revenue recognition and service contracts

Appendix 2

List of international accounting standards (IASs and IFRSs) and IFRIC interpretations

International Accounting Standards – applicable for 2005

IAS 1	Presentation of financial statements
IAS 2	Inventories
IAS 7	Cash flow statements
IAS 8	Accounting policies, changes in accounting estimates and errors
IAS 10	Events after the balance sheet date
IAS 11	Construction contracts
IAS 12	Income taxes
IAS 14	Segment reporting
IAS 16	Property, plant and equipment
IAS 17	Leases
IAS 18	Revenue
IAS 19	Employee benefits
IAS 20	Accounting for government grants and disclosure of government assistance
IAS 21	The effects of changes in foreign exchange rates
IAS 23	Borrowing costs
IAS 24	Related party disclosures
IAS 26	Accounting and reporting by retirement benefit plans
IAS 27	Consolidated and separate financial statements and accounting for investments in subsidiaries
IAS 28	Investments in associates
IAS 29	Financial reporting in hyperinflationary economies
IAS 30	Disclosures in the financial statements of banks and similar financial institutions
IAS 31	Interests in joint ventures
IAS 32	Financial instruments: Disclosure and presentation
IAS 33	Earnings per share
IAS 34	Interim financial reporting
IAS 36	Impairment of assets
IAS 37	Provisions, contingent liabilities and contingent assets
IAS 38	Intangible assets
IAS 39	Financial instruments: Recognition and measurement
IAS 40	Investment property
IAS 41	Agriculture

IFRS 1   First-time adoption of International Accounting Standards
IFRS 2   Share-based payment
IFRS 3   Business combinations
IFRS 4   Insurance contracts
IFRS 5   Non-current assets held for sale and discontinued operations
IFRS 6   Exploration for and evaluation of mineral resources

IASB statements

Preface to international financial reporting standards
Framework for the preparation and presentation of financial statements.

Interpretations – SICs and IFRICs

SIC 7   Introduction to the euro
SIC 10   Government assistance – No specific relation to operating activities
SIC 12   Consolidation – Special purpose entities
SIC 13   Jointly controlled entities – Non-monetary contributions by venturers
SIC 15   Operating leases – Incentives
SIC 21   Income taxes – Recovery of revalued non-depreciable assets
SIC 25   Income taxes – Changes in the tax status of an enterprise or its
          shareholders
SIC 27   Evaluating the substance of transactions involving the legal form of a
          lease
SIC 29   Disclosure – Service concession arrangements
SIC 31   Revenue – Barter transactions involving advertising services
SIC 32   Intangible assets – Web site costs

IFRIC 1   Changes in existing decommissioning, restoration and similar liabilities.
IFRIC 2   Members' shares in co-operative entities and similar instruments
IFRIC 3   Emission rights
IFRIC 4   Determining whether an arrangement contains a lease
IFRIC 5   Rights to interests arising from decommissioning, restoration and
          environmental rehabilitation funds

Index

Accountancy Foundation, 60
Accountancy Investigation and
    Discipline Board, role, 60
accountants
  professional bodies, 55, 56
  role in transactions, 62–3
accounting
  meaning, 3–4
  terms, 6–9
  trends, 69–74
accounting policies
  company law, 42
  departure from, 36
  disclosure, 5, 11
  group accounts, 43
  mergers, 99
  selection, 10–11
  specification, 8
  statements, 5, 11
accounting principles
  accruals concept, 36–7, 130
  aggregate amounts, 37
  break-up basis, 35
  company law, 34–7
  consistency, 35–6, 131
  departure from, 35, 37, 165
  disclosure of liabilities, 36
  going concern basis, 35
  matching, 37
  materiality, 42–3
  prudence, 36, 125
  realised and unrealised profits, 36
  v. rules, 71–2
  substance over form, 48, 50
accounting standards
  company law obligations, 22–8
  disclosure of departure from, 26–7
  and DTI, 21

enforcement, 59–60
EU regulation, 16, 17–19
international harmonisation, 14–15
recent activity, 70
and taxation, 21
United Kingdom, 9–10, 12–14
Accounting Standards Board (ASB)
  creation, 12–14, 49, 56
  FRSs. *See* Financial Reporting
    Standards
  Reporting Standard, 178–9
  role, 9, 58
  Statement of Principles, 13
  statements, 196
Accounting Standards Committee, 9, 12,
  49, 57
accounts. *See* annual accounts
accruals accounting
  accounting principle, 36–7
  meaning, 6, 7
  operating leases, 130
acquisitions. *See* mergers and
  acquisitions
adjusted earnings numbers, 67–8
aggregate amounts, principle, 37
AIM, 18, 181
alternative accounting rules, 39–41
analysts, 65, 66, 68
annual accounts
  approval, 27–8
  company law obligations, 24–8
  distribution, 27–8
  exemptions, 28
  filing, 27–8
  formats, 29–34
  groups. *See* group accounts
  IFRS obligations, 27
  revision, 28, 59

201

.